Tunisia's National Intelligence

Tunisia's National Intelligence
Why "Rogue Elephants"
Fail to Reform

Noureddine Jebnoun
With a Foreword by George Joffé

New Academia Publishing in association with

The Center *for* Contemporary
Arab Studies
Georgetown University

NEW ACADEMIA
PUBLISHING
Washington, DC

Library of Congress Control Number: 2017943156
ISBN 978-0-9986433-2-8 paperback (alk. paper)

NEW ACADEMIA
PUBLISHING

New Academia Publishing, 4401-A Connecticut Ave. NW, #236,
Washington, DC 20008
info@newacademia.com - www.newacademia.com

Cover image: By Noureddine Jebnoun. May 2015: Police personnel escorting two individuals dressed in Salafī fashion style on Avenue Habib Bourguiba next to the Interior Ministry.

*To the memory of all the brave citizens
who endured tragic fates at the hands of
the Arab mukhābarāt*

Contents

Diagrams and Tables

Acknowledgements

I thank Professor Osama W. Abi-Mershed, the director of Georgetown University's Center for Contemporary Arab Studies (CCAS) for his support of this project. I am grateful to the CCAS for sponsoring this research. I acknowledge colleagues at the CCAS—Professors Emad El-Din Shahin, Rochelle A. Davis, Belkacem Baccouche, Fida Adely, and Marwa Daoudy—who have offered both friendship and encouragement. I am particularly indebted to both Professor Emeritus Clement M. Henry and Professor Robert Springborg for their constructive and substantive feedback and invaluable insights on this work. I am thankful to Professor George Joffé, whose engagement with the manuscript has been an important throughout. I am grateful to the three anonymous reviewers who reviewed the manuscript for New Academia Publishing-CCAS and offered extremely valuable feedback. I owe a profound debt of gratitude to those among Tunisian military and security personnel, both retired and still in active duty, who accepted to be interviewed and shared their thoughts and experiences. While I have benefited tremendously from my conversations with them, the responsibility for any errors or emissions in this final product is mine. I extend my deep appreciation to Samantha Brotman who read the first draft of the manuscript and provided thorough stylistic guidance. Finally, I thank Vicki Valosik, the CCAS Multimedia and Publications Editor, for her help in editing the manuscript.

Note on transliteration

For the Arabic names listed in this book, I used a transliteration system based on the guidelines of the *International Journal of the Middle East Studies* (IJMES). Arabic names and words have been transcribed in a consistent way. I have used full diacritical marks in the transliteration, indicating the "ayn: ع" as ['] and the hamza as [': ء]. The vowels with a line on top [¯] have been used to indicate that they are long. However, one exception has been made to the IJMES system by using the French spelling for President Habib Bourguiba, whose name is spelled identically in both French and English literature.

Abbreviations

ATCE (French acronym): Tunisian External Communication Agency
ATI (French acronym): Tunisian Internet Agency
BND: German Federal Intelligence Service (Bundesnachrichtendienst)
BOP (French acronym): Brigade of Public Order
BTS (French acronym): Territorial Saharan Brigade
CC: Crisis Cell
CDPS: Coordination Directorate for Public Security
CDSS: Coordination Directorate of Specialized Services
CITFR: Crisis Intervention Team for First Responder
CMC: Consultative Military Committee
CNI: Spanish Centro Nacional de Inteligencia
CSC: Command and Staff College
DES: Directorate of External Security
DGSE (French acronym): General Directorate for External Security
DGSM (French acronym): General Directorate of Military Security
DIA: Defense Intelligence Agency
DII: Directorate of Intelligence and Investigations
DISA: Defense Intelligence and Security Agency
DLSTC: Defense Language School and Training Center
DMA: Defense Mapping Agency
DMI: Egyptian Military Intelligence and Reconnaissance Administration
DRS (French acronym): Algerian Department of Intelligence and Security
DSS: Directorate of State Security
DSS: Directorate of Strategic Studies
G2: Military Intelligence Directorate of the Army
G3: Operations Directorate of the Army
GDER: General Directorate of External Relations
GDIIS: General Directorate of Intelligence and Internal Security

GDNG: General Directorate of the National Guard
GDNS: General Directorate of National Security
GDPSPPO: General Directorate of Presidential Security and Protection of Prominent Officials
GDSC: General Directorate for Securing Communications
GDSS: General Directorate of Specialized Services (Ministry of the Interior)
GDSS: General Directorate of Specialized Services (Ministry of the National Defense)
GFS (French acronym): Special Forces Group
GIA (French acronym): Islamic Armed Group
HUMINT: Human Intelligence
ICC: International Criminal Court
IFC: Intelligence Fusion Cell
IPCP: Individual Partnership Cooperation Program
ISF: Internal Security Forces
ISP: Internet Service Provider
JCTP: Judicial Counterterrorism Pole
MMD: Military Medical Directorate
MTI (French acronym): Islamic Tendency Movement
NAIS: National Agency for Information and Security
NCA: National Constituent Assembly
NCTC: National Counterterrorism Committee
NDC: National Defense Council
NDI: National Defense Institute
NFA: National Frequencies Agency
NG: National Guard
NGSU: National Guard Special Unit
NSC: National Security Council
NSFTE: National Strategy to Fight Terrorism and Extremism
NSS: National Security State
NTA: National Telecommunications Authority
NWC: National War College
OSINT: Open Source Intelligence
PCMA: Permanent Committee for Monitoring Armament
PSD (French acronym): Dustūrian Socialist Party
PSG: Presidential Security Guard
PSSDI: Presidential Security Sub-Directorate of Intelligence

SDECE (French acronym): French External Documentation and Counter-Espionage Service

SIGINT: Signals Intelligence

SIMS: School of Intelligence and Military Security

SISMI: Italian Servizio per le Informazioni e la Sicurezza Militare

SM (French acronym): Military Security

SPCOC: Security Pole for Counterterrorism and Organized Crime

TAF: Tunisian Armed Forces

TND: Tunisian Dinar

UGTT (French acronym): Tunisian General Labor Union

VNSAs: Violent Non-State Actors

Foreword

Noureddine Jebnoun's masterly study of independent Tunisia's intelligence and security services, both before and after the fall of the Bin ʿAlī regime, is highly illuminating, not least because it demonstrates that so little has changed since the revolution in January 2011. What is somewhat more depressing is that it seems that little will change in the immediate future, even though Tunisia's security services have recently come under international and hostile scrutiny. At the start of 2017, a coroner's inquest in Britain commented very unfavorably on the security service's behavior at Sousse in July 2015 when a tourist hotel was attacked, with 38 tourists, mostly British, being killed. Yet there has been no evidence in Tunisia that significant reforms are planned as a result.

One of the most striking aspects of the behavior of the intelligence and security services that emerges from Dr. Jebnoun's account is the incompetence that they have continuously demonstrated in terms of guaranteeing the security of the state and in uncovering threats to its survival. Thus they failed to uncover the network plotting the Gafsa armed uprising in 1980 even though it had moved from Libya into the Tunisian town several weeks before the insurrection actually occurred. They were unaware of Algerian designs on the border village of Hazoua in late 1991 until Algerian forces actually crossed the border. They were unable to protect Muhammad Brāhmī from assassination in July 2013, even though the CIA had warned them beforehand of a plot to assassinate him. Nor did the security forces identify the amateurish beginnings of the Soliman Group until its members began to actually train on the ground. There has been a similar failing over the security forces' ability to contain contemporary terrorism—in Sousse or in the Jebel Ash-Sha'nabī region, where they have had to rely on Algerian and American support to contain the threat.

Alongside their incompetence was the complete illegality in which they operated. There was never a proper legal structure to establish their political accountability, certainly not before 2011. Indeed, on one occasion, the head of military intelligence felt so liberated from legal constraint that he even took it upon himself to organize a completely illegal search of the office of the Minister of Defense, his ostensible superior! And, even after the revolution, the constant changes to organizational structures of both the intelligence and the security services had much more to do with technical issues of management and operational control than they did with legal accountability. The result is that, even today, an appropriate process of accountability and control is still lacking, even though proper civil-military relations are an integral part of the democratic process, particularly where the security and intelligence services are involved.

Allied to this was their astonishing organizational ability to proliferate new and ever more complex management structures as time went by, particularly under the Bin 'Alī regime. Of course, some of this complexity has been shorn away in the wake of the revolution, as the more explicitly political and illegitimate aspects of the organizations concerned have been eliminated, but much of the complexity still remains in place. There had also been external pressure on the interim al-Nahḍah led-government and its caretaker successor to reform both security services and intelligence services, whether military or civilian, as there has been on the Qā'id al-Sabsī regime as well. But even here, it is sad to have to note that that pressure has really been directed toward technical reform, not toward the political and legal environment in which such services should operate. Furthermore, many of those technical reforms resonate with American paradigms now that Tunisia houses American drones, to considerable Algerian disgust. And Algeria today is Tunisia's other significant security partner.

There is, of course, an explanation which Dr. Jebnoun provides early on in his account and which has to do with the purpose for which the intelligence and security services were originally designed, certainly after the "medical coup" of November 7, 1987, which removed the octogenarian Habib Bourguiba from power. Tunisia's security and intelligence services were truly part of the "deep state" that the Bin ʿAlī regime constructed with the purpose of protecting the regime from the state—not at all to guarantee the security of the state. They were there to coerce, intimidate, and repress the population so that it would never threaten the regime that ruled over it, not to guarantee its own security from external or domestic threat. That was the reason why the intelligence and security services existed in a legal vacuum and why so little professional attention was paid to what was ostensibly their primary purpose, whether in the civil or the military sphere. Military intelligence monitored the army, not the threats that the armed forces faced, whilst civilian intelligence and security conditioned the civilian population through direct action and a veritable army of informers, irrespective of the security threats it really faced.

Given the lack of thorough legal and political reform since the revolution, such motivations have persisted, particularly as the personnel involved seems largely to have remained in place and maintained the same attitudes to the tasks before it as it had done in the pre-2011 epoch. In part, this has been because of the very real and immediate dangers that the country faces and in part because Tunisia's politicians either lack the experience or hanker for the same certainties that their predecessors before the revolution enjoyed. Nonetheless, real reform will be unavoidable if democratic transition is to succeed, not least because Tunisia's intelligence and security services ultimately failed their biggest challenge—protecting the regime from the revolution itself! It remains to be seen, as the remnants of the former regime reassert themselves through contemporary political institutions, whether this is an objective that they really wish to achieve or whether a reversal to the *status quo ante* is their ultimate objective. If it is the former, then little time remains for fundamental change to be achieved. If it is the latter then, tragically, everything remains in place for that to be the outcome.

George Joffé
Department of Politics and International Studies
University of Cambridge, UK

Introduction

Tunisia's popular uprising, which erupted unexpectedly following an altercation between a street vendor and a municipal policewoman in December 2010, has propelled Tunisia's security sector to the center stage of the country's political transition. This transition has occurred in the aftermath of the overthrow of the country's autocratic ruler of 23 years, Zayn al-ʿAbidīn Bin ʿAlī (1987–2011). Interestingly, the public debate on security sector reform (SSR) since 2011 has failed to define the framework, objectives and outcomes of such reform. Rather, SSR has become just one narrative among others in the transitional process, used by both international actors advancing their own agenda in a "tyranny of experts"[1] often disconnected from locally grounded realities[2] and Tunisian policymakers who seem primarily concerned with the consolidation of their power and their cynical political calculus.

The upsurge of security challenges amidst rising violence within Tunisia and across the Middle East has fortified the government's counterterrorism agenda and reduced pressure on the security sector to reform. Moreover, the legacy of more than five decades of authoritarianism—punctuated by serious violations of human rights—and the absence of transparency with regard to the structures, legal mandate, mission and operations of security forces, are all major impediments to the development of any comprehensive reform. Although scholars agree that SSR is critical to the success of the country's transition to democracy, they have not given any attention to the subfield of intelligence reform as one of the key prerequisites for the consolidation of democracy in Tunisia. This missing piece could be explained by the lack of reliable data in the realm of intelligence and the difficulty of shedding light on the role played by the intelligence and security services in the regime's dark web of coercion in strengthening its authoritarian resilience under the rule of Habib Bourguiba and Bin ʿAlī. The ambiguous role of Tunisia's intelligence and security services in the post-uprising era is far from being an independent professional instrument of citizen protection and is even less of an informative tool for public authorities in an imperiled time of uncertainty and anxiety. The absence of mechanisms of accountability and oversight of the intelligence and security apparatus constitutes a deficit in democratic control over such services and throws into question their effectiveness and compliance with the law. Increasing dysfunction, abuses, and unlawful activities have turned Tunisia's intelligence services into rampageous "rogue elephants."

The US Senator Frank Church first used the expression "rogue elephants" during his examination of American intelligence agencies in the aftermath of the Watergate affair to describe the illegal domestic spying activities of the CIA, NSA and FBI. In 1975, the Senator led the eponymous Church Committee, which disclosed a broad range of illegal intelligence actions and found in "three days of hearings on the intelligence agencies' illegal mail-opening program ... that the CIA had opened more than 200,000 letters and had photographed the outside of 2.7 million pieces of mail sent to and from the Soviet Union during its nearly twenty year program. The FBI had operated a similar project."[3] Although the scope of flagrant violations committed by the American "rogue elephants" is incommensurable with those inflected by their Tunisian counterparts on Tunisian citizens, Tunisia's intelligence apparatus' ruthless methods, intrusive security activities, abuse of power, and unaccountable questionable practices nevertheless suggest that Church's metaphor of "rogue elephants" is relevant to investigate Tunisia's national intelligence architecture.

Drawing on extensive fieldwork and original data,[4] this book is intended to fill the gap in the overlooked field of intelligence reform and democratic security governance in post-authoritarian Tunisia. The first chapter lays out its theoretical framework on intelligence in comparative case studies and discusses the democratic control of intelligence. The prerequisites of such control entail a clear definition of intelligence services: their mandate, power and competence; their supervision and oversight; their professionalization based on the respect of the rule law; and their protection of human rights and accountability. The second chapter sheds light on the dynamics of intelligence and security services in Tunisia's post-independence era and focuses on their growing political function as a means of regime control and suppression of dissents. The third chapter highlights the role of intelligence and security services under the fallen regime, showing that the latter had manipulated the intelligence security apparatus to the extent that it created a *de facto* police security state[5] that sought to inhibit any democratic alternative to it. Finally, the fourth chapter investigates the factors delaying the reform of the intelligence sector and demonstrates that intelligence in the Tunisian transitional context is experiencing more of a mending than a "democratic reform" process per se. This process has so far meant bolstering the capabilities of the intelligence services rather than holding them accountable to citizens and new institutions.

Chapter One

A Comparative Theoretical Framework on Intelligence and State Violence

The role played by military institutions—and to some extent the security apparatus—in the wave of upheavals that struck the Arab world in 2010–11 has generated a new literature on civil-military relations that differs from the social science literature on that topic from the 1960s and 1970s. The earlier literature emphasized the potentially positive involvement of the military as an agent of social change in the state-making process in countries such as Egypt, Syria, Algeria, and Libya in the post-independence era.[6] In contrast, the current literature tries to investigate and assess the Arab military's behavior in the face of massive popular mobilizations under authoritarian regimes and to highlight their critical role in negotiating the ongoing political transition.[7] While the post-Arab uprisings have witnessed a growing volume of literature on SSR, the role of intelligence services has been virtually absent as a topic in academic studies, as scholars have largely disregarded the impact of such services on both the resilience of authoritarianism and on the disquiet of the transitional process.[8] Instead, scholarly research has been directed toward police reform in the Arab world as a major component of the internal security apparatus.[9]

Needless to say, further research on the role of intelligence within Arab autocracies is crucial, as theoretical literature on the topic is not particularly well developed. Western literature tends to conceptualize intelligence as a "subset of civil-military relations"[10] because "military still plays a predominant role in intelligence," whether in emerging or full-fledged democracies.[11] This literature also makes an analogy between civil-military relations and civil-intelligence relations. Such a comparison includes the civil democratic control over both the military and intelligence, the definition of the roles and missions to perform, and the effectiveness and professionalism of these organizations.[12] Although this comparative approach may be relevant in a liberal democracy, it seems somewhat problematic within the Arab context, as civil-military relations and its intelligence subset are embedded within regime patronage networks and "shaped by communal or regional loyalties, making their cohesion and effectiveness hostage to those loyalties."[13] These patterns are discernible in most of the memoirs published by many former Arab senior military officers, security officials, ministers, and diplomats after leaving office, and mainly following the death or ouster of the leader under whom they served. These memoirs, as Sassoon demonstrates, are fascinating accounts that begin to lift the thick veil of secrecy within the inner circles of several Arab authoritarian regimes by shedding light on internal power dynamics, the decision-making rationale, and, most significantly, the functioning of their coercive apparatus.[14] Few retired intelligence professionals in the Arab world have written their memoirs, and those that do exist are of little value for scholars of democratic control of intelligence as they are very selective often biased in recording their experiences, and prone to political amnesia.[15]

In fact, the history of the Arab intelligence (also known as *mukhābarāt*) raises, as Sirrs points out, the "paradox" of power. Arab regimes seek to "project strength and fear" through their secret services that aim to intimidate or harm political dissents. At the same time, these services "reveal their profound weaknesses, such as lack of popular legitimacy."[16] These same services engage in coup-proofing strategies by employing, among other means, "informant rings" as "the most dedicated" and "powerful defenses against insurrection" and conspiracies.[17] Intelligence agencies are the most secretive dimension of these states, where lawlessness, systematic repression, and abuses against the regimes' own people are the tools of governing,[18] the exact opposite of the principles of a democratically controlled intelligence sector. In most Arab countries, torture is the preferred tool utilized by the intelligence services for the "extraction of [useful] information" from those considered "the die-hard enemy of the nation." Intelligence services employ a wide range of techniques that include, among others, "mutilation, emasculation, eye-gouging, and amputation of arms and legs."[19] In addition to the regular use of torture, intelligence services work tirelessly to infiltrate the state, its bureaucracy, and institutions at all levels, and to monitor the armed forces and each other in order to ensure the regime's survival and durability. They exert endless effort and means to penetrate and manipulate political parties, civil society, universities, and the media in order to ensure maximum control over society. Intelligence services can also infiltrate target groups as a means of manipulation by manufacturing false flag violent activities, seeking to further drag them into violence while weakening their cohesion and discrediting them among their grass-roots supporters. Allegedly, Algeria experienced the same manipulation scheme during its civil war in the 1990s, as was claimed by a former defector from the country's Department of Intelligence and Security (DRS). The former official openly accused the DRS of systematically infiltrating and manipulating the Islamic Armed Group (GIA) to commit massacres against civilians.[20] In short, Arab intelligence services have a reputation of being a "state within a state," since "no man can stay in power without their support."[21] The pervasiveness of Arab intelligence services, which is a key pillar of the centralized "security complex,"[22] has contributed not only to shaping state-society relations but also to defining, to some extent, the political identity of the state itself.[23]

Lack of accountability, infringement on people's fundamental rights, and large-scale intrusion into their private lives and all spheres of society are not specific to Arab intelligence services. The abuses of secret services under the then communist totalitarian system are legendary, yet "the problem of evil" has not been completely confronted.[24] Still, there is an abundant literature delving into the culture of repression and impunity that was the principal *modus operandi* of these services.[25] Since 1989, however, post-communist countries have followed generally positive paths of transitions. They have developed a variety of constitutional mechanisms of intelligence oversight and strived to depoliticize secret services and state bureaucracy to prevent misuse of intelligence. One should acknowledge that Western regional organizations such as the European Union (EU) and NATO played key roles in this process as they designed the criteria for former communist countries seeking membership, chief among them the reform of their intelligence services.[26]

In contrast, Latin America experienced the National Security State (NSS) or the so-called "garrison state,"[27] which shaped its history during the Cold War as a security paradigm that was inspired by, and exported from, America in the post-Second World War. The NSS under the United States' global banner of anticommunism orchestrated covert operations through coups and counter-coups, death squads, extrajudicial killings, human rights abuses, and genocidal violence.[28] In this crusade, intelligence turned into a key element of Latin American governments' NSS doctrine. This was clearly corroborated by Mares:

> ... the national security doctrine highlighted the ability of the internal threat to hide among the population and spread the revolutionary message among students, within unions, and to landless peasants. In this context, intelligence became an important tool to fight against subversion. French and US counterinsurgency doctrines emphasized the fundamental importance of timely intelligence to defeat the internal threat. Secret US CIA and Army training manuals were revealed which advocated and trained in the use of abduction and assassination as well as medical, chemical, and electrical techniques during interrogation.[29]

Notwithstanding the tragic implications of NSS for Latin America and the changes within the security sector, the "third wave" of democratic transitions has severely weakened the excesses of secret services. Indeed, countries such as Brazil and Argentina have undergone substantial structural reform of their intelligence services, and have achieved major progress in terms of demilitarization, civilianization, oversight, and accountability as a part of the ongoing democratic consolidation.[30]

In Africa, the intelligence sector has traditionally focused on regime survival aimed at securing the clientage of its Cold-War sponsors. The proliferation of military coups across the continent strongly impacted the structures and purposes of the African intelligence apparatus by highly militarizing their organizations and politicizing their missions. African post-coup military juntas reshuffled these services to maintain loyalty, secure the new regime, and pre-empt further coups.[31] Despite the persistence of "coup syndrome" in shaping Africa's security,[32] many African countries succeeded in overcoming this syndrome by moving away from regime-centric security and developing new democratic norms governing intelligence. One might point to the case of Ghana, where the Security and Intelligence Agencies Act of 1996 (Act 526) governs all of the country's intelligence actors. In this example, intelligence was established by legislation rather than by executive order. It is independent from the military and the police, has a specific role in policymaking processes, and is subjected to civilian democratic control and judicial and parliamentary oversight.[33] In this same vein, South Africa's intelligence services went through immense restructuring (though not without challenges), shifting from an apparatus designed to defend a white minority and supremacist regime in the context of Apartheid to more accountable bodies serving within the framework of a new legitimate constitution.[34] Despite the establishment of the 1994 Intelligence Service Act regulating the country's intelligence community, the heavy legacy of the Apartheid era is still alive in the public mindset. Yet, this charged legacy of violations was "an opportunity to accelerate reforms" and "overcome the difficulties of transformations." [35]

Interestingly enough, intelligence abuses are not a characteristic exclusive to authoritarian regimes, be they in Africa, the Middle East, former people's democracies of Eastern Europe, or former military dictatorships in Latin America. In established democracies such as the United States, intelligence regarding the assessment of Iraqi weapons of mass destruction (WMD) was distorted and politicized, on the eve of the invasion of Iraq.[36] The "Global War on Terror" has shown the public the dark side of American intelligence, which relies on a broad range of ruthless techniques. The CIA has reportedly used waterboarding, rectal rehydration, rectal feeding, confinement, sleep deprivation, sexual humiliation, arbitrary detention in undocumented "black sites,"[37] rendition, abduction to pursue its mission. The 525-page executive summary released by the U.S. Senate Select Committee on Intelligence portrayed these methods as "enhanced interrogation techniques" to avoid using the word torture.[38] The report showed how the organization impeded internal as well as Congressional and executive oversight. It misled the judiciary body and engaged in systematic misinformation campaigns with the media on the torture issue. These cases illustrate the constant tension between democracy and intelligence, freedom and security, and prove that institutional reforms are necessary but insufficient. Without active citizen awareness and support, "rogue elephants" will continue to operate above the law and without any control or accountability.[39]

In the above surveyed literature on intelligence, there is a strong consensus that "most intelligence services have more than information; they have guns as well."[40] Tunisia is not an exception, as intelligence under the fallen authoritarian regime lacked any legal framework and acted in a gray era of lawlessness. This is still the case with the emerging democratic system. The main features of Tunisia's current intelligence services are violations of human rights; brutality by security services; corruption; and opacity with regard to the structures, the legal mandate, the budget, and absence of oversight over the missions and operations. Yet strands in the literature tend to conceptualize intelligence as a subfield of civil-military relations because of the military's hegemonic role in countries in transition to democracy. This is a serious shortcoming in existing investigations of Tunisia's intelligence, as the role of the military within the intelligence architecture is marginal in comparison to the civilian intelligence and security bureaucracy. Thus, it is imperative to research the country's intelligence from the SSR perspective. Although SSR does not substantially differ from civil-military relations, as both focus on state security and civilian control and oversight, it reflects some levels of inclusiveness with regard to "human" and citizen security as opposed to state-regime centered security. The Organisation for Economic Co-operation and Development (OECD) defined SSR as a "security system" that consists of

> **Core security actors**: armed forces; police service; gendarmeries; paramilitary forces; presidential guards; intelligence and security services (both military and civilian); coast guards; border guards; customs authorities; and reserve or local security units (civil defense forces, national guards, militias).

Management and oversight bodies: the executive, national security advisory bodies, legislative and legislative select committees; ministries of defense, internal affairs, foreign affairs; customary and traditional authorities; financial management bodies (finance ministries, budget officers, financial audit and planning units); and civil society organizations (civilian review boards and public complaints commissions).

Justice and the rule of law: judiciary and justice ministries; prisons; criminal investigation prosecution services; human rights commissions and ombudsmen; and customary and traditional justice systems.

Non-statutory security forces: liberation armies, guerrilla armies, private security companies, political party militias.[41]

Reform of intelligence services in Tunisia cannot be addressed separately from the above security puzzle, as it constitutes a critical component of SSR and has the potential either to move reform forward or to fall behind. The OECD inclusion of a variety of actors in SSR shows that the debate on intelligence cannot be confined to the narrow loci of demilitarization, civilianization and professionalization. Like democratization, intelligence reform is a continuing process that involves every political, economic and cultural aspect of society, and intelligence is a dimension that impacts all of these areas.

Chapter Two

Mapping the Evolution of Tunisia's Intelligence and Security Apparatus (1956–1987)

Domestic Intelligence and the Genesis of the State Coercion System

Shortly after independence, Tunisia started building its intelligence and security apparatus. The services emerged within a bloody civil war that pitted Bourguiba against his Neo-Dustūr Party rival, Ṣālaḥ Bin Yūsuf. The two leaders had irreconcilable political visions for post-independence Tunisia. Bourguiba's vision favored dialogue and gradualism as the way to achieve the country's independence. He sought to build Tunisia's future with France, rather than against it, by shaping the country's identity within the framework of radical secularism and Westernization. In contrast, Bin Yūsuf subscribed to the belief that Tunisia should achieve immediate independence and that employing armed struggle was the means by which to attain it. He conceived of Tunisia as a part of its Arab environment where Islam must be the main foundation of its identity. In March 1956, Tunisia became a sovereign state and Bourguiba triumphed over Bin Yūsuf's partisans, most of whom were physically suppressed by the French army that had aligned with the former against the latter. Those who survived were captured, tortured, and executed by Bourguiba's nascent security services backed by both the Neo-Dustūr Party's militia "Vigilance Committees" and the "Dustūrian Youth."[42] The Royal Decision of March 31, 1956 legalized the existence of these militia organizations as "Vigilance Councils," operating under the authority of the Interior Ministry whose aim was to "assist [the Interior Ministry] in securing public order and searching for criminals [namely Bin Yūsuf's partisans]."[43] Less than one month later, the Grand Vizier (Head of the Government) Bourguiba signed a new royal decree that authorized granting the "Vigilance Councils" members financial compensation for their services and inclusion of their salaries and wages into the security personnel payroll of the Interior Ministry.[44] In August 1961, Bin Yūsuf, who was already expelled from the party and stripped of all his political responsibilities, was assassinated in a hotel in Frankfurt by two operatives who were hired by both Bourguiba's party henchman, Bashīr Zarg Laʿyūn, and the Minister of Interior, Tayyab al-Mhīrī. The latter, also known as the "Tunisian Beria" for his iron-fisted oppression of the Yūsufists, was the key mastermind of the murder. This political assassination marked the beginning of the interaction between the state's security services and party apparatus, and their becoming the main players in the country's political arena, which they did through joint, ad hoc security cooperation, and penetration of all segments of Tunisian society.

In newly independent Tunisia, intelligence and security services became interchangeable and inseparable, as the line between them blurred in terms of their authority, such as the power to arrest and search homes, and their areas of responsibility, which included gathering information, conducting criminal investigations, and carrying out operations. Later, these overlapping areas became a constant variable in the ways these services operated under both Bourguiba and his successors. However, the emergence of intelligence and security apparatus in the wake of independence was a reaction to an improvised chain of events rather than the outcome of a rational and planned policy on this matter. In fact, these services were rudimentary and relied on personnel who served under the French colonial rulers. The new Tunisian bureaucracy was short of competent manpower in the security field. Many of the superintendents, chief inspectors, and inspectors were subject to suspicion by the new Tunisian bureaucracy that constantly questioned their loyalty to the post-colonial independent state.[45] French civil servants, like many other Europeans who belonged to the French administration under the protectorate's colonial regime, consented to work in Tunisia's different departments within the framework of "technical cooperation." Some of these French citizens operated within an espionage network that was built by the French External Documentation and Counter-Espionage Service (SDECE) and sought to gather information on the Tunisian leadership, as well as the activities of the Algerian National Liberation Front (FLN). In 1959, the intelligence and security services of Tunisia's Interior Ministry succeeded in debunking the SDECE's "Magenta" network and arrested 14 of its French operatives, some of whom were embedded in the Ministry of Post and Communications, where they tapped phone conversations, including the private ones of Bourguiba.[46] The dismantling of the Magenta network allowed Bourguiba to hit two birds with one stone. Besides flattering Tunisia's nascent intelligence and security services for its awareness and effectiveness, Bourguiba sought to embarrass the French government, and mainly General Charles de Gaulle, showing that despite its independence, Tunisia was not treated as an independent state. Rather, the French intelligence services continued to target the Tunisian government through covert operations carried out against the FLN. Moreover, this operation provided Bourguiba with the opportunity to undermine the FLN's Yūsufist wing by confirming to the Algerian leadership that his support to their cause was unequivocal.

Given the magnitude of the Magenta episode and the complicity of many Tunisian security operatives, the Signals Intelligence (SIGINT) service, attached to the Office of the Minister of Interior and tasked with gathering intelligence by intercepting signals and communications, was subjected to reorganization. Three decrees outlined in this reorganization detailed the status of the personnel, the oath of office, the obligation of secrecy, and the disciplinary measures for breach of confidentiality.[47]

Over the following decade, the intelligence and security apparatus increased its repression to meet the regime's growing challenges. The execution of 11 civilians and members of the alleged military plotters, as well as arrests among their networks followed the December 1962 aborted coup against the regime. The security services, mainly the then infamous State Security Brigade (turned the Directorate of State Security or DSS) under the leadership of Ṭāhir Muqrānī, employed brutal interrogation techniques that included "beating with whip, using electric shocks applied to genitals, cigarettes burning, rape with bottle, waterboarding and the like to extract information and confessions [from the prisoners]."[48]

Quickly, the campaign of repression was extended to include young students returning from Middle Eastern countries and suspected of being Arab nationalist militants in the Yūsufist sphere. Belhassen cogently describes this oppression:

> Since 1963, a wave of arrests hit students. It is one of the rare times when Bourguiba proceeded to preventive, ruthless and systematic repression. The objective of students' torture was to gather information on financing networks. In this specific case, security services took over intelligence from the Tunisian diplomatic missions abroad whose mission was to thwart the formidable means mobilized not only by the [pan-Arab] ideology but also by the Arab states [against Bourguiba regime].[49]

The late 1960s were characterized by the failure of the country's planned economy and increasing civil turmoil, mainly from the leftist students who had started openly defying Bourguiba's authoritarian style. Putting blame for the socio-economic failure on his close collaborators, discarding any criticism, and denying the right for peaceful dissent, Bourguiba resorted to increased coercion. In this regard, the Interior Ministry's security services were reshuffled and upgraded in 1967 without any legal framework outlining the scale or objectives of their reorganization. For the first time since their creation during the wake of independence, the police and the National Guard (NG) were unified into one organization called General Directorate of National Security (GDNS) within the Ministry of Interior and under the command of a general director, a position that was assumed for the first time by al-Ṭāhir Balkhūjah. With the assistance of the United States, Balkhūjah established a new anti-riot police force to remedy the deficiencies of the police during the popular riots in the wake of the June 1967 War.[50] The new unit, the Brigade of Public Order (BOP), played a critical role in the repression of students and organized labor demonstrations during the major crises the country experienced. The BOP used excessive force and employed lethal crowd-control tactics to the point that the security apparatus was named in popular discourse after the general director as "al-Ṭāhir BOP." Balkhūjah, however, acknowledged that one of the most important challenges he faced during his tenure was the need to improve the security officers' analysis and reporting assessment skills. Indeed, he conceded that intelligence reports delivered by both police and NG were politicized, full of misinformation and fallacies, and irrelevant to the policymakers.[51] Notwithstanding assertions of success, Balkhūjah failed to achieve this task for obvious reasons. It is difficult, even impossible, under authoritarian rule to introduce even limited technical "reforms" that would affect the intelligence and security services capabilities, as their primary mission is to strengthen the regime-centered security at the expense of the population. Like their counterparts in the Arab world, Tunisia's security apparatus draws its illegitimate legitimacy from the regime itself by targeting its perceived and imaginary opponents, tailoring intelligence reports that reflect the authoritarian mindset of the leadership, and supporting its preconceived policy.

In the late 1970s and the early 1980s, Tunisia experienced further social unrest. Riots across the country were expressed through arm wrestling between the powerful Tunisian General Labor Union (UGTT) and the government, which was backed by the Dustūrian Socialist Party (PSD), whose involvement was motivated by the policy of party control over the UGTT and its opposition to the workers organization autonomy and strong leadership.[52] The struggle reached its apex on January 26, 1978, during what was known as "Black Thursday." Since the police failed to maintain public order, the government resorted to army intervention, which caused hundreds of deaths and injuries among the rioters. This crucial crisis shook the regime's foundations, threw into question its legitimacy among the population, and even intensified the dissension within the PSD.[53] The crisis also showed the failure of the intelligence services and the security apparatus to better understand and assess society's dynamics and to provide the government with relevant information with regard to policymaking in order to ease tension and prevent social upheaval. Significantly, the crisis brought to the forefront a man of providence, Bin 'Alī, as head of the GDNS, a position that he held for almost two years before being dispatched as ambassador to Poland as a result of his failure to prevent a Libyan-backed insurrection in the mining city of Gafsa in January 1980.[54] The insurgents who came from Libya via the Tunisian-Algerian border spent three weeks in Gafsa before launching their assault, while internal security services failed to detect their presence.

It was only after the "bread riots" from December 1983 to January 1984 that the security apparatus underwent in-depth reorganization. Ironically, such reorganization coincided with the reappointment of Bin ʿAlī as the GDNS's general director who, one year later, was promoted to the rank of Minister of State and attached to the Prime Minister for National Security. Presidential Decree 1244 of 1984 signed by Bourguiba, though not exhaustive, is the most comprehensive decree promulgated to date on the Interior Ministry's organization and the purposes of each one of its departments.[55] Besides the administrative organization of the Interior Ministry, the decree identifies the GDNS and the General Directorate of the National Guard (GDNG) as two separate security entities under the authority of the Minister of Interior. According to Article 11 of the decree, the GDNS has three main missions: "maintaining public order, monitoring borders and foreigners, and investigating all aspects of political, economic, social and cultural fields and reporting on them."[56] Interestingly, the decree issued a legal mandate for the Internal Security Forces (ISF) (i.e., police and NG) for the first time since their creation, with a mission of gathering information on the society. In other words, the surveillance and intelligence penetration of Tunisian society was openly endorsed by the 1984 presidential decree. The GDNS was organized into two major components: personnel and supporting services, and operational and investigative directorates. The supporting services component was organized around the Directorate of Procedures and Legal Studies, Organizational and Work Design Unit, Central Secretary, Service of Social Work, and Coordination Directorate of Joint Services. The operational and investigative component was structured mainly around the General Inspection of the National Security, General Directorate of Presidential Security and Protection of Prominent Officials (GDPSPPO), Operations Room, Directorate for Professional Training, Sub-Directorate of Computerizing, Coordination Directorate of Specialized Services (CDSS), and Coordination Directorate for Public Security (CDPS). The CDSS was considered the GDNS's center of gravity, as it performed all kinds of operations, including intelligence, counterintelligence and covert operations. It encompassed the ruthless DSS (with two sub-directorates and six services); the Directorate of Technical Services broken into two sub-directorates and five services; the Directorate of External Relations divided into two sub-directorates and six services; and the Sub-Directorate of Borders composed of a Travel Documents Service, Service of Aliens, and Service of Borders Control. Article 11 also authorized CDSS to "use operational and active groups as well as cells and networks which their missions and organizations have to be regulated by a ministerial circular." This very controversial branch within the GDNS played a critical role in tracking dissidents, whether inside or outside the country, and it became an extended arm of the autocratic system insofar as it operated within a gray area of intelligence. As for the CDPS, it served at the core of the GDNS's power as one of its key operational pillars. It managed the state security's system interaction with the population on a daily basis. It was divided into four directorates and one sub-directorate, all of which were broken into a variety of services and sub-directorates and operated through territorial units and urban intervention units. These included the BOP Directorate, the Directorate of Regional Police, the Sub-Directorate of Traffic Police, the Directorate of Security District of Tunis, and the Directorate of Judiciary Police. All of the GDNS's directorates, sub-directorates, and services were connected to a plethora of security apparatuses at the regional and local levels.

Initially, the National Guard was created by royal decree on September 6, 1956 as "an organization helping in maintaining security and implementing laws and arrangements under the direct authority of the Minister of the Interior."[57] However, it emerged in the post-independence period as a security organization, drawing together the former *fallāqahs* (i.e., Neo-Dustūr's armed fighters), who used to crack down on the Yūsufists. During the 1960s, the Guard stretched its capabilities from strictly an apparatus of border control to a major element of the internal security system. It was revamped in the same way as the police. In 1984, Colonel Ḥabīb 'Ammār, Bin 'Alī's classmate at the French École Spéciale Militaire of Saint-Cyr, was promoted to the rank of Brigadier and appointed as Commandant of this paramilitary force. Article 12 of the afore-mentioned 1984 presidential decree has defined six principal missions for the GDNG that revolved around "maintaining public order, protecting land and maritime borders, intervening throughout the country as a force of 2nd category,[58] gathering intelligence in the field of politics, investigating the social and economics fields, and providing civil protection."[59] Similar to the GDNS, the GDNG was tasked with an intelligence mission, which consisted of the securitization of the public and private life by widening the traditional range of intelligence activity to the intrusive function of monitoring all aspects of society.

The GDNG was structured around three major branches that included the personnel and logistics services, the NG staff, and operational directorates. The personnel and logistics services were organized around the Secretary, Service of External Relations, Directorate of Joint Services, Directorate of Studies and Professional Training. The NG staff was assigned to a Chief of Staff assisted by the NG Commandant. The Chief of Staff's missions were to coordinate between all the directorates and the units by issuing orders and directives and to ensure their execution by these services. The operational component was broken into Operations Room, two major directorates, and one sub-directorate. First, the Directorate of Territorial Units was organized around three major sub-directorates that included the Sub-Directorate of Public Security with three services; the Sub-Directorate of Traffic Police with four services; the Sub-Directorate of Borders with three services; the Sub-Directorate of Security District of Tunis; and the Sub-Directorate of Intervention Units that comprised of Logistics and Command Service, Service of Specialized Units, and the Service of Critical Infrastructure. The second operational directorate was the Directorate of Special Units organized around a Logistics and Command Sub-Directorate broken into a Logistics and Command Service, Service of Armored Vehicles, National Guard Special Unit (NGSU) also known as Commando Special Unit, and Aviation Service. The third operational element, namely the Sub-Directorate of Intelligence and Investigations (SDII) divided into three services. Like the CDSS, the SDII was charged with widespread surveillance, monitoring, and harassing political dissidents. Later this sub-directorate was turned into a

Directorate of Intelligence and Investigations (DII) while its three services became sub-directorates. It should be noted that all of the GDNG's organizations were formalized at the regional and local levels.

The Ministry of Interior and its main security directorates experienced a series of opaque reorganizations under Bin ʿAlī's rule amending decree 1244. None of the decrees governing these restructurings have ever been published, as will be documented later in this study. The sophistication and complexity of Tunisia's security apparatus, which came as a result of the 1984 presidential decree under Bourguiba, was rivaled only by the rise of the country's intelligence capabilities. The revamped intelligence and security machine was first applied against the Islamists, mainly the members and militants of the Islamic Tendency Movement (MTI) in the 1980s. Bourguiba's use of oppression and his rejection of any compromise with the Islamist awakening precipitated the demise of his reign. Most importantly, Bin ʿAlī, who spearheaded this bone-breaking battle, never lost sight of nurturing intelligence relations with Tunisia's Western partners, mainly the United States. This obsession was clearly described by Eric Rouleau who served as the French Ambassador to Tunisia in the mid-1980s while Bin ʿAlī served as Interior Minister:

> General Bin ʿAlī was an enigma to the French. Under various pretexts, he declined to meet with French officials such as the ministers Edith Cresson and Pierre Bérégovoy–and, more surprisingly, the head of the French counterespionage, i.e., the General Directorate for External Security (DGSE), General René Imbot. The ultimate humiliation occurred when the French Defense Attaché, Colonel (then General) Yvan de Lignières informed me that Mr. Bin ʿAlī boycotted him for weeks while he was meeting regularly with the Tunis CIA station chief. … The information, was of course, passed on to Paris through a secret cable to a limited number of senior leaders in the Quai d'Orsay and the Élysée palace. … It was only the day of my final mission in Tunisia, and during a courtesy visit that I paid to Mr. Bin ʿAlī, that he asked me in raging anger why do I consider him as a CIA

agent ... Bin ʿAlī quoted word for word the confidential ca-
bles that I sent to the Quai d'Orsay ... The French embassy
was not spared by his espionage network.[60]

The ascending power of domestic intelligence and intricacy of
the security apparatus were matched only by the weakening and
inefficiency of the military intelligence. The latter was the poor
cousin of the country's security architecture.

Powerless Military Intelligence against Foreign Threats

Ironically, it was during the last years of the monarchy's rule that
the installation of the military intelligence's basic infrastructure
was endorsed. Ṭāhir Bin ʿAmmār, then the Grand Vizier (Head of
the Government) of Muhammad VIII al-Amīn Bey, the last king
of Tunisia, signed the Royal Decree of January 19, 1956, authorizing the building of a "military intelligence communications system
tasked with the defense of the [country's national] territory."[61] The
communications system was designed to connect Tunis to both
the neighboring areas of Bizerte and other locations next to the
Tunisian-Algerian border, mainly the village of Ghar ad-Dimaʾ.[62]
The choice of these locations was not coincidental, as France held a
strong military presence in the northern part of the country and the
FLN and its armed wing, the National Liberation Army (ALN), had
established their headquarters in the region of El-Kef. Thus, this
new military intelligence device sought to monitor the French military presence around Bizerte and ultimately to keep an eye on the
FLN-ALN's activities. Later, Grand Vizier Bourguiba signed two
other royal decrees that established the organization of the Ministry of National Defense, which included a National Defense Council (NDC) presided over by the Head of the Government[63] and were
followed one month later by the creation of the Tunisian Armed
Forces (TAF).[64] These two decrees said absolutely nothing about the
organization, status, or missions of the new military intelligence.
Meanwhile the NDC sought, according to Article 6 of the January
19 decree, "to acquire the necessary means that would enable Tunisia to assume its responsibilities in the fields of defense and security."[65] Besides the permanent membership of the major depart-

ments' heads (i.e., defense, interior, foreign affairs and finance), a Consultative Military Committee (CMC) was instituted by the Royal Decree of May 3, 1956.[66] The CMC was comprised of TAF's various components and was tasked with the mission of providing the NDC with defense and security expertise.[67] In 1970, the composition of the NDC was amended and this institution passed under the authority of the Prime Minister, while the CMC was removed as a result of this reorganization.[68] However, during Bourguiba's rule, the NDC did not play any role in the country's national security and fell quickly into destitution.

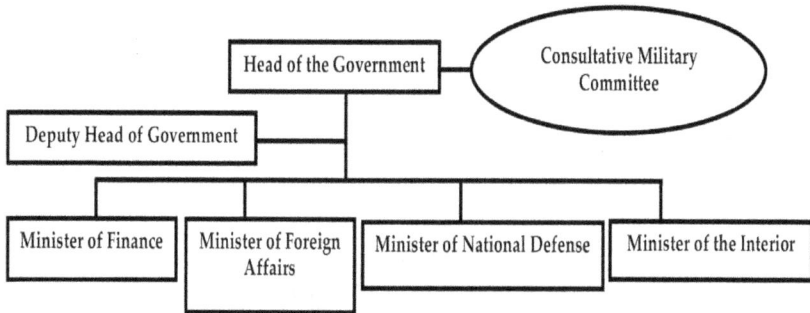

Figure 1: Tunisia's National Defense Council (1956)
Royal Decree of May 3, 1956, *OJT*, n° 36, May 4, 1956, 823–824.

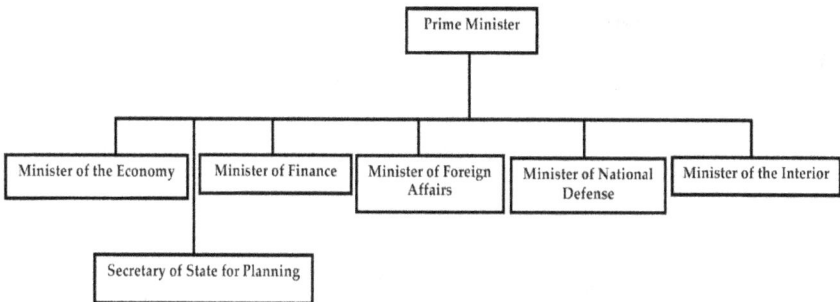

Figure 2: Tunisia's National Defense Council (1970)
Decree n° 61, February 21, 1970, *OJRT*, n° 10, February 24, 1970, 218.

Shortly after independence, an embryonic military intelligence apparatus under the leadership of Captain Ḥassān Bin Lanwar was established within the Ministry of Defense, also known as Military Security (SM),[69] and later attached to the Office of the Minister of Defense.[70] Upon completing a Military Intelligence Officer Basic Course of the U.S. Army Intelligence Center and School at Fort Holabird in the United States, Bin ʿAlī was appointed a chief of the SM in 1964, a position that he held until 1974.[71] Bin ʿAlī owes this appointment to his powerful father-in-law, General Muhammad al-Kāfī, the then Army Chief of Staff. Bin ʿAlī was a politically reliable officer of dubious military competence, and lacked any understanding of the military intelligence's primary role. Military intelligence should provide a sound assessment of risks, external threats, and opportunities. Military intelligence should also assist policymakers in defining the country's national interests, and in developing a relevant national security policy and national and military strategies that suit the missions of the TAF. In contrast, Bin ʿAlī turned the SM into a tool tasked with monitoring the TAF's internal security and with gathering information on the private lives of military personnel, "including his comrades, with the purpose of blackmailing them when Ben Ali thought it would be to his advantage to do so."[72] In fact, the SM became another internal security apparatus operating in parallel with those within the Interior Ministry. Bin ʿAlī's long tenure as chief of the SM made it difficult for his successors to question the rules he established.[73]

Captain Ḥassān Bin Lanwar	...–1964
Colonel Zayn al-ʿAbidīn Bin ʿAlī	1964–1974
Major General Abū-Bakr Bālmā	1974–1984
Brigadier ʿAmmār al-Kharījī	1984–1985
Brigadier Yūsuf Bin Slīmān	1986–1988

Figure 3: Tenure of Military Intelligence Chiefs (1964–1987)

However, the missions of the SM, for the first time since its founding, were explicitly clarified under the tenure of Colonel (then later Major General) Abū-Bakr Bālmā, who served as head of the organization for almost ten years. Article 11 of 1979 Presidential Decree defined the SM's mission as one that would "ensure the protection of military personnel, documents, equipment and installations against any interference and to promote the acquisition and exploitation of military intelligence. In addition, the SM [was] tasked with handling and preserving the archives of the Ministry of National Defense."[74] According to the same decree, the SM's internal organization was defined by an undisclosed ministerial decision.[75] Notwithstanding, the SM's security priorities directed toward Algeria and Libya were perceived as "a potential threat to Tunisia because of sharp differences in political orientation and Algerian and Libyan military superiority,"[76] which the military intelligence directorate failed to anticipate and ultimately prevent the 1980-Gafsa attack. The failure to assess and understand the threats within Tunisia's geopolitical regional context became a constant characteristic of the SM. To remedy the country's military intelligence deficiencies, Bālmā sought to provide the TAF with allegedly more efficient means of support from the U.S. Department of Defense by signing an agreement with the U.S. Defense Mapping Agency (DMA). The DMA agreement was aimed at establishing "cooperation and mutual assistance in mapping, charting, and geodesy, as well as the exchange of maps, charts, aerial photography and related data."[77] Brigadier General ʿAmmār al-Kharīji, Bālmā's successor, saw further organizational inefficiencies when the PLO headquarters, located at Hammam-Lif (12 miles south-east of Tunis), were bombed by Israeli warplanes in October 1985. The Tunisian military learned that its friendly relationship with the United States and France, and their alleged security "umbrellas," were useless and inoperable when it came to protecting Tunisia from external aggression. Adding insult to injury, the SM did not anticipate such an attack, nor did the air force retaliate. The frustration of Tunisian officers about the powerlessness and "blindness" of their military intelligence deserves to be emphasized.[78] A retired high-ranking officer who commanded a mechanized infantry regiment, in the early 1980s in the northwestern part of the country, near the

Tunisian-Algerian border, expressed such a sentiment:

> When I was in charge of this command for almost four years, I was kept in the dark about the capabilities of the Algerian military deployed in the other side of the border. During my entire tenure, I never received from the SM or the G2 (Military Intelligence Directorate of the Army) any information with regard to the equipment, readiness, training and deployment of the Algerian troops in the area of my responsibility. I spent my time guessing about the Algerian capabilities by relying on open sources. I know that Algeria's 5th Military Region has a joint command, with units organized in a Russian fashion but with undeniable air and land superiority. As I studied in Western military schools the Russian doctrine at the operational and tactical levels, I was able to understand how such forces could be organized. However, I was unable to assess their operational capabilities, their posture or their intentions.

This weakness of the military intelligence, as outlined above, was matched only by the obsession of the SM with monitoring the TAF and reporting on them—as it was anecdotally highlighted by the same officer:

> One day, I received a memorandum from the SM indicating that a corporal serving under my command was caught by SM's plainclothes operatives, selling sheep in the town's weekly market, located in the area where the regiment is based. Such case requires disciplinary measures. I summoned the corporal to my office and asked him about the reasons behind his act. He argued that his low income of the equivalent of US$125 monthly allowed him to barely survive with a family of six members. He pointed out that the police and NG agents were getting rich from illicit activities and contraband with Algeria. He concluded from his perspective that it is better to sell sheep outside of the office hours than selling the ammunition of the regiment.[79]

Likely, it is the toothlessness of the military intelligence that convinced Bin ʿAlī not to give any importance to the TAF's attitude toward his "medical coup d'état" of November 7, 1987. The TAF's leadership, including the head of the SM Colonel (then Brigadier) Yūsuf Bin Slīmān, were informed about "what was already a fait accompli," rather than being involved in staging the coup.[80] This bloodless coup paved the way for the institutionalization of Bin ʿAlī's police security state. He then made the dual intelligence and security functions the foundation of his new regime.

Chapter Three

Bin ʿAlī's Myth of Absolute Security
(1987–2011)

Domestic Intelligence and the Obsession with Security Control

The first act taken by Bin ʿAlī in the aftermath of Bourguiba's ousting reflected the regime's security priorities to the core. In November 1987, he established a National Security Council (NSC) that canceled out the NDC. The NSC was tasked with the mission "to collect, study, analyze, and assess all information and security data related to national security within the realms of domestic policy, foreign affairs, and defense policy in order to protect the state's internal and external security and consolidate its foundations."[81] It was chaired by the president and included as permanent members the Prime Minister, the Minister of State for National Defense, the Minister of Foreign Affairs, the Minister of the Interior, the Deputy Secretary of the Ministry of the Interior, the Chief of Staff of the Armed Forces, and the Director of SM, also known as General Directorate of Military Security (DGSM). The NSC met once a week or as needed. In November 1988, the Presidential Decree 252 gave the GDNS's General Director the status of permanent member in the NSC.[82] In accordance with this decree, the NSC was provided with a permanent Secretary General in charge of preparing the work sessions' agendas, drafting the minutes of meetings, following-up on the council's decisions, and keeping the president informed about the implementation of the NSC's decisions. The NSC also experienced an in-depth reorganization that created seven specialized committees (i.e., intelligence, national defense, civil defense, food security, transportation security, infrastructure security, and energy security) to help the president in his decision-making. Presidential Decree 1195 of 1990 attributed the committees' chairs to different government departments. Unsurprisingly, the Intelligence Committee that included representatives from the Interior Ministry, the Defense Ministry, and the Foreign Affairs Ministry was placed under the direction of the Interior Ministry.[83] Such a decision illustrated the priorities of the new leadership in giving the Interior Ministry a central and exclusive role in the field of intelligence. Though this monopoly of intelligence enabled the regime to control large segments of the Tunisian society during Bin ʿAlī's reign, it actually weakened the regime. The regime was relying on one source that manipulated and politicized intelligence. The Interior Ministry's monopoly over the intelligence sector provided its services with relatively strong autonomy and power that goes with their activities. It created a dependent relationship between the regime and its services, and it allowed the former to rely on the latter to secure its survival. This monopoly encouraged the intelligence services of the Interior Ministry to operate with unrestrained and unchecked power to entertain the regime's fear. The fear of falling to potential coups persuaded Bin ʿAlī to take some preventive measures as a part of coup-proofing mechanisms. Less than three months after his November 1987 coup, Bin ʿAlī separated the GDP-SPPO, also known as the Presidential Security Guard (PSG), from the Ministry of Interior. The PSG that was in charge of security for the presidential palace on the night of November 6–7, 1987 was pulled out of action by the NGSU under the leadership of Ḥabīb ʿAmmār, the coup's main executor. Presidential Decree 250 of 1988 established the GDPSPPO as an autonomous directorate within the presidential office and under the direct command of the president himself.[84] Later, this apparatus under the leadership of General ʿAlī Ṣariātī turned into a force of 3,000 armed personnel, equipped with highly sophisticated military hardware, and organized into subunits with different purposes. As the ultimate shield of the regime, the GDPSPPO was provided with its own system of intelligence, the Presidential Security Sub-Directorate of Intelligence (PSSDI), tasked with gathering intelligence critical for the regime's security. Given the regime's broad definition of security, the PSSDI was allowed to gather information deemed sensitive from all the governmental departments, including the Interior and Defense Ministries.[85]

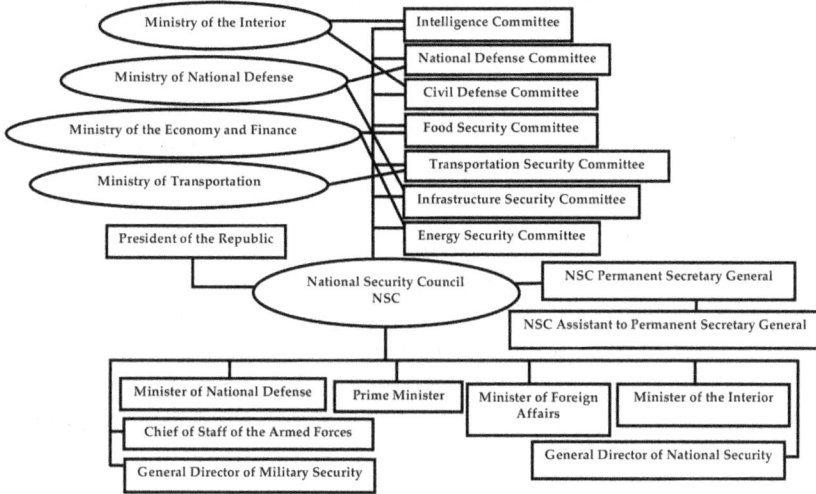

Figure 4: Tunisia's National Security Council
Decree n° 1195, July 6, 1990, *OJRT*, n° 48, July 20, 1990, 965–966.

Bin ʿAlī regime was obsessed with security and control over everything and sought absolute centralization. This obsession was facilitated by the acquiescence and indulgence of Tunisian elite to what was considered the regime's security imperatives as a bulwark against the potential recurrence of the Algerian scenario. The latter was used as a pretext to strengthen the regime's social control through the party's monitoring mechanisms, such as *lijān al-yaqaẓah* (Awakening Committees) and *lijān al-aḥyāʾ* (Neighborhood Watch Committees).[86] In addition to these committees, Presidential Decree 147 of 1993 established *al-Muwāṭin ar-Raqīb* (the Watchdog Citizen) that was tasked with spying on the administration. The same decree allocated a monthly allowance of 100 Tunisian Dinars (TND) to TND150, which an amendment increased to between TND170 and TND250 in July 2006, to the "watchdog citizen" for his/her service.[87] Ex-political prisoners, especially those among the al-Nahḍah rank and file, were subjected to daily harassment and pressure from the intelligence services that sought to recruit them as informants. These practices ranged from intimidation and oppressive security surveillance, to preventing them from obtaining employment and resuming their normal lives, to threats targeting their family's members.[88] In the same vein, Tunisian expatriates living overseas—mainly in France—were subjected to large-scale surveillance through complex informant networks operated by the General Directorate of Specialized Services (GDSS) and benefitted from the complicity of the French government.[89] In Tunisia, the number of wiretaps had increased from around twenty in the mid-1980s—with half of them devoted mainly to foreign diplomatic missions—to almost 5,000 in 2004.[90] Moreover, all the appointments within the Interior Ministry (i.e., superintendent, principal superintendent, director, general director) were subjected to Bin ʿAlī's own discretion and signed by presidential decrees.[91] Although Bin ʿAlī was addicted to the daily intelligence reports submitted to him by the GDNS and GDNG's general directors, he relied mainly on specific reports from the GDSS[92] within the GDNS, the GDNG's Directorate of Intelligence and Investigations (DII),[93] and the PSS-DI. Rather than contributing to diversifying the sources of intelligence, this reliance on those services resulted in centralization of assessments and managing informants. This dependence further led to the manipulation of intelligence, which generated mistrust between services and failed to produce professional assessments. The lack of information sharing between different services and the vertical siloing of these services weakened their understanding of the intelligence dynamism and its inherent risks and uncertainties. Nearly every directorate within the Interior Ministry had its own connection with the Carthage palace and Bin ʿAlī's inner circle (i.e., Bin ʿAlī's in-laws, and his wife Leila Tarābulsī's clan). Most of the Interior Ministry's senior security officials were part of a corrupt framework and connected to Bin ʿAlī's entourage. These officials provided Bin ʿAlī's associates with protection for their businesses in return for financial benefits. Security officials who worked in the border areas were to some extent involved in cross-border illicit trafficking and had to share some of their illegal income with their superiors in Tunis in order to keep their positions. Corruption that was once pervasive within the security sector under Bourguiba became a structural problem under his successor.

President of the Republic

General Director of Presidential Security

General Directorate of Presidential Security and Protection of Prominent Officials
(GDPSPPO)

Presidential Security Sub-Directorate of Intelligence
(PSSDI)

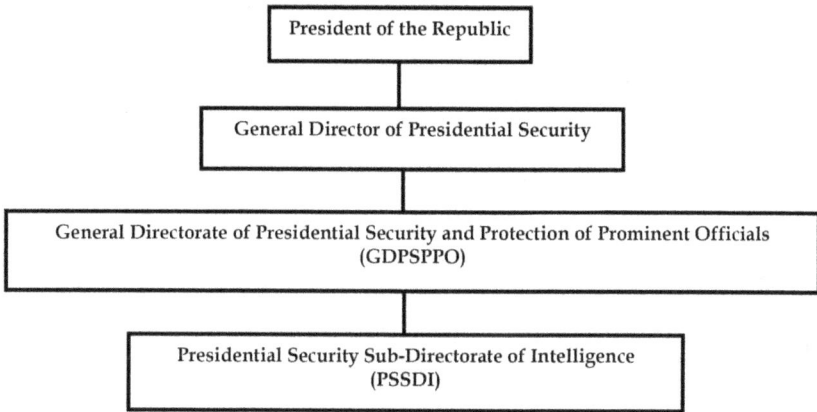

Figure 5: Presidential Security Sub-Directorate of Intelligence
(1988 to present)

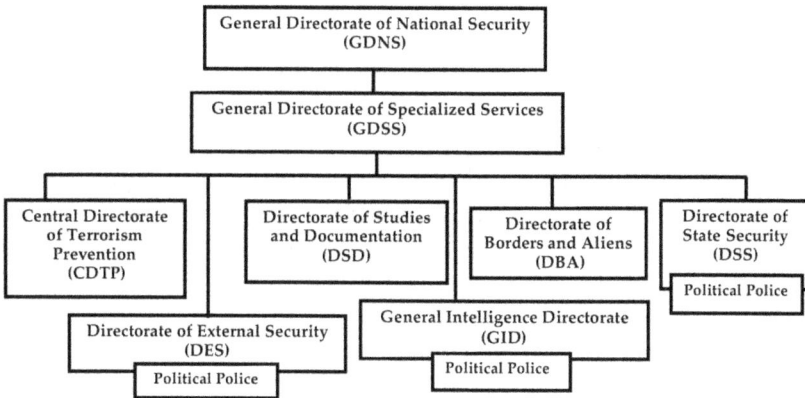

General Directorate of National Security
(GDNS)

General Directorate of Specialized Services
(GDSS)

Central Directorate
of Terrorism
Prevention
(CDTP)

Directorate of Studies
and Documentation
(DSD)

Directorate of
Borders and Aliens
(DBA)

Directorate of
State Security
(DSS)

Political Police

Directorate of External Security
(DES)

Political Police

General Intelligence Directorate
(GID)

Political Police

Figure 6: General Directorate of Specialized Services (1984–2011)

```
┌─────────────────────────────────────────────┐
│   General Directorate of the National Guard  │
└─────────────────────────────────────────────┘
                      │
┌─────────────────────────────────────────────┐
│   Directorate of Intelligence and Investigations │
│                   (DII)                       │
└─────────────────────────────────────────────┘
                      │
    ┌─────────────────┼─────────────────┐
┌─────────────┐ ┌─────────────┐ ┌─────────────────────┐
│ Sub-Directorate of │ Sub-Directorate of │ Sub-Directorate of Intelligence │
│ Investigations     │ Counterterrorism   │ (SDI)                           │
│ (SDIV)             │ (SDCT)             │                                 │
└─────────────┘ └─────────────┘ └─────────────────────┘
```

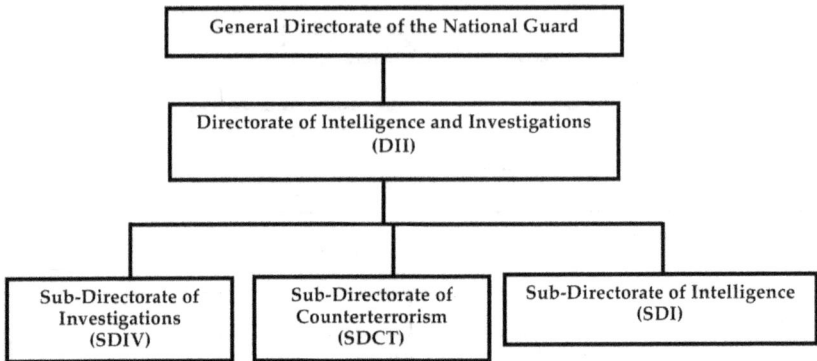

Figure 7: Directorate of Intelligence and Investigations (1984 to present)

Bin ʿAlī's securitization of power gained in scale. His presidential convoys became a major constraint for people who found themselves stuck in traffic. These convoys were protected by heavy security measures that included deployment of security forces in addition to the PSG, plainclothes police, and helicopters. The main roads were blocked to regular traffic in order to secure maximum safety for these convoys. Disarmed policemen from different services were dispatched along different potential itineraries that could be used by the presidential convoy for the purpose of deception. This security obsession was a substitute for Bourguiba's policy that revolved around a subtle manipulation of Tunisia's political arena, a mix of coercion and compromise, and a kind of direct communication and contact with the population through his constant trips across the country. Bin ʿAlī's progressive securitization of power centralized the country's political system around the presidential circle that relied mainly on police control and repression. These trends became tangible after the failure of political overture and the return of heavy-handed repression against the al-Nahḍah movement in the spring of 1991. In the summer of 1991, the political climate degraded further when the TAF were hit by an arbitrary purge of 244 officers—commissioned and non-commissioned—who were falsely accused of conspiring against the regime. They were arrested based on fabricated intelligence and delivered by the DGSM to the Ministry of Interior's DSS where they withstood torture and psychological abuse in what was known as the Barraket al-Sahel affair;[94] a forged conspiracy staged by the then Minister of Interior ʿAbdullah Qallāl. Qallāl sought to "decapitate the army," in the words of the late Minister of Defense Ḥabīb Būlaʿrās.[95] In the aftermath of this "decapitation," the Defense Ministry was compelled to keep the Interior Ministry informed about any military exercise, the size of the forces involved, their area of deployment, the timeframe, and the type of the ammunition employed. Then the Interior Ministry would deploy its informants to verify that the military operated accordingly. This tragic affair saw the "shifting balance from the Defense to the Interior Ministry during the early phases of Ben Ali's rule" in terms of budget, influence and prestige in such a way that in the wake of the 2010–11 uprising, the Interior Ministry budget was 1.4 times that of the Defense Ministry.[96]

It is not within the aim of this book to survey all the abuses committed by the security services under Bin ʿAlī's rule, as these have been thoroughly documented by dozens of reports published by human rights organizations.[97] However, the increasing oppression went hand in hand with the constant reorganization of the ISF. These reorganizations were characterized by a strong opacity about the structure, legal regulations, role, and functions of these forces. Indeed, all the legal texts of these successive reorganizations have been kept secret.[98] The level of opacity of the internal security sector is met only by the absence of its accountability and its omnipotence over society. Although there were an estimated 9,000 associations categorized as civil society actors dominated by state controlled organizations, they operated more as government-organized non-governmental organizations (GONGOs)—a government tool that sought to maintain control over civil society, promote the government's propaganda discourse on democratization and its commitment to human rights, and discredit the work of dozens of independent civil society actors. However, GONGOs were not able to operate freely without the complicity of the Interior Ministry and the so-called political police, as was highlighted by a general director within the Interior Ministry:

Under the fallen regime, the Interior Ministry did not have a special organization called *police politique*. However, hundreds of policemen were dispatched to almost all the department's directorates and services in charge of monitoring all categories of associations, to harass and intimidate human rights activists, to pressure the rebellious, to dissolve those who sought to politicize their activities (i.e., criticizing the regime for the lack of civil liberties and violations of human rights), and to empower those (i.e., GONGOs) who promoted the regime's interests. The fact that these associations must obtain a formal authorization from the Interior Ministry as proof of their registration, this procedure provides the political police and other intelligence services with tremendous data about the organizations' members, their funding, their usefulness, and their foreign partners. This precious data is a kind of barometer that allowed Bin ʿAlī regime to better gauge the society-mindset and to keep it under control.[99]

The former French ambassador to Tunis Yves Aubin de La Messuzière confirmed this assessment. He wrote:

In March 2005, I was summoned to the office of the new Minister of Foreign Affairs, ʿAbdulbāqī Harmāssī who during our meeting raised the issue of the French diplomats' interactions with members of the opposition and civil society actors. He pointed out a lunch between the embassy's political counselor Jean Hannoyer and Mr. Najīb Shābbī, the Progressive Democratic Party's secretary general. The minister identified the name of the restaurant. I strongly protested and told the minister: "I have the impression that you are reading a police report. It is unacceptable ... I know that my colleagues and I are under permanent surveillance. At least, we now have a very clear evidence of such surveillance."[100]

The surveillance of foreign diplomats and journalists, mainly those from EU countries, allegedly for their criticism of the regime's human rights record, was well documented.[101] Moreover, the few Arab journalists who dared to inquire about and report on the country's human rights situation were treated even more harshly as they often lacked effective support from international human rights activists while their Western colleagues enjoyed strong mobilization under the same circumstances. They faced constant harassment and intimidation from intelligence operatives. In November 2006, a journalist of the Algerian daily *El Watan* who interviewed Munṣif al-Marzūqī, a human rights activist then living in his residence in Sousse (87 miles south of the capital), was closely followed by plainclothes policemen during his travels across the country while his hotel was surrounded by police and his "actions and words spied on, and his movements monitored."[102] While de La Messuzière devoted 21 pages of his book to such activities,[103] the U.S. embassy in Tunis acknowledged "the strict covert and overt Tunisian surveillance against foreign missions."[104] However, this surveillance was relatively soft by the country's surveillance standards, as was explained by a retired officer who ran the Tourist Security Directorate within the NG:

> Beyond securing the main tourist infrastructure across the country, a mission that we had difficulty performing, my service was tasked with spying on the legally recognized members of the opposition. The effectiveness of such mission required some basic rules. My operatives started identifying the meeting locations, mainly cafes and hotels visited by our targets. Once the location was identified, contact with the managers or owners was initiated. Very specific questions were asked on the frequency of these meetings, time, and even beverages ordered. Managers and owners were often cooperative but were unable to provide us with further information. Then, we dispatched some of the operatives to verify the gathered information and identify the waiters working in these spaces. Afterwards, and based on clandestine photos taken of the waiters, we started checking their backgrounds. Based on collected information obtained from their background check we tried to identify the most vulnerable waiter (i.e., family problems, financial debts...). Once our potential informant was selected, we approached him with specific requests. With or without the manager's

consent, we assigned the waiter to the table of our targets and tasked him with the specific mission to report to us the content of their discussions. We drafted our intelligence reports based on these reports.[105]

The increased surveillance power of the country's coercive security and intelligence apparatus was extended to monitoring Internet activities. Dissatisfied with the stifling press freedom, Bin ʿAlī regime established the Tunisian Internet Agency (ATI) in 1996. Acting under the authority of the Ministry of Technology and Communications, the ATI was tasked with operating the country's Internet infrastructure and managing the Internet Service Provider (ISP). As a state-controlled gateway, ATI centralized Internet infrastructure and efficiently filtered all connections running to and from ISPs. In fact, the ATI became quickly a tool of cyberspace control by assisting the Interior Ministry's GDNS in tracking, monitoring, infiltrating, and censoring cyber-dissent websites, as well as breaching their email accounts, thus turning the country into one of the main notorious "Internet enemies" constantly listed and denounced as the most "repressive in the world."[106] A number of high profile activists and Tunisian out-of-country opposition websites such as the National Council of Liberties in Tunisia, *Réveil tunisien*, *Tunisnews*, and *Takriz* came under constant aggressive cyber-attacks. In addition, sites of international human rights organizations such as Amnesty International, Reporters Without Borders, and the Committee to Protect Journalists, were inaccessible from Tunisia thanks to "surveillance products of U.S. origin, such as SmartFilter technology created by McAfee and used in Tunisia since 2002 to block access to parts of the Internet."[107]

Conscious of the powerful social and political force of the Internet, Bin ʿAlī's autocratic rule sought to muzzle online freedom of speech by targeting bloggers. The first victim of such policies was Zuhair Yaḥyāwī, the founder and administrator of an online unauthorized blog *TUNeZINE*, which was known for its dissent activities and sarcastic criticisms of the regime. Yaḥyāwī not only organized an online referendum in which he invited Tunisians to cast their ballot on whether or not Tunisia was "a republic, a kingdom, a zoo, or prison,"[108] but he also hosted on his blog an open letter from his uncle and dismissed judge Mukhtār Yaḥyāwī addressed to Bin ʿAlī, in which the judge strongly criticized the absence of an independent judiciary in Tunisia. Arrested and jailed for "spreading false information and misusing telecommunication lines," Yaḥyāwī was "tortured in pre-trial detention and served 18 months of his sentence before being released. In March 2005, at the age of 36, he died of a heart attack."[109] Another case that ended less tragically is that of lawyer Muhammad ʿAbbū — a member of the then-unrecognized political party, Congress for the Republic (CPR) — who published an article in *Tunisnews* in August 2004 in which he "denounced torture in Tunisian prisons, noting a parallel with the abuses endured by Iraqi prisoners in Abu Ghraib."[110] In an article posted on the *Tunisnews* website in February 2005, ʿAbbū expressed his strong disagreement with the decision of the Tunisian government to extend an invitation to the then Israeli Prime Minister Ariel Sharon to participate in the World Summit on the Information Society held in Tunis in November 2005. ʿAbbū denounced the decision in powerful words by drawing a striking parallel between Bin ʿAlī and Sharon: "the two [men] have common characteristics: they are both military, both experts in repression of uprisings and both are afflicted with family members involved in crimes of corruption. What's more, they are in perpetual quest for international support."[111] Soon after, ʿAbbū was abducted by plainclothes policemen from the streets of Tunis and handed a three-year prison sentence for "insult to the judiciary," "inciting the population to break the country's laws," and "publishing articles inclined to disturb public order."[112] Repression continued to curb both cyberspace freedom of expression and information. In 2002, young Internet users — most of them in their early twenties — from the southeastern coastal town of Zarzis were convicted and sentenced to long prison terms based on fabricated confessions extracted from them through torture.[113] They were accused of using the Internet to join a militant group connected to al-Qaʿida and planning to wage terrorist attacks across the country "although no evidence was ever presented in support of this claim. Their use of the Internet was the pretext for their conviction."[114] In 2004, their sentences were slightly reduced from 19 years to 13 years in prison.[115] Released in 2005, the Zarzis group was denied the right to education, subjected to constant police harassment, and put under house arrest until the fall of the dictator in 2011.

This wave of suppression targeting cyber-activists was coupled with the development of a repressive and broad arsenal of legal ammunition for excessive regulation of the Internet. Presidential Decree 501 of 1997 stated the "definition of the terms and conditions for the implementation and the provision of valued-added such as Internet" is the most coercive in the legal regulatory framework.[116] It required all ISPs to obtain a formal license from the Ministry of Communications, valid for three years and renewable, in accordance to the regulations (Art. 7). Also, the applications to operate an ISP service had to be submitted to a "Commission on Telecommunications Services" chaired by the Minister of Communications and include representatives of the Defense and Interior Ministries, as well as other members assuming positions related to communications and information technology (Art. 8).[117] In accordance with Article 14, "each ISP must appoint a director responsible for the content of the web pages and sites that the ISP has to host in conformity with the Press Code."[118] Additionally, providers were required to submit the list of their customers to the public operator (ATI). Similarly, the use of encryption services must be subject to approval from the Minister of Communications (Art. 11, paragraph 2). The ISP provider was not permitted to introduce any change on the provided service unless the Minister of Communications authorized it (Art. 10). The Ministerial Decision of September 9, 1997 regulating the "conditions for encryption use in the provision of value-added telecommunication services," further intensified control over cyberspace by requesting from people or ISP providers, who seek to use service encryption, "to obtain a prior authorization to establish and use encryption" (Art. 2).[119] Applications thus had to be submitted to the Ministry of Communications with the "required keys to decrypt the data" (Art. 3). The encryption authorization was granted by the Minister in Charge of Communications only after "consulting the Commission on Telecommunications Services" and "on an individual basis, non-transferable to a third party, except by express authorization of the Minister in Charge of Communications" (Art. 4).[120]

Subsequently, the introduction of the 2001 Telecommunications Code widened state control and monopoly over all communications sectors that included cyber-activities, networks, and infrastructures.[121] ISPs were required to collect data on their customers (i.e., names, physical addresses, and phone numbers) (Art. 14), to release their customers' data for security purpose (Art. 15), and to make all technical, functional, financial, and computational data of each of their networks and services available to the Ministry in Charge of Communications. In addition, they had to be "receptive to national defense and public security requirements" (Art. 26), even though those requirements were not defined.[122] Article 63 established the National Telecommunications Authority (NTA) in charge of settling disputes over interconnection and network access. The NTA was also tasked with reviewing the disputes related to conditions of joint use of existing networks (Art. 67). Settlement sessions were confidential and not accessible to the public (Art. 69). The Code defined the terms and conditions under which the state could concede some communication services to private operators. However, the Defense and Interior Ministries were the only entities authorized to validate the transfer of any communication assets to private actors (Arts. 52 and 56). Article 47 instituted the National Frequency Agency (NFA) in charge of "preparing a national plan of radio frequencies, monitoring the technical conditions of radio equipment, and supervising use of frequencies in accordance with provided authorizations."[123] Thus, existing private radio broadcasters, formerly not subjected to official regulation, faced a five-year term of imprisonment if they did not acquire prior authorization from the NFA (Art. 82). The same sentence was imposed on anyone who had no prior authorization from the agency while operating public or private communication networks, who providing communication services through satellite or phone (Art. 82), and to anyone who operated encryption software or services without disposing of a prior authorization (Art. 87).

The passing of the 2004 law on the creation of the National Agency for Information and Security (NAIS) strengthened this liberticide legal framework.[124] The NAIS was tasked with the protection and audit of networks and information systems. In case of attacks targeting to country's computer information systems, infrastructures, and computer networks, the agency, after obtaining approval of the Minister responsible for Information Technology, would be required to shut down the Internet system while coordinating the appropriate protective measures with the Defense and Interior Ministers (Art. 11). In fact, the Tunisian government abusively used this article to simply block the users' Internet in an attempt to control civil society activists and monitor their electronic communications.

Interestingly, the tremendous resources squandered by the regime in monitoring and putting cyberspace under siege would have been more valuable had they been invested in beneficial projects, thus providing job opportunities to the most disenfranchised country's graduate youth. Most significantly, Bin ʿAlī regime engaged in cyber arm-wrestling with the rights of citizens to free access to online information, to voice their criticism of government policies, and to expose the regime's abuses, which was a losing battle anyways. Not only did this paranoid approach divert funds from improving networks to upgrade surveillance or censorship capabilities, but it also failed to crackdown on the online insurgency that strongly delegitimized the regime and contributed to its demise. Its Internet firewalls were breached because the techniques used to access censored websites were advancing as quickly as those used to perform Internet censorship, rending the censorship tools increasingly inefficient. Diana clearly highlights this lost battle in a similar context:

> History teaches us that dictatorships are afraid of words, so dictators censor books, imprison, torture and kill the 'producers of word.' But the word is spread from heart to heart, from mind to mind, overcoming any censorship and any prison.[125]

Notwithstanding the magnitude of police security and state control under Bin ʿAlī's rule,[126] Tunisia's domestic intelligence and security services experienced obvious failure—a failure caused by the inability of these services to understand regional dynamics—as Algeria's civil war was used to curtail Tunisians' civic and political freedoms, shifting "the country into a vast surveillance camp."[127] In February 1995, Algerian GIA militants attacked a NG forward station located in the Tamaghza area close to the Algerian border just minutes before the Ramadan fast was to be broken.[128] The assault ended with the beheading of seven NGs. The NGs were then stripped of their military fatigues, boots and rifles, and their bodies were abandoned. The assailants stole the NG's vehicle and some food supplies. Through its propaganda tool, the Tunisian External Communication Agency (ATCE),[129] Bin 'Alī regime tried to hide the story from the national and international media, attempting instead to portray the event as a traffic accident. Moreover, the kidnapping of two Austrian citizens in February 2008 in Tunisia, who were freed nine months later in Mali,[130] was another example of the intelligence failure. At the time, the embarrassing silence of the Tunisian government after the crisis began was explained by its concern regarding the seven million tourists flocking to the country and the risk that its image as the "safest" place in the region would be tarnished. There is no doubt that the location of the kidnapping was significant as well. The fact that it occurred within Tunisian territory begs the questions (regarding the December 2006-January 2007 armed confrontations around Soliman's city): How were the infiltration operations carried out by the Tunisian jihadist group? How were trainings conducted and weapons smuggled across the Algerian border? And how did they establish such an organized network? Undoubtedly, Soliman's group had opted for violence based on newly prepared guerilla tactics, a *modus operandi* largely developed by the Algerian Islamist insurgents in the early 1980s. The group's reliance on irregular warfare methods was at the heart of the matter and was what had justified such a "panic in high places of the Tunisian regime," in the words of an officer who was involved in the operations.[131] Additionally, the ease with which the Soliman's group had recruited militants and carried out its operations despite the infamously close surveillance of the security services in Tunisia had shaken the Bin 'Alī regime. Already in April 2002, following a deadly attack on a synagogue in the island of Jerba, for which al-Qa'ida claimed responsibility, the Tunisian regime tried to convince its people (as well as its Western partners) that the attack was an isolated incident. The regime was later forced to retract that statement under pressure from Germany and France, both of which lost citizens in the attack.[132] Contrary to the dominant discourse that emerged in the post-Bin ʿAlī era—a discourse that sought to depict the rise of insecurity and violence as a direct consequence of the disorganization of the country's intelligence and security apparatus—the above security events demonstrated that these services were ineffective prior to the fall of the regime in January 2011. Indeed, the services failed due to their lawlessness and their systematic reliance on brutality and torture, which also created an environment ripe for such a lack of security.

Military Intelligence Blindness: Policing and Failing the Tunisian Armed Forces

The military intelligence was not substantially different from their ruthless domestic counterparts. The DGSM gained prominence in the aftermath of Bin ʿAlī's coup, particularly during the Barraket al-Sahel affair, during which time the then-senior military officers (i.e., Army Chief of Staff General Bin Ḥassīn, Military Intelligence Chief General Farza, GDNS's General Director General Ṣariātī) and senior security officials (GDSS's General Director ʿAlī Ganzūʿī, DSS's Director ʿAzzadīn Janayyaḥ) were identified by the victims as the primary individuals responsible of the TAF's purge. However, it was mainly under Farza's leadership that the military intelligence became another internal security service similar to those operating within the Interior Ministry but tasked with policing the TAF.[133] His successors further strengthened this pattern.[134]

Given that Bin ʿAlī was an artillery officer by training but never commanded any military unit, the DGSM became, after his 1987-coup, an artillery officers' fiefdom. As an artillery officer, Farza ran the organization for a decade. Although the artillery consisted of only three regiments within the army, which was dominated by the infantry, most of the artillery officers' behavior was arrogant toward the infantry officers. They had a Napoleonic complex.[135] Farza developed a very sophisticated system of surveillance within the TAF through informants and wiretaps. Most of the defense ministers who served during Farza's tenure were monitored by the DGSM while their secretariat staff was infiltrated by military intelligence operatives, as will be highlighted later. Although security officers' functions were institutionalized at the level of regiments

Brigadier Yūsuf Bin Slīmān	... −1988
Brigadier Muhammad Hādī Bin Hassīn *	1989–1990
Brigadier ʿAlī Sariātī	1990–1991
Major General Hafīz Farza	1991–2001
Senior Colonel Rashīd ʿAmmār**	2001–2002
Brigadier Muhammad al-Muaʾddib	2002–2009
Brigadier Ahmad Shābīr	2009–2011

Figure 8: Tenure of Military Intelligence Chiefs (1987–2011)
* In 2001, he retired with the rank of Lieutenant General as an Army Chief of Staff and appointed by Bin ʿAlī as GDNS's general director in 2002.
** In 2013, he ended his career because the age limit with the rank of Lieutenant General as TAF Chief of Staff.

and brigades, respectively known as S2 and B2 and responsible for security within the army, it was believed that many military personnel (i.e., officers and NCOs) operated undercover on behalf of the DGSM. Tunisian defense attachés did not escape security rules. They were forbidden to use emails in communicating with their counterparts in the countries where they were assigned. Rather, they were required to use the fax machine connected to the Defense Ministry in Tunis. The ministry could therefore access the communications of any Tunisian defense attaché around the world. The Interior Ministry used similar encryption techniques to monitor the Tunisian embassies' activities abroad. Senior Colonel Mukhtār Hashāyshī, then Defense Attaché at the Tunisian embassy in Washington, D.C. (2000–2003), pointed out to me in one of my visits to the U.S. that his Pentagon counterpart strongly recommended the use of email rather than fax since faxes had been phased out in the Pentagon. The defense attachés performed their duties as DGSM's correspondents abroad and had to write a monthly report on the security, political, and economic situation of the country of their residence. However, those who served in Western capitals had easier access to information on Tunisia from open sources than their colleagues dispatched to other countries. Thus, they were inclined to self-censor by not communicating such available information to the DGSM to avoid jeopardizing their careers, especially if the information was not in line with the regime's positions.[136] The DGSM's surveillance system was expanded to military higher education institutions, such as the National War College (NWC), Command and Staff College (CSC), and the National Defense Institute (NDI). At these institutions, professors' lectures were recorded, videotaped, and screened for security purposes. Intelligence officers could easily report on any professor if they thought that the content of the lecture or the topic addressed was incompatible with the department's official line. Given the civil war in Algeria, the topics of low-intensity conflicts and guerillas were forbidden from the curriculum. As a professor at the NWC (1998–2004), I had to argue with the then NWC Commandant, Senior Colonel ʿAzmī Maḥjūb (1996–2000)—who himself had written a memorandum to the DGSM—for the need to discuss the changing nature of the threats in order to get approval to incorporate these topics into the academic program. The DGSM's obsession with policing the TAF reached unbearable levels when Senior Colonel Tawfīq Lakhwā, then the director of NDI and a well-educated, talented and wise military leader, was dismissed overnight from his command after having disseminated an academic article to NDI's 2000-person class in which the author, an American scholar, criticized the rise of Tunisia's police state.[137] These class participants were senior leaders from different governmental departments that included the Presidency and Ministries of the Interior, Defense, and Foreign Affairs. Later, NDI's personnel discovered that some of these participants had reported Lakhwā.

Though the DGSM succeeded in keeping the TAF at bay, it failed to provide forces in the field with relevant intelligence about potential risks and threats. The DGSM's incompetence dangerously impacted the security of the country and jeopardized the safety of deployed forces. The obvious incompetence of the military intelligence was thoroughly reported by a retired high-ranking officer who then was a Brigade Commander, whose account merits extended attention:

In the late 1980s, I was a commander of, at that time, the Territorial Saharan Brigade (BTS), it was the strongest and largest military unit within the TAF controlling a third of the country. The area of responsibility and deployment of this unit covered almost the entire south of the country. The BTS was made-up of almost 7,000 military personnel and organized around 2 territorial regiments, 1 motorized infantry regiment, 1 artillery regiment, 1 support/logistics regiment, 1 armored reconnaissance regiment and 1 intervention battalion. The posture of the brigade was directed to confront any military action coming from Libya. On September 29, 1991, I was flying from Remada (south) to al-Aouina Air Force Base in Tunis to attend a session at the NDI. When my military jet landed, I saw the then Army Chief of Staff, General Hādī Bin Ḥassīn waiting for me. I understood that something serious had occurred somewhere in the south while I was flying to Tunis. He informed me that an Algerian military force made an incursion into the region of Hazoua located at the Tunisian-Algerian border. This force accompanied bulldozers from Algeria's National People's Army (ANP) Corps of Engineers that destroyed a road and temporarily occupied the area of Hazoua. He ordered me to fly immediately and inquire about the situation. Hazoua is a border village in which some agricultural projects had been developed by the Tunisian government for the benefits of its inhabitants. It is separated by less than 19 miles from the city of Tozeur. However, Algeria disputed Tunisia's sovereignty over Hazoua. While I was flying, I thought that the incursion could be a preliminary diversion operation for a large-scale attack that could force us to move our prepositioned forces from the border with Libya to the Algerian border. Such movement could have facilitated any attack from Libya, with ease, especially since Qadhdhāfī's tone became more aggressive during that time toward his Tunisian and Egyptian neighbors as a prelude to the imposition of United Nations embargo on him resultant of the Lockerbie bombing. I strongly recommended to the Army Chief of Staff not to move any forces from the south and to provide

me with units from the north to organize a defense around
Hazoua. The incursion was a surprise for us as we never
imagined that the Algerians who started fighting a ruthless civil war will make such a move. However, DGSM's
failure to inform us about Algeria's intentions was obvious.
When the incursion occurred, I only had a sergeant and 9
soldiers in Hazoua who were forced to withdraw. When
my helicopter landed, I was surprised to see that the ANP
engaged more than 40 armored personnel carrier (Russian
made BTRs) and field artillery. The deployment of such a
heavy force had one main objective which was to intimidate
us since the occupation of Hazoua did not require such im-
pressive force. However, I knew if the ANP was able to deploy this force in the first echelon as a reconnaissance force,
it meant for me that it would have been able to engage its
available reserve in the area which could be 4 to 5 times the
initial deployed force. I spent 25 days on the ground living
in a wrecked vehicle. During this timeframe, I was able to
organize defense positions with a task force of 400 soldiers
equipped mainly with American TOW anti-tank missiles,
French MILAN anti-tank missiles, 12.7 mm machine guns,
and mortars. During this period of escalation, I did not re-
ceive any valuable intelligence from both the DGSM and the
G2 (Military Intelligence Directorate of the Army) about the
intentions of the Algerians and the movement of their forces
in the area. In other words, the DGSM and the G2 kept us in
the dark as if they were hit by a kind of paralysis. Though
the crisis de-escalated at the political level, I felt for the first
time in my whole career that the military intelligence had
failed us and left us barefaced in the fog of war. I still carry
a bitter taste from this crisis.[138]

Later, General Khālid Nizār, the then Algerian Minister
of Defense explicitly admitted in his memoirs that he personally mounted and organized the whole operation by engaging a
large- scale-force, likely a brigade, under the command of General
ʿAbdul-Ḥamīd Jawwādī, the then commandant of Algeria's 4th
Military Region. He asserted that the objective of the operation was

not to invade Tunisia "nor to express any bellicose attitude toward the great Tunisian people who helped us tremendously during the Revolution."[139] Rather, he aimed at responding to what he called "the Tunisian provocations," while blaming the Tunisian government for "refusing to divide Hazoua between the two countries."[140]

The Hazoua crisis perfectly illustrated not only the blindness of Tunisia's military intelligence but also the divergence of priorities between those of the DGSM and those of the TAF. The DGSM policed the Tunisian military rather than providing them with appropriate assessments of real and potential threats at the national and regional levels to better prevent and ultimately mitigate any crisis. DGSM's surveillance of the TAF was a key characteristic of Bin ʿAlī's tenure. The Hazoua crisis cost the late Defense Minister Ḥabīb Būlaʿrās his position, though he was appointed Parliament President in October 1991. Būlaʿrās, a well-versed politician, strongly recommended that Bin ʿAlī seize upon this crisis by modernizing the TAF. He warned Bin ʿAlī that he would be unable to manage further humiliations inflicted upon the TAF or predict their consequences on the political stability of the country. As a last stand before leaving his office, Būlaʿrās invited the then Commander of the BTS, accompanied by the Army Chief of Staff, to a meeting where he congratulated the former for his commitment and dedication to his duties, though he acknowledged that the means placed at his disposal for the mission were limited. However, Farza, whose services failed to help the army better manage this crisis, was confirmed in his position and shortly after was promoted to the rank of Major General. The message sent by Bin ʿAlī to the TAF was clear: the regime was grateful to those who contributed to policing the TAF and securing the regime regardless of whether or not they were competent.

It was only when Dālī al-Jāzī, a jurist and one of the founding fathers of the Tunisian League of Human Rights and its first Secretary General, was appointed as the Minister of Defense in January 2001 that Farza definitively lost his position. Al-Jāzī took over the Defense Ministry and brought with him his personal secretary from the Ministry of Higher Education. He suspected that the secretariat staff of his predecessors in the Defense Ministry had been infiltrated by the DGSM. Thus, he was determined to stop such illegal practices. As Farza lost his spy network and any insight about the activities of the new minister, he decided to cross a "red line" and tasked one of his operatives with searching the minister's office. The intrusion into the office of al-Jāzī occurred on a Sunday, a non-work day. On Monday morning, when al-Jāzī entered his office, he realized that it had been searched and that someone had tried to force open the drawer of his desk. He knew that Farza's services were behind such an illegal act. He summoned the general to his office and confronted him with the facts. Farza denied that he had anything to do with the intrusion, though it was evident that he did, as the protection of the ministry's buildings legally fell under the DGSM's responsibility. Then, al-Jāzī ordered a review of the CCTV camera in his office and caught the intruder, a DGSM operative. Notwithstanding Bin ʿAlī's commitment to support men who played a key role in the survival of his regime, the Brutus of Carthage regretfully sacrificed General Farza following the discovery.[141]

The demise of Farza's era led to a limited reorganization of the DGSM. In March 2002, al-Jāzī issued Ministerial Decision 562 to create a Permanent Committee for Monitoring Armament (PCMA).[142] Article 1 assigned the direction of the PCMA to an officer with a rank of colonel and placed the committee under the authority of the DGSM. Article 2 authorized the PCMA to hold regular monthly meetings. The innovation that came out of Article 3 approved the appointment of civilians within military intelligence for the first time since its founding in the wake of the country's independence. In fact, among the nine members composing the PCMA and those who represented the Army, Air Force, Navy, Military Medical Directorate (MMD), and the Directorate of Armament and Ammunitions, two members were professors at higher education military institutions. Given al-Jāzī's academic background, he likely thought that the presence of academic faculty would contribute to more pragmatic approaches and original analyses from the committee. The PCMA was tasked with submitting to the Minister of Defense a monthly report in accordance with Article 4. Notwithstanding the vagueness of the committee's mission, its generic name suggested that al-Jāzī had deliberately intended to broaden it, seeking to incorporate any issue that he would have considered critical for the country's national security. In this regard, the PCMA was tasked with studying the regional arms race and investigating the new military acquisition and procurement among Tunisia's neighbors. The PCMA worked on assessing the evolution of the regional geopolitical context in shaping Tunisia's security, while only external factors were considered decisive in affecting the country's stability. The PCMA delved into Libya's WMD program and even explored potential regional consequences of a power vacuum if Qadhdhāfī were to die. Despite foreign and domestic challenges, the durability of the Libyan regime had never been questioned and most of the scenarios assumed that its continuity likely would have been secured by the Brother Leader's informal inner circle. Given the growing risk of biological and chemical attacks in the aftermath of 9/11, the PCMA recommended providing TAF units with NBC capabilities and the creation of the Crisis Intervention Team for First Responder (CITFR) to address both natural and human-made disasters. With regard to the NBC capabilities, al-Jāzī agreed that the shortcomings in terms of equipment and training were salient within the TAF. Due to the scarcity of resources allocated to the Tunisian military, he decided to devote some of these resources to the formation, preparedness, and readiness of an NBC platoon that later, if the means allowed, would be turned into a company or perhaps a battalion. As result, an NBC platoon was created and quickly expanded into the size of a company and attached to the Army Corps of Engineers, whose main mission was to intervene in situations of terrorist attacks or human disasters involving chemical or biological hazards. The CITFR was promptly established and placed under the command of the MMD. During the 2011 Libyan civil war, the CITFR was deployed in the forefront of the country's mobilized means and effectively succeeded in handling the waves of refugees crossing the Tunisian-Libyan border, regardless of the logistical nightmare.

Despite some of the PCMA's valuable achievements, the departure of al-Jāzī from the Ministry of Defense in November 2004 negatively impacted the committee's activities, which rapidly fell into destitution. From the beginning of the PCMA's inception, the DGSM was reluctant about al-Jāzī's decision to appoint its members from outside the military intelligence, not to mention the presence of civilians within the committee. The DGSM felt most of the topics addressed by the PCMA should be tackled in-house, not only for alleged security breaches,[143] but mainly to gain control of the security agenda, priorities and recommendations that could leverage the minister's decisions. Rather than seeing the PCMA's activities as a complement or a competitor challenging the DGSM's overwhelming conformism, the committee was considered a rival structure trying to interfere in the military intelligence's reserved domain. Indeed, elements within the military intelligence asserted, without tangible proof, that PCMA's assessments overlapped with DGSM's work, as well as with the reports submitted by the Tunisian defense attachés residing in the neighboring countries. Moreover, the crisis of confidence that punctuated the late al-Jāzī's relationship with the DGSM erupted subsequent to the dismissal of Farza and characterized the then Minister of Defense's four-year tenure. Likely, this was another reason behind the abortion of al-Jāzī's attempt to alter the military intelligence *modus operandi*.

Given the state and evolution of Tunisia's post-independence intelligence and security services analyzed above, to what extent could this coercive apparatus that operated for more than five decades within the realm of lawlessness, abuses, and opacity be amenable to reform in the post-uprising era? The following chapter tries to explore this challenge.

Chapter Four

Lost in Political Transition: The Dilemma of Intelligence Reform

Internal Intelligence and Stalled Reform

Although the 2011 popular uprising was directed against Bin 'Alī's political system and his entourage, it primarily targeted the core symbols of his regime: the oppressive security institutions for which the fallen dictator justified the use of live ammunition against the demonstrators as a "legitimate right of self-defense."[144] While the fall of the autocratic regime shook its coercive apparatus, it did not revolutionize this key sector in the same way that the country's political institutions experienced democratic transition in the post-authoritarian era. Some progress has been made with regard to the Interior Ministry's withdrawal, including its monitoring and interference in the electoral process, the amendment of the ISF legal framework with regard to arrest and detention powers, and the inscribing of human rights provisions into the ISF regulations. However, opacity has remained the main feature of the security sector. There is still a lack of transparency around the fundamental requirements for effective reform, such as the organizational charter of the Interior Ministry, and the roles, missions, and legal mandates of different security services.[145]

The disbanding of the dreaded DSS and the deactivation of political police did not remove the veil of opacity.[146] Rather, this entrenched opacity has been strengthened in the post-uprising era with the amendment and adoption of new, unpublished legal texts regarding the structures, size, organization, and operations of the ISF.[147] The United Nations Human Rights Council Special Rapporteur further emphasized this lack of transparency:

[He] highlighted the lack of publicly available information in which several security organs of the State performed, including the secrecy surrounding decree n° 246 of 15 August 2007, which purportedly clarified the structure of the internal security forces under the Ministry of the Interior, but was not a publicly available document. ... The Special Rapporteur regrets the fact that he was not provided with a copy of the decree during his visit despite the assurances of the Minister of the Interior to the contrary. ... The Special Rapporteur regrets that he has been unable to establish the existence, nature of and content of a "Decree n° 246 of 15 August 2007" during his two missions, which only confirmed his previous findings: namely that it was this secrecy that was an important element that contributed to the shield of impunity behind which the actors of the Tunisian security apparatus under the Ben Ali regime could operate. In transparent States, all functions and powers of the security organs are regulated by publicly available laws. Such transparency prevents not only the creation of myths about what these agencies do but also ensures their accountability when these agencies commit illegal acts.[148]

Later, this obsession with secrecy led the United Nations Human Rights Council Special Rapporteur to strongly criticize the lack of tangible reform of the security legislation, which "remains unpublished," and constitutes "an obstruction to the process of transition."[149] The United States also voiced its growing criticism regarding the entrenched opacity in Tunisia's security sector governance despite the American indulgence toward client regimes in developing countries like Tunisia that traditionally benefit from U.S. security assistance. Seemingly, the United States' main reproach revolves around the reluctance of Tunisia's Ministry of Interior to communicate "details on its budget and number of police personnel, limiting the ability to provide assistance."[150]

This absence of transparency was aggravated by the deterioration of the relationship between the security sector's personnel and citizens as a result of the abuses inflicted with complete impunity by the former onto the latter under the fallen regime. This lack of

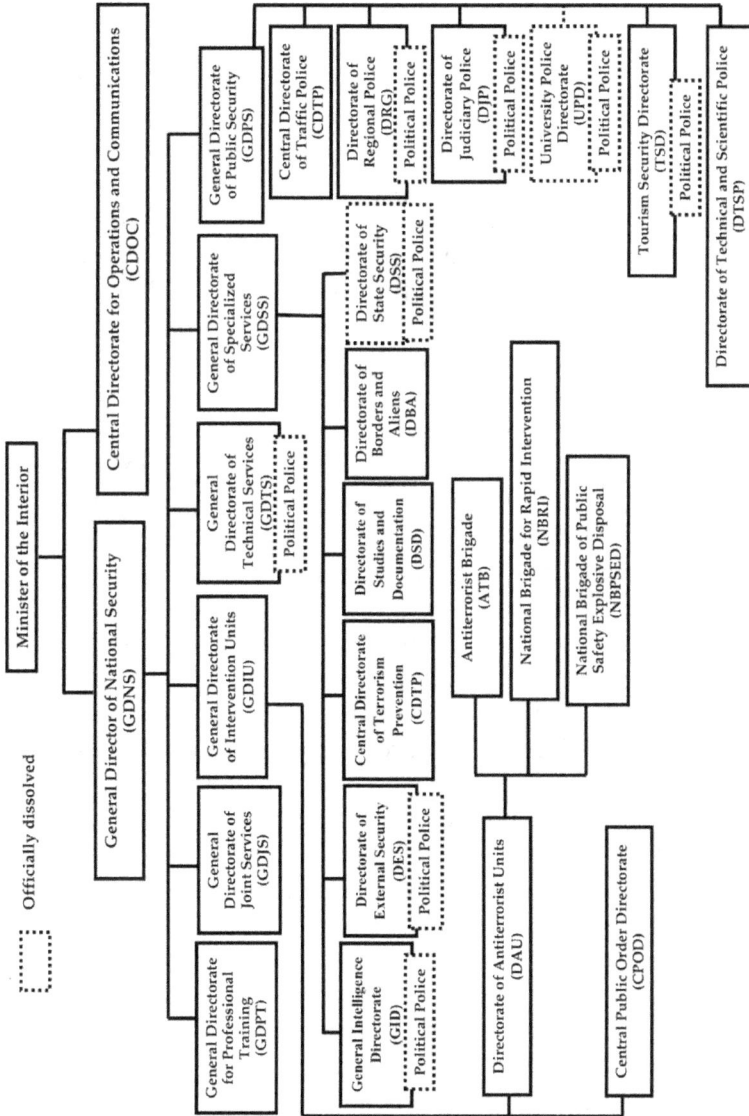

Figure 9: Post-2011 GDNS organizational chart

trust between most of the Tunisian people and their ISF led some members within the security sector to seize the window of freedom while promoting the idea of victimhood. Rather than questioning their role as perpetrators of oppression, they equated themselves with victims who suffered gross human rights violations at the hands of security services. This new discourse was translated into practice through the establishment of security unions. The unions' purposes have expanded beyond promoting professional rights to meddling in the country's security affairs to the point that they have been considered in the words of the Minister of the Interior Hādī Majdūb, "a major hindrance to any serious attempt of reform" and "a salient way of politicization of the security sector."[151] This growing politicization, though inherited from Bin ʿAlī's era, has become a constant factor in the post-uprising security debate with the rise of terrorist attacks, political assassinations, and insecurity across the country and the region. Some of these unions, "believed to be manipulated by occult corrupted business lobbies,"[152] intimated to the media the existence of a "parallel security apparatus" working for al-Nahḍah.[153] While it is not easy to confirm these assertions, one can argue that the al-Nahḍah led-coalition government appointed individuals to many Interior Ministry key positions who were known for their close ties with the Islamist leadership. These politicized appointments could be explained by the Islamist movement's obsession with thwarting any threat emanating from the department responsible for their oppression under the autocratic rule. Most importantly, these unions strongly condemned the decision to disband the DSS, echoing many senior security officials who considered such a decision a "criminal" act.[154] To this day, these unions keep arguing about the security vacuum created as a result of this decision and allege that the DSS played a pivotal role in gathering intelligence on all kind of threats to the country's security. However, the exaggerated role of the DSS in the national security architecture has been assessed by a general director within the Interior Ministry who served in the 2000s within the Directorate of External Security (DES) in Europe:

> It is true that most of the directorates within the GDSS focused on major security threats that would have negative

impact on the country's stability. Although the major task of the DES is the exchange of information with its intelligence foreign counterparts, most of the data gathered and exchanged during Bin ʿAlī's tenure focused on Islamists movements. This data was not restricted to groups who relied on violence and represent a threat to the country but also included those which made the choice to engage peacefully in politics (i.e., al-Nahḍah). This kind of intelligence privileged by the fallen regime's security priorities was exclusively communicated to the DSS through the GDSS general director. It allowed the DSS to update its own data on the Islamists inside Tunisia and likely to amplify the perceived threat for its own agenda. However, the DSS had its own sophisticated informers' networks also known as Human Intelligence (HUMINT), which penetrated the country's social fabric as well as the bureaucracy. The recruitment and motivations of informers discredited the value of the information. The demise of the regime severely disorganized these networks. As a result, informers who were mostly forced into these networks regained like other Tunisians their freedom and sought to dissociate themselves from the most heinous and feared security apparatus in the country. Moreover, the DSS's reliance on torture and heavy-handed treatment distorted the processed information. Thus, rather than the DSS dissolution decision per se that affected the country's security, it was more the nature and the performance of this organization that bore the germs of its demise. Such organization that operated for more than four decades within the realm of lawlessness cannot survive to the fall of an authoritarian regime. Indeed, accountability, transparency and oversight are at odd with its narrow security lexical.[155]

Needless to say, the structural dysfunctions, outlined above, regarding the way information was collected causes one to deeply question the legitimacy of the intelligence and security services activities. While distorted information was inherent to the intelligence services under Bin ʿAlī regime, there is a tendency for information to be overlooked in the post-uprising era. Indeed, intelligence and security apparatus failed to provide protection to the late member of the National Constituent Assembly (NCA), Muhammad Brāhmī, who was assassinated by an Islamic State's operative on July 25, 2013. The DES received an intelligence warning from the CIA on July 14—eleven days before his murder occurred—about a potential threat against Brāhmī's life. Two months later, the then Minister of the Interior Lotfī Bin Jiddū confirmed receiving the warning and acknowledged the failure of his services in a statement before the NCA and confirmed by the media outlets.[156] Most of the analysis attributed this failure to the disorganization endured by the intelligence and security apparatus in the post-uprising, as well as to the political crisis and security pressure in a country experiencing a fragile transition. However, the aforementioned interviewee is more nuanced about the failure of the intelligence services to detect and prevent Brāhmī's murder:

> The official discourse attributed the failure in protecting Brāhmī to technicalities issues, chief among them the lack of capacity, weak inter-services coordination, and inadequate organization. However, this discourse overlooked the fact that Tunisia's intelligence apparatus functioned as a tool for regime survival and stability along with increasing politicization for more than five decades. Thus, these services are still suffering from this syndrome and the focus on technicalities alone cannot overcome it. The key challenge these services face is more about the difficulty to operate a paradigm shift from state-centric security, which was equated with the securitization of the regime in power and the prominent role of the political police within the society to the human-citizen security approach.[157]

Yet, these "technicalities" have been at the core of failed "reform" attempts initiated in the post-authoritarian era. In fact, this vision is enshrined in the so-called *White Book*, which was drafted by a team of experts led by Lazhar ʿAkarmī, the then Delegate to the Minister of the Interior in Charge of Reform, and released in 2011.[158] Rather than promoting the principles of democratic governance of the security sector (i.e., democratic control, accountability, transparency and oversight), the book focused on strengthening the operational capabilities of the security sector to overcome the country's security challenges (i.e., terrorism, organized crime, illegal migration, money laundering, etc.). The book even recommended an increase in size of the ISF and a redirection of foreign security assistance to improve the ISF's operational efficiency. The document briefly stressed the need for the creation of a national intelligence agency tasked with collecting and analyzing information critical to the country's national security. While it raised the basic principle of oversight, it did not explain how the intelligence might best be controlled (i.e., executive, legislative, and judicial powers; and control mechanisms incorporating media, civil society actors and citizens), nor did it highlight the legal framework that would regulate intelligence activities. This narrow approach to reform was "more of an over-securitization in reaction to risks and threats rather than a professionalization [of the security sector] seeking to align with international standards."[159] It was facilitated by both the country's hybrid security conditions and the obvious indifference of the NCA to enforcing democratic oversight over security. In fact, most of the NCA's members "lack[ed] professionalism [and expertise] in terms of drafting security legislation or oversight [of] intelligence agencies" and "suffer[ed] security illiteracy."[160] This trend was further consolidated with the ratification of the 2014 constitution, in which intelligence was one of "the missing-link[s]" of the constitutional process.[161]

Since 2014, the consecutive governments have failed to initiate any comprehensive reform of the country's security complex, nor have they asserted any democratic control over "The Invisible Government."[162] There are serious critical impediments to the democratization of Tunisia's internal intelligence. These include: the authoritarian legacy entrenched within the intelligence security apparatus; the negative implications of the "bargained competition" between al-Nahḍah and the fallen regime's loyalists;[163] the lack of security professionalism and competence; the pervasive corruption within the security sector; the absence of political vision for sustaining reform momentum and prioritizing its objectives; the obsession of secrecy often used to cover up wrongdoing and abuses; and the opacity with regard to the structure of intelligence services, missions, and budget;[164] among other factors. Furthermore, the growing mistrust between security sector actors, the public and political elite, the continued reliance on torture for the purpose of abusing citizenry,[165] the restrictions on fundamental liberties,[166] and the socio-economic post-transition anxiety have relegated the intelligence and security reform to the bottom of the list of priorities for policymakers. The absence of effective mechanisms and structures governing the field of intelligence are palpable in the way security crises have been managed.[167]

Meeting Dates	Events
February 2, 2012	President Munṣif al-Marzūqī chaired a security meeting in the aftermath of a series of clashes between security forces and Salafist jihadist militants in Bir Ali Bin Khalifa.
September 15, 2012	President al-Marzūqī chaired an "exceptional" security meeting after Tunisian demonstrators stormed the U.S. embassy on September 14.
February 17, 2014	President al-Marzūqī chaired a National Security Council (NSC) meeting to inquire about the security situation following a 20 hour-gun battle between security forces and Islamist insurgents in the northern suburb of Tunis (i.e., district of Raoued).
May 29, 2014	President al-Marzūqī chaired an NSC meeting to inquire about the security situation in Mount Ash-Shaʿnabi after gunmen killed four policemen in an attack on the Interior Minister's home Lotfī Bin Jiddū in Kasserine on May 28.
June 28, 2015	President al-Bājī Qāʾid al-Sabsī chaired an NSC meeting in the aftermath of the mass shooting attack that targeted tourists in the resort town of Sousse on June 26.
November 26, 2015	President Qāʾid al-Sabsī chaired an NSC meeting in the aftermath of a suicide attack on PSG bus on November 25.

Figure 10: Selected Reactive Security Meetings in Response to Recurrent Attacks

The above-listed attacks illustrate the absence of intelligence as an informational function in helping the decision makers better understand, detect, anticipate, and ultimately, prevent threats. There is no intelligence supervisory body; such a body should be subjected to executive, parliamentary, and judicial oversight, in charge of both daily coordination of the activities of all intelligence services and ensuring the dissemination of accurate information to the appropriate actors. This absence proves the amateurism and unpreparedness of the political leadership in dealing with the country's emerging threats. This amateurism translated into bitter fiasco during the 2015 Sousse terror attack that the intelligence services failed to detect and prevent. Even worse, the UK inquest into the Sousse attack portrayed the security services response as "at best shambolic, at worst cowardly."[168] The investigation solemnly condemned the reckless and unprofessional behavior of some members of security forces who "fainted through terror and panic."[169] It critically accused one officer of "having taken off his shirt to hide the fact he was an officer."[170] The inquiry concluded that Tunisian security services "had everything they required to confront the gunman and could have been at the scene within minutes," however, their "delay [to intervene] was deliberate and unjustifiable."[171]

Needless to say, the nonexistence of an intelligence code of ethics that emphasizes legitimacy, competence, integrity, morality, professionalism, a defined scope of activity, intellectual independence, and impartiality in informing policymakers, among other ethical principles, is at the heart of Tunisia's domestic intelligence crisis. Thus, it was not a surprise that the aforementioned listed security crises were met with improvisation and incompetence, leading the European Parliament to solemnly request "the need to reform the country's intelligence services while respecting the rule of law and human rights conventions."[172]

Desperately seeking to minimize the successive oblivious failures of its intelligence apparatus, the Tunisian government exaggerated the role played by its security services in the raid that targeted Khālid Shāʾib (alias Loqmān Abū Ṣakhr), the Algerian head of the ʿUqbah ibn Nāfiʿ group, at the end of March 2015. During the raid, an ambush was organized by the NGSU, and technicalities were once again at the core of the government's discourse. Indeed, Ḥabīb al- Ṣīd, the then Head of the Government, strongly commended the "qualitative and complex operation carried out exclusively by Tunisian resources."[173] However, he "did not reveal the pivotal role that the U.S. Special Operations forces had taken in helping to design and stage the operation."[174] Backed by a CIA team, the U.S. Special Operations forces intercepted and tracked the militant's communications, and planned the execution of the operation. While it "unfolded, an American surveillance aircraft circled overhead and a small team of U.S. advisers stood watch from a forward location."[175] Such assistance, rather than cooperation that entails equal partnership, displayed the absence of Tunisia's autonomous intelligence capabilities, despite official discourse, and its reliance on foreign actors. Moreover, the involvement of the CIA in such a raid sends the wrong signal to its Tunisian intelligence counterparts and risks enabling the latter to move further from a role of informing policy decisions to a more controversial policy-making function, an approach that is central to CIA activities. Yet this way of performing international operational and tactical intelligence cooperation risks jeopardizing Tunisia's constitutional standards, as it enables loose and informal cooperation that uses technical arrangements to sidestep democratic control and oversight of intelligence activities.

Tunisia's "Known Unknown" Implications of International Intelligence Cooperation

Tunisia has long-standing military and intelligence ties with the United States, which have been further strengthened by the post-uprising political context. In May 2015, the signature of the "Memorandum of Understanding" between Tunisia and the United States inaugurated a new era of multidimensional cooperation between the two countries,[176] though such cooperation is still a work in progress. However, U.S. security assistance has become problematic for a country struggling with its tenuous, and to some extent, volatile transition. In May 2015, the designation of Tunisia by Washington as a non-NATO major ally has deepened the U.S. security involvement with Tunisia while enabling its "integration ... into a militarized political and economic order" that likely will strengthen "the development-security nexus" and "contribute to the depoliticization and denationalization of both economic and security concerns."[177] This new status extends the U.S. military assistance beyond the traditional delivery of military equipment and provision of training for Tunisian military personnel to include "additional funding to joint counterterrorism research and development projects for Tunisia."[178] The designation will prioritize "the delivery of Excess Defense Articles (EDA)—military equipment granted or sold at a reduced cost to foreign governments to modernize partner forces."[179] Furthermore, it will remove the limits on the procurement of U.S. military hardware, "allowing Tunisia to possess War Reserve Stockpiles in territories outside of U.S. military establishments in the country."[180] Most importantly, the substantial shift in the security relationship between the two countries occurred during the second bilateral session of the U.S.-Tunisia Strategic Dialogue that was held in Tunis and chaired by President Qā'id al-Sabsī and U.S. Secretary of State John Kerry in November 2015. This dialogue brought to the table very sensitive topics that were discussed in secrecy by these two men. In this regard, the Tunisian side agreed, in principle, to acquire intelligence, surveillance, and reconnaissance (ISR) capabilities from the United States for the benefit of the TAF.

While the agreement was under discussion, a memorandum from the Diplomatic Section within the Tunisian Presidency that was leaked by a Tunisian whistleblower website and summarized the main points discussed by both Qā'id al-Sabsī and Kerry indicated clearly that the Tunisian party insisted on the "necessity to tackle with full details all the political, legal, and security aspects of the ISR."[181] The Tunisian concerns seem motivated by the potential linkage that could exist between the delivery of the ISR capabilities to Tunisian military and the unfolding negotiations on the Status of Forces Agreement (SOFA), which would involve the deployment of American troops in Tunisia as well as the security implications regarding the use of Tunisian military facilities by the U.S. military, mainly through the deployment of U.S. drones that could be employed for reconnaissance, battlefield surveillance and target acquisition. It should be pointed out, however, that former U.S. Secretary of Defense, Donald Rumsfeld, who discussed this issue with Bin 'Alī during his visit to Tunis in February 2006, had previously launched talks over SOFA.[182] However, the new security landscape in the Sahel-Sahara region that emerged following the 2011-U.S.-European military intervention in Libya's ensuing descent into chaos, and Tunisia's desperate need for military assistance to secure its borders in times of growing regional insecurity, enabled U.S. diplomacy to pressure its Tunisian counterpart to accept negotiating a new SOFA. The latter would enable the U.S. military personnel to establish a "foothold" under "the sovereign control of the host government" seeking to position and operate unmanned aerial vehicles (UAVs) to fill the intelligence gap on the "blind spots" of the radical militant groups in the region, "provide the U.S. military and spy agencies with real time intelligence on Islamic State activities in Libya," and ultimately "project U.S. power in the vast area."[183] In the meantime, the United States provided Tunisia with US$250 million in security assistance in the aftermath of the 2015 terror attacks to boost the country's counterterrorist capabilities while paving the way for the deployment of "U.S. service members ... with Tunisian security forces for counterterrorism [with whom they] are sharing intelligence from various sources, to include aerial platforms."[184] In September 2016, the Tunisian president, during his visit to the United States, agreed to further strengthen Tunisia's security relationship with Washington.[185] He praised the U.S. security assistance that he called a "very good cooperation on combatting terrorism, and it is working."[186] In October 2016, an anonymous, official source within the U.S. government affirmed that American UAVs "began flying out of the Tunisian base in late June [2016] and have played a key role in an extended U.S. air offensive against the Islamic State stronghold in neighboring Libya."[187] The same source further explains the patterns of the U.S. government's decision to use Tunisian military facilities for its Air Force Reaper drones:

> Obama administration officials ... have tried to shore up Tunisia's fledgling democracy and position the country as a key counterterrorism partner in the region. Although the drones operating out of Tunisia conduct only surveillance missions, ... they could be armed in the future if Tunisia gives the United States permission. ... The Obama administration has kept its negotiations over access to the base secret for more than a year because of concerns that Tunisia's

young democracy, worried about closely associated with outside military power, would pull out of the talks, or that militants would step up attacks in the North African country. … Tunisian officials negotiating the drone deal were particularly concerned about a public backlash over cooperation with a foreign power and wanted to avoid the appearance that they were party to U.S. military operations in a neighboring country. At the same time, Tunisian officials were eager to secure additional U.S. support for their counterterrorism fight at home. Tunisian officials were especially worried that an eventual assault on Islamic State hideouts in Libya could send militants streaming across the border into Tunisia.[188]

The above considerations behind using a Tunisian military base that "clearly functions as an American outpost,"[189] and operates as a launchpad for U.S. UAVs seem motivated by both domestic and regional dynamics. However, these considerations prove that the American discourse on security sector reform, aimed at enabling Tunisia to "address threats effectively and accountably,"[190] is an empty shell. The secrecy that surrounded Tunisia's signature, in April 2016, of a "Technical Agreement" (TA) drafted by the U.S. Africa Command (USAFRICOM) on the United States' use of a Tunisian military base for surveillance operations illustrated American willingness to privilege the operational and technical aspects of the agreement over any political accountability.[191] Reportedly, USAFRICOM operatives have full operational control (OPCON) over the deployed UAVs. OPCON is defined as "the command authority that may be exercised by commanders at any echelons."[192] Such function entails "organizing and employing commands and forces, assigning tasks, designating objectives, and giving authoritative direction necessary to accomplish the mission."[193] However, the Tunisian military is not privy to systematic access to intelligence collected by the U.S. drones in the region — mainly captured critical data that provides real-time security analysis and trends. Rather, the Tunisian counterpart is allowed only to access select, filtered intelligence after final approval from the USAFRICOM.[194] Significantly, President Qāʾid al-Sabsī kept Tunisia's democratically elected legislative body in the dark about the negotiations over the TA, which was neither informed of the negotiations nor offered any oversight of intelligence activities. These activities resulted in what could be seen as clandestine intelligence operations led by a global foreign power employing its intelligence assets and using a sovereign country's military facilities to achieve its worldwide strategic interests with unpredictable consequences for the host nation. Notwithstanding the denial of the existence of a foreign military base on Tunisian soil by the Tunisian Minister of Defense Farḥāt Ḥorshānī,[195] the latter has failed not only to allay Tunisians' anxiety about such a foreign presence in a country that is still struggling with its fragile transition, but also to lessen the regional implications of such a presence. The most widely circulated Tunisian newspaper *al-Ṣabāḥ* emphasized the ambiguity of the Tunisian government toward its Algerian neighbor on the issue of the American military presence:

> The growing embarrassment in the Tunisian-Algerian relationship has been caused by the obscurity in the Tunisian official statement with regard to the establishment of an American drone base in Tunisia, and its oscillation between the denial and the lack of frankness with the Algerian partner in regard to the procedures and the truth about the accords signed by Tunisia with the American counterpart that are still subjected to suspicion from the Algerian authorities who deal with the Western interventions in North Africa with extreme sensitivity. [196]

At this stage of the analysis, it is too early to assess the impact of Tunisia's decision to harbor and expand the U.S. drone network across North Africa and the Sahel-Sahara region on the bilateral Tunisian-Algerian relationship, which was perceived by Algeria as a "stab in the back."[197] Although Algiers continues to express its profound apprehensions with regard to the American and Western intentions in the region,[198] the extension of U.S. war drones to the North African tier of the Sahel-Sahara region will certainly further exacerbate the regional discord. In late November 2016, President Qā'id al-Sabsī unexpectedly acknowledged that he personally authorized the deployment of 70 U.S. military personnel operating American UAVs in order to "prevent any potential attack from the Islamic State across the Tunisian-Libyan border." He did this without confirming whether the drones were flying over Tunisian airspace or beyond the country's borders. However, he strongly refuted the existence of any disagreement with Algeria about such a decision. He even asserted that Algiers was informed about it beforehand and he would not question any of his neighbor's sovereign decisions if the Algerian authorities "decided one day to deploy Russian militaries on their soil."[199]

Given the secrecy that surrounds the TA clauses, only the evolution of the regional security dynamics could determine the future status of the U.S. "foothold" in Tunisia. American military move would likely compel Tunisia to embrace the American regional security agenda within the "globalizing national security" context,[200] and to become one of many pawns in the U.S. global game of unaccountable and unlawful drone operations. Strikingly, the U.S. government has never published any serious study on the strategic efficiency of the lethal drone attacks or its extrajudicial assassination drone program.[201] Since the establishment of the USAFRICOM in 2007 as an independent regional combatant command, the U.S. Pentagonization of the African continent through military installations, deploying both drones and Special Operations forces, and spreading American shadow wars has tremendously increased. *TomDispatch* blog has thoroughly investigated this policy by accessing "highly classified internal AFRICOM files ... obtained via the Freedom of Information Act."[202] The examined documents confirmed this trend and showed that the "36 U.S. outposts scattered across 24 African countries" according to the 2014-USAFRICOM strategic posture, expanded, in 2015 to "46, including '15 enduring locations'... that already provided the U.S. military with unprecedented continental reach" of drone and surveillance network.[203] Interestingly, the declassification of the 2014-USAFRICOM secret map on the U.S. military deployment across the African continent designated 15 African countries among them Tunisia as a "high threat-high risk facility."[204] Such designation has coincided with the U.S. escalation of its active military engagement across the Sahel-Sahara region. Likely, Tunisia will be exposed to more lethal violence, as the U.S. "footprint" in this country could become a magnet for violent non-state actors (VNSAs) who not only aim to undermine the country's democratization process but also seek to delegitimize it by emphasizing its irrelevance while also associating it with the American military expansionism across the Middle East and Africa. Moreover, this presence could compromise any potential role that Tunisia would have to play in the settlement of the Libyan crisis. Ultimately, Tunisia could be held accountable for breaching basic principles of international law if drones operate from Tunisian territory armed with Hellfire missiles or Viper strike bombs or cause unintended civilian causalities in Libya or elsewhere.

The absence of clear safeguards and arrangements for a country experiencing a fragile democratic transition in authorizing and subjecting international intelligence cooperation to adequate rules of accountability and transparency could plunge the Tunisia-US cooperation into what the former U.S. Secretary of Defense Donald Rumsfeld called the "known unknowns" category. Indeed, such cooperation could deepen the "unknowns" if Tunisia's intelligence still operates unobtrusively and away from rigorous oversight with the complicity of American power. More importantly, this cooperation risks raising legal and ethical issues with regard to secrecy, sharing information, and respect for human rights standards between Tunisia, a member of the International Criminal Court (ICC),[205] and the United States, which does not recognize the ICC's jurisdiction.[206] Apart from the international intelligence cooperation and accountability that require the right legal conditions and oversight for such cooperation—which are beyond the scope of this book—it is important to assess the state of "reform" within the military intelligence in the post-uprising era.

Military Intelligence and Limited "Reform"

On January 15, 2011, less than 24 hours after Bin ʿAlī fled the country, the French Chief of the Defense Staff contacted General Rashīd ʿAmmār, the then Army Chief of Staff, to inquire about any assistance the Tunisian counterpart might need. General ʿAmmār, a former head of the DGSM, who was familiar with the weaknesses of the country's military intelligence, requested that the French general keep him informed about the unfolding situation in Libya.[207] 'Ammār was concerned about any subversive action that could have been staged by Qadhdhāfī in seeking to abort the popular uprising. In the summer of 2013, General 'Ammār announced his retirement on a TV broadcast interview, and acknowledged that the difficulty the TAF was facing in fighting a low-intensity conflict against Islamist insurgents operating in the Mount Ash-Sha'nabi was a result of the intelligence's impotence and the lack of cooperation between the country's intelligence services tasked with fighting transnational threats.[208]

Although the powerlessness of the military intelligence was the main characteristic under Bin 'Alī's rule, its increasing politicization during the transitional process was a new trend that further undermined its effectiveness. In early February of 2011, General 'Ammār appointed General Aḥmad Shābīr, the DGSM's chief, as general director at GDNS. 'Ammār considered Shābīr the right man to manage this troubled, coercive labyrinth and improve its operational capabilities. Shābīr, like his mentor 'Ammār, was an artillery officer who served as a defense attaché in France and ran the military's intelligence apparatus. His appointment to the highest security position within the Interior Ministry likely would have provided the Army Chief of Staff with more insight into the complex dynamics within the internal security apparatus, while the TAF were facing new security challenges created by the demise of the authoritarian rule. However, Shābīr likely thought that this new appointment was a demotion that sought to drive him away from the TAF, especially since serving within the previous position as the DGSM's chief was considered less risky for an officer who enjoyed a linear career within the army than assuming the volatile direction of the GDNS in the post-uprising era. Shābīr, who spent only a few weeks as the head of the GDNS (February 1-March 3, 2011), quickly regained his former position as the Chief of Military Intelligence. His reinstatement coincided with the Libyan revolt that broke out in mid-February 2011, during which General 'Ammār and the then Prime minister Qā'id al-Sabsī played a key role in facilitating the transit of weapons across the Tunisian-Libyan border. Indeed, United Arab Emirates (UAE) and Qatar's C-17 Globemaster, an aircraft designed for strategic airlift missions, carried out most of the weap-

ons delivered to Libyan rebels based in the Nafusa mountains. After being transported to the Tunisian military air force base located
in the town of Remada, close to the Libyan border, military convoys
under the protection of the Tunisian army dispatched these weapons to the Libyan rebels. Other shipments of weapons delivered
by vessels to the Zarzis maritime port in the country's southeast
quickly found their way to the anti-Qadhdhāfī's rebellion. Qatari,
Emirati, and Jordanian Special Forces joined the Libyan rebels via
the Tunisian territory. Although both Tunisian political and military authorities endorsed this covert action, Shābīr felt that he had
been kept in the dark and was not a part of these decisions. Shābīr
started questioning the wisdom of this covert action and required
a formal authorization from the political authority to enable the
landing of Emirati and Qatari military transport aircraft. He also
requested that all the transited weapons be inspected and subjected
to the military intelligence's inventory. Shābīr's effort to assert his
authority over the clandestine conveyance of weapons into Libya
put an end to his career in the early summer of 2011.[209]

The appointment of Shābīr's successor, Commodore Kamāl
ʿAkrūt,[210] promoted later to the rank of Rear Admiral, accelerated
the pace of the weapons delivery to Libyan rebels. However, the
relationship between President al-Marzūqī and the military leadership became intense as a result of the degradation of the security
climate across the country, mainly after the rise of attacks against
military personnel in Mount Ash-Shaʿnabī. Lacking any military
or security expertise, al-Marzūqī appointed Senior Colonel Ibrāhīm
Washtātī to the position of Adviser to the President in Charge of
Military Affairs in September 2012. Washtātī, a director of NDI
and former defense attaché in Washington, D.C., is considered by
many to be a shrewd and calculating person. He came to his new
position with two principal objectives: get promoted to the rank
of Brigadier General, and undermine ʿAmmār's power, which he
considered an impediment to reforming the military institution. To
this end, he needed to provide al-Marzūqī with in-depth insight
about the dynamics within the Ministry of Defense. Rather than
advising the president, Washtātī exacerbated the growing tension between the commander-in-chief and the military leadership.
Washtātī sought to weaken the DGSM's chief, seen as ʿAmmār's

protégé, by questioning the way the department sought to address the rising insecurity in borderlands. However, the security failure was beyond the scope of the military leadership. It was structurally inherent to the status and role of military intelligence profoundly marginalized under the fallen ruler. In fact, the DGSM struggled to adjust to the new security context. Moreover, the TAF was neither trained nor prepared to face asymmetric warfare. This tension reached new heights when the president's entourage, primarily his Chief of Staff and spokesman ʿAdnān Manṣar, alerted the media to an alleged attempted coup against al-Marzūqī in the aftermath of Brāhmī's assassination in July 2013. An attempted coup would have threatened a repeat of the Egyptian scenario that followed the ouster of President Muhammad Morsī, but in Tunisia. Despite these dangerous allegations, Manṣar failed to give tangible proof about the involvement of military and security leaders in what he called a "political-military-security attempted coup."[211] Manṣar, who built his assumptions on fantasies, further fueled al-Marzūqī's phobia of imaginary coups. Later, Manṣar retracted and argued that the media misconstrued his statement. However, his accusations left a deep resentment among the military leadership who strongly condemned Manṣar's assertions and asked permission to investigate them.[212] Later, ʿAzīz Krīshān, a former adviser to al-Marzūqī, acknowledged that the alleged coup was a fictional story invented by Manṣar to draw the sympathy and support of the Islamists for al-Marzūqī, a prerequisite to his success in the presidential elections.[213] On June 24, nine days before Sīsī's coup and one month prior to Brāhmī's murder, ʿAmmār decided to voluntarily retire from the military because of the age limit. To this day, no one has been appointed to the position of Chief of Staff of the TAF. A deep reshuffling of the TAF's top command (i.e., Army, Air Force, and DGSM) designed by Washtātī followed ʿAmmār's departure. Seemingly, ʿAkrūt's discharge from the DGSM was motivated by his decision to keep the military intelligence away from any politicization. Reportedly, al-Marzūqī expressed "unwarranted anger" toward ʿAkrūt when the latter refused to brief him on the country's security situation in the presence of some members of al-Marzūqī's party, the CPR. As a military intelligence professional, ʿAkrūt argued that he was not allowed to share sensitive information with

individuals who did not belong in the sphere of governmental security decision-making.[214] Sanctioned for his ethical leadership,
'Akrūt was appointed a defense attaché in Libya, a position that
he fervently declined as he believed—not without reason—that
he would have been assassinated for the role that he had played
in toppling Qadhdhāfī's regime. As an alternative to his initial as-
signment, 'Akrūt was appointed as a defense attaché in the UAE.
Seemingly, the Emiratis, aware of the ramifications of the Arab uprisings,[215] were very pleased to have the former head of Tunisia's
military intelligence assigned to their country. For obvious reasons,
the Emiratis expedited 'Akrūt's agreement, paving the way for his
new position.

Aside from the structural challenges inhibiting the function of
the DGSM, the new military intelligence chief, General Nūrī Bin
Ṭāwiss,[216] was at the center of a new struggle about the control of
the military intelligence apparatus that opposed the two main executive branches. Bin Ṭāwiss sought to facilitate the flow of information between his department and the presidency to overcome
any quid pro quo arrangements with al-Marzūqī. From August
2013 to January 2014, he was often solicited to brief the president
about the country's security challenges. However, Bin Ṭāwiss acted
with complete autonomy from the Minister of Defense, as he did
not feel compelled to keep the minister informed about his meetings with the commander-in-chief. Ghāzī Jarībī, the new minister of
defense in the Mahdī Jum'ā caretaker government, strongly questioned this way of interacting with the presidency. Furthermore,
the security prerogatives of both the president and the Head of the
Government, as stated in the new 2014 constitution, created further confusion with regard to executive control over security and
the armed forces in both peacetime and wartime.[217] Thus, Jarībī
decided to change the rules and assert his constitutional rights as
the main individual responsible—even before the president—for
defense issues, including intelligence. Bin Ṭāwiss interpreted the
minister's new move as a subtle tactic seeking to take over intelligence and undermine his prerogatives. Although Bin Ṭāwiss was
backed by al-Marzūqī through Washtātī, Jarībī did not hesitate to
dismiss him. In the meantime, the rise in ambushes, the systematic use of improvised explosive devices against military personnel

operating in the Mount Ash-Sha'nabi area, the growing casualties among military, and the increasing pressure imposed by the media on the military to deliver victory against the insurgents, despite the creation of a border buffer zone and a military operations zone,[218] pushed the new Army Chief of Staff, General Muhammad Ṣālaḥ Ḥāmdī, to resign after just one year of his appointment. Ḥāmdī, justified his resignation by citing his disagreement with the Minister of Defense in assessing and tackling the threats. A former officer of Special Forces, also known as Special Forces Group (GFS), Ḥāmdī spent his whole career within this elite corps and relied excessively on the GFS in his counterinsurgency effort. He assessed that the infantry was not trained to tackle irregular warfare. However, he seemingly used GFS in routine clear-and-search operations instead of being employed in very specific missions, such as raids and collecting tactical intelligence. Such misuse of the GFS raised the rate of casualties among its personnel.[219] Moreover, the lack of tangible intelligence on the insurgents' movements forced the army to rely on artillery and warplanes in targeting the Ash-Sha'nabī area.

The degradation of the country's security situation and the political polarization went hand in hand with the deterioration of the relationship between al-Marzūqī and Jum'ā. Both men disagreed over the appointment of senior security officials, chief among them the head of military intelligence. While the former refused to endorse the appointment made by the Head of the Government, the latter used his constitutional prerogatives to create a Crisis Cell (CC).[220] The CC was tasked with keeping the head of the government informed about the country's security situation. Jum'ā held CC's meetings at the Head of the Government's Office, to which the Ministers of Defense, Interior, and Foreign Affairs were convened. In addition to the heads of key security departments, the DGSM, GDNS, and GDNG chiefs attended these meetings. Although the CC was considered a micro-NSC that sought to compete with the president's security team, its main goal was to coordinate the activities of the joint operations led in the field by components of army and security forces. This coordination also sought to overcome the climate of suspicion and mistrust between the Interior and the Defense Ministries' personnel, a climate that had prevailed since the post-independence period and was deepened after the uprising. To overcome the constitutional blockage between al-Marzūqī and Jumʿā, a compromise between the former and the latter was reached; as part of the compromise, an acting director, Senior Colonel Tawfīq Raḥmūnī, was appointed to manage the DGSM's activities on a daily basis.[221] The newly emerged majority of the 2014 legislative and presidential elections would have to decide the final appointment of the military intelligence chief.

Rear Admiral Kamāl ʿAkrūt	2011–2013
Brigadier Nūrī Bin Ṭāwiss	2013–2014
Brigadier Tawfīq Raḥmūnī*	2014–2017
Brigadier Ḥabīb al-Ḍīf**	2017–...

Figure 11: Tenure of Military Intelligence Chiefs (2011 to present)
* Graduated from the Tunisian National War College, class of 2002
** Graduated from the Tunisian National War College, class of 2004

Given the legislative electoral momentum that saw al-Marzūqī's CPR roundly defeated and al-Nahḍah's loss of control of the new parliament, the Head of the Government used his constitutional rights and issued a decree related to the establishment of a new military intelligence apparatus. He convened a cabinet meeting that promptly endorsed a decree on the creation of the Defense Intelligence and Security Agency (DISA) on November 20, 2014. Article 1 of the decree acknowledges the DISA as "a public institution of administrative character that enjoys legal status and financial independence."[222] The same article tasked the agency with "the mission of protecting the personnel, equipment, installations and secrecy of the Ministry of National Defense."[223] Article 1 also assigned to the DISA the mission of "gathering intelligence on the potential threats able to endanger the security of the armed forces, and the country's security in general."[224] The DISA contributes to "preventing and combatting terrorism" and to "advising the military leadership and the Minister of National Defense."[225] Ironically, the decree above, which was issued during a new era of democratization, is much too broad and ill-defined, and poorly lays out the principal functions of the DISA. At the procedural level, an executive decree exclusively created the DISA instead of being the result of extensive legislative debate and parliamentary process that would have incorporated it into a clear legislative framework for the military intelligence role, missions, and legal mandate. The text is also silent about oversight of the agency and the role of the executive, legislative, and judiciary bodies, as well as civil society actors in performing such oversight to ensure that there is transparency and accountability in military intelligence activities. Additionally, the text does not provide any details about the organization of the new agency, nor does it provide any clear definition of terrorism.[226] Some key concepts in the decree are imprecise, such as "potential threats" and the "country's security in general."[227] These phrases are not defined, and their meaning depends on different political interpretations. Furthermore, the counter-intelligence functions are vaguely implied and do not cover the spectrum of countering hostile intelligence operations, subversion, treason, sabotage, etc. The decree is devoid of any legal regulations and directives that would deter military intelligence officers from infringing upon citizens' constitutional rights. Moreover, the decree does not specify the role of the DISA within the country's national security architecture or the agency's interaction with other services and the NSC. Last but not least, the decree confined the DISA's functions to narrow traditional threats (i.e., terrorism) and overlooked the human and holistic approach of security. Overall, this decree was scantily designed and echoed the authoritarian context where technicalities are critical to the intelligence and security services. Tunisia's embryonic democracy still has a long way to go before it can incorporate the basic rules of accountability and transparency into legislation governing its military intelligence sector.

The DISA was awarded TND1 million (US$0.4 million) for the 2016 fiscal year.[228] On February 20, 2015, Raḥmūnī was promoted to the rank of Brigadier General by a presidential decree.[229] Although the DISA emerged as a new military intelligence entity, its structure is still driven by the old DGSM's scheme.[230] Indeed, most of the directorates have been upgraded from simple directorates to general directorates. The DISA General Director oversees four major general directorates, a language training center, and an intelligence training school: the General Directorate of Intelligence and Internal Security (GDIIS), the General Directorate of External Relations (GDER), the General Directorate for Securing Communications (GDSC), the General Directorate of Specialized Services (GDSS), the Defense Language School and Training Center (DLSTC), and the School of Intelligence and Military Security (SIMS). The GDIIS is tasked with securing the military personnel, equipment, and installations. This directorate is seemingly expanding its range of actions beyond the military sphere to include domestic intelligence through investigative work on the domestic ramifications of VNSAs. However, GDIIS has its own network of HUMINT and it is difficult to assess its efficiency. Given the scale of armed attacks targeting the TAF in the post-uprising years, some of the military intelligence interviewees asserted their determination to build strong and independent domestic intelligence gathering-capabilities as a part of the adaptation process of the army's doctrine to the new irregular threats in both urban and remote areas. However, they failed to explain how such capabilities could be developed without engaging in domestic covert operations that could jeopardize the security and constitutional rights of citizens. Such an approach could also be seen by the ISF as an intrusion of the military intelligence into a realm that traditionally was a fiefdom of the domestic intelligence services within the Interior Ministry. As for the GDER, it supervises the activities of the defense attachés abroad that rely fundamentally on Open Source Intelligence (OSINT). Also, Tunisian defense attachés complement their OSINT with "protected" information that they gather from their foreign counterparts in their countries of residence. The GDER also acts as a liaison between the foreign defense attachés in Tunis and the Ministry of Defense. The GDER interacts with its foreign military counterparts such as the U.S. Defense Intelligence Agency (DIA), the French DGSE, the Italian Servizio per le Informazioni e la Sicurezza Militare or SISMI, the Spanish Centro Nacional de Inteligencia or CNI, the German Federal Intelligence Service (BND or Bundesnachrichtendienst), the Algerian DRS, and the Egyptian Military Intelligence and Reconnaissance Administration or DMI, among others. The GDSC is in charge of securing military communications and directing the military's SIGINT activities. The GDSS is responsible for the maintenance of intelligence infrastructure and logistics. The DLSTC encompasses language institutes and labs (English, Italian, German, Spanish, Greek, Turkish, and Arabic). Arabic is taught to Western foreign officers, mainly those from intelligence agencies, who seek to polish their Arabic. The other foreign languages are taught to both Tunisian officers and NCOs who have to perform their military training abroad. In June 2016, an unpublished Presidential Decision established the SIMS and was as one of the major measures taken to celebrate the 60th anniversary of TAF's creation. Its role is "to train specialized servicemen according to modern programs and modern tools."[231] No details, so far, have emerged from the presidential decision with regard to the SIMS mission, legal mandate, and organization. Reportedly, the creation of such professional training institution should focus on the profession of intelligence by remedying the lack of intelligence technical skills among NCOs. Throughout specialized courses on military intelligence, SIMS should provide NCOs with adequate tools of critical analysis to better understand the intelligence dynamic in "real time" at the tactical level, which is critical to the success or failure of unfolding military-security operations.[232] Located next to al-Aouina Air Force Base, the construction of the SIMS infrastructure was largely funded by the United States.[233] Finally, the creation of the Directorate of Strategic Studies (DSS), one of the GDER's sub-divisions, was an innovative step. The DSS will "play a critical role in informing the decision maker at the strategic and the battlefield levels" through "the development of in-depth prospective analysis about the surrounding geopolitical context," in the words of General Raḥmūnī.[234] The DISA will seek to "improve its analytical capabilities by recruiting analysts with different academic backgrounds and appropriate skills who are able to turn information into knowledgeable intelligence vital to managing the rising uncertainties."[235] The process of "skillful civilianization," though "constitutes a limited approach, it will lead to critical innovation within the agency."[236] Yet the DISA leadership is more concerned with strengthening the capabilities of the new military apparatus than the meaning of intelligence within a democratic context. Understandably, the failure of the military intelligence to perform its missions efficiently since the country's independence has haunted all those who assumed the direction of such an apparatus in the post-authoritarian era. They find it challenging to create a symbiosis between efficiency, effectiveness, and legality. However, they are also aware that the prevailing "culture" of abuse within the intelligence military apparatus has to be tackled by disseminating suitable ethical standards throughout the new agency.

Figure 12: Defense Intelligence and Security Agency Organization

The creation of the DISA did not fill the intelligence gap for the troops engaged in operations against Islamist insurgents. The unfolding operations across the country, mainly in the borderland areas, required an improvement of the army's intelligence system at the tactical and operational levels. Moreover, it has become obvious that the DISA is unable to keep the military consistently informed about the situation in the field, as it does not have access to field information in real-time. Indeed, the agency's *modus operandi* is still influenced by decades of centralization, and is seemingly stuck in a time when the information was controlled, filtered, and passed downward. Thus, the army has started a process of revamping its intelligence capabilities by introducing, at the tactical level, the concept of the Intelligence Fusion Cell (IFC).[237]

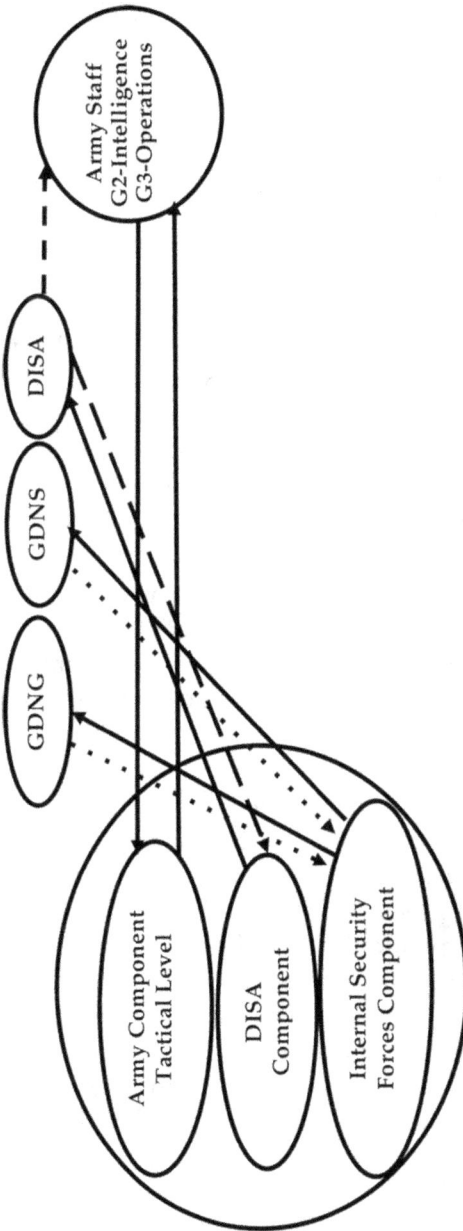

Figure 13: Intelligence Fusion Cell (IFC) Structure

In July 2016, the international multilateral cooperation over the IFC suddenly surfaced to the Tunisian public, while the NATO Secretary General Jens Stoltenberg, during the 2016-NATO Warsaw summit, announced "NATO is providing advice to the Tunisian authorities on the development of a Tunisian Intelligence Fusion Centre and will provide training to Tunisian Special Forces."[238] Seemingly, this announcement was in line with the signature of the Individual Partnership Cooperation Program (IPCP) between NATO and Tunisia in 2014. It should be pointed out that IPCP covers a broad range of security cooperation areas, including but not limited to, "intelligence exchange, counter-terrorism, cyber defense, and border control."[239] As with the episode of U.S. drones operating from Tunisian soil, the Tunisian Ministry of Defense denied the existence of NATO's IFC in Tunisia, while it affirmed the creation of IFC "in the Defense Department, [which has been] funded by Tunisian investments and directed by Tunisian military skills" since 2014.[240] In the meantime, the department acknowledged that the Atlantic Alliance would cooperate with Tunisia in areas of intelligence collection and data analysis directed toward the fight against terrorism.[241] Although the aforementioned NATO statement did not make any explicit reference to the presence of an Atlantic Alliance's IFC in Tunisia, the Tunisian government denial of the existence of such a structure on its soil shows its obsession to prove its control over a sensitive field—considered a symbol of national sovereignty—to outspoken civil society actors traditionally suspicious of such cooperation.[242] Most importantly, this denial aims at eclipsing the lack of transparency related to the international intelligence cooperation. As such, cooperation is subjected to neither parliamentary or independent oversight, nor judiciary scrutiny.

The IFC's design, organization, and *modus operandi* cannot deny that this structure is an American operational concept experienced in both the Iraq and Afghanistan wars, and was recommended by a former member of the U.S. Special Operations forces who served as a DIA officer. He graduated from the Tunisian CSC in 2002 and has been an adviser with a dozen U.S. military contractors to the Tunisian GFS since 2014.[243] Notwithstanding the American origins of this concept,[244] the U.S. Department of Defense does not provide a specific definition of IFC. Its Joint Intelligence manual defines fusion as: "In intelligence usage, the process of managing information to conduct all-source analysis and derive a complete assessment of activity."[245] More specifically, "Fusion Cell" is defined as:

> a collaborative effort of 2 or more Federal, State, local, or tribal government agencies that combines resources, expertise, or information with the goal of maximizing the ability of such agencies to detect, prevent, investigate, apprehend, and respond to criminal or terrorist activity.[246]

This definition of a fusion cell involves the existence of an organization in which the efforts, resources, and means of different structures are combined in an interactive fashion to better achieve the assigned mission. In the Tunisian context, the IFC is, at the tactical level, organized around three components: the army, the DISA, and the ISF (i.e., police and NG). The interagency coordination is supposed to be at the center stage of the IFC's activities by fusing the different analyses of these components into one integrated intelligence assessment. The latter is meant to be directed to the chain of command within the Defense and Interior Ministries in order to give the military and the security apparatus' decision makers a better picture of the dynamic situation in the field and adjust their decisions accordingly. Instead, each component continues to draw its own assessment that it submits to its counterpart within the different ministries. The army in the forefront of the counterinsurgency effort interacts energetically with the IFC's army component through its G2 and G3 directorates (i.e., Intelligence, Operations). The DISA, currently undergoing a process of restructuring, is still struggling with the legacy of centralization, where its strong hierarchical organization strives to adapt to the bottom-up intelligence process. As for the key security directorates within the Interior Ministry—GDNS, GDNG—they are still operating in a way that privileges the information processed and directly emanated from their services, such as the GDSS and DII and their respective sub-directorates, rather than information passed to them from the IFC. The absence of a synergetic holistic approach within the IFC could be explained by the mistrust between the different components at the tactical level. Reportedly, such mistrust is palpable, especially with regard to the reliability of information in the field. It is salient in the borderland areas, and is dangerously affecting the country's stability, as "state security actors are helping to smuggle weapons over the borders that another part of the military is contending with."[247] Moreover, competition between the different and very divided intelligence services within the Interior Ministry and between these services and the DISA is another factor behind the weakness of this fused intelligence approach. Rather than helping to accurately assess the complexity of the security environment, this limited tactical "reform" further fragmented intelligence at all levels, and enabled each service to manipulate the information for political purposes by biasing and shaping their analyses to support decisions that have already been made by policymakers. Furthermore, the IFC's integration into Tunisia's military intelligence system showed that the country's foreign sponsors are more interested in upgrading its intelligence capabilities falling within a technicalities discourse than strengthening its "democratic security sector governance."[248]

A Broken and Ineffective National Intelligence Architecture

The intelligence fragmentation at the tactical level is reflected at the political level. In fact, the NSC deals simultaneously with at least four major intelligence and security directorates: GDNS, GDNG, DISA, and GDPSPPO.[249] Each of these services seeks to draw the attention of the president to perceived threats by providing him with contradictory, weak, and inaccurate assessments on specific issues (i.e., VNSAs, security operations). These assessments lack any strategic analysis. The NSC does not play its typical multi-functional role of advising the decision-maker, interacting between officials, coordinating policies, communicating with a legislative body on security issues, integrating and evaluating intelligence, and building consensus and processes for team decision-making, among others. Rather, it operates in a "Soviet politburo" fashion way, to paraphrase an attendee of one of President Qāʾid al-Sabsī's meetings on the country's security situation. In this meeting, Qāʾid al-Sabsī made some security parallels between his past experiences as Interior Minister and Defense Minister, shared some of his priorities,

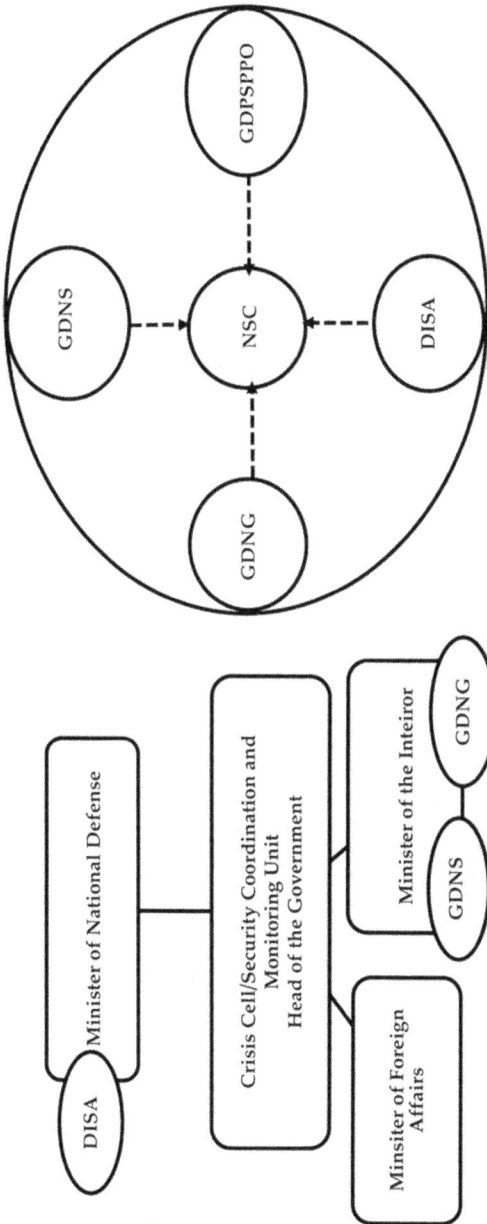

Figure 14: Tunisia's National Intelligence Architecture in Post-Popular Uprising

and then opened the floor to some of the NSC members who reiterated what the president had said. Afterwards, some of them highlighted the achievements of their security services and advanced some ideas for which they pushed the other NSC members to endorse without prior discussion or consultation. These ideas were often expressed in a way to impress the head of the state and the NSC attendees, rather than to convince them, a sort of soft "shock and awe."

Yet, the NSC's intelligence fragmentation and segmentation is obvious in the absence of a national assessment that is sufficiently evaluated and integrated like the U.S. National Intelligence Estimate (NIE). The NIE model, despite its limits in assessing uncertainty, still "highlight[s] the 'Best Estimate' or 'Key Judgments,'"[250] while it is produced by competitive and diverse analytical approaches. Reportedly, President Qā'id al-Sabsī expressed his resentment when the country's intelligence services reported facts without providing him with useful analysis in the aftermath of the suicide attack that targeted the PSG's bus in late November 2015. Rather than questioning and identifying challenges by "speaking truth to power" in a professional fashion, these services tend to support politics as "intelligence to please." In fact, the unspoken rules of the Tunisian security bureaucracy are that the high-ranking officials within the intelligence and security apparatus have incommensurable power over both the flow of information and their subordinates. Thus, to avoid jeopardizing their power and their career, these senior intelligence and security officials opportunistically embrace the official political line of policymakers while they allow their intelligence and security services to operate based on political stereotypes, where profiling targets driven by baseless assumptions is still a primary piece of their *modus operandi*. Parker clearly outlines this aspect:

> There is much talk of reforming Tunisia's security sector, with the help of Western money and training. ... But the old habits of a police state persist–during my time in Tunis, I was watched at my hotel, and my interpreter was interrogated on the street. ... The old methods of surveillance are returning. ... antiterrorism law [has] allowed the police to round up suspects and hold them for as long as two weeks

without charges. According to the Tunisian Interior Ministry, a hundred thousand Tunisians–one per cent of the population–were arrested in the first half of 2015.[251]

Amnesty International's investigations are consistent with the
above findings, which are reminiscent of the repressive methods
employed under Bin ʿAlī regime. The human rights organization
published a report in early 2017 stating that "human rights violations persist" and "that not enough has been done to break with the
patterns of violations that were common" under the fallen regime
to "make Tunisia the success story it is often portrayed as."[252] Six
years after the demise of the autocratic rule, the country's human
rights record remained poor, and the security apparatus persist in
perpetrating serious abuses, including the use of "torture and arbitrary and incommunicado detention" and other ill-treatment in
response to threats from VNSAs.[253] Although the report noted the
failure to reform the country's intelligence and security services in
the aftermath of the 2011 popular uprising, it highlighted the leaning of the security forces toward the abuse of laws ensuing the state
of emergency. The report describes in details some of these abuses:

> … home raids and searches were carried out at different
> times of the day or night by a large number of armed offi-
> cers. … security forces were masked and armed with rifles,
> and used excessive and unnecessary force. They broke doors
> down and pointed rifles at residents, including in the pres-
> ence of children, and in some cases opened fire into the air.
> … It appears that, in many cases, house searches were arbi-
> trary and discriminatory, based on little evidence pointing
> to the involvement of the residents in activities that would
> warrant a search. … security forces conducted door-to-door
> searches storming into most homes in the area, breaking
> down doors without identifying themselves or presenting
> warrants and pointing guns at residents, including some
> who were still sleeping. Many of those arrested were taken
> away while still wearing their nightclothes and slippers.
> Some were beaten during transfer to the police station for
> questioning. … repeated house searches and raids have

had long-term consequences on the mental and physical health of the entire family. In some instances, the affected individuals were rushed to hospital due to the shock they felt following the violent intrusion by armed security forces into their homes. ... wives had miscarried or were severely affected as a result of the fear and stress caused by forceful or repeated home raids.[254]

In addition to these ruthless counterinsurgency tactics, the report shed lights in full detail the torture techniques of the security forces:

Detainees were tortured and otherwise ill-treated during interrogation to coerce them to give false confessions: some were subjected to electric shocks, including on the genitals or a stress position known as the roast chicken, whereby their hands and feet were cuffed to a stick, while some were slapped, deprived of sleep, forced to undress or threatened with a female family member being raped or otherwise harmed.[255]

Moreover, the report showed that intelligence and security services conduct arrests in discriminatory and arbitrary manners, which are mainly based on profiling alleged targets:

Bearded men and those dressed in clothing such as a *kamis* (a long shirt usually worn in Tunisia by religious Muslims) and women wearing a *niqab* (a full-face veil) appear to be particularly targeted based on their physical appearance ... stopped in the street or taken off public transport by security forces and then transferred to police stations where they were kept for several hours and questioned about their reading habits, what television shows they watched, where they had studied and how often and where they prayed. ... they were usually made to sign a written statement recording their answers to questions but often were not allowed to read the contents.[256]

The report solemnly held Tunisian authorities responsible for misusing the emergency laws and turning a blind eye to "their international obligations by violating the absolute prohibition of torture under any circumstances."[257] Furthermore, the report denounced Tunisian security forces' increasing heavy-handed tactics, which "have violated people's rights to liberty and to a private life, hindering their ability to lead a normal life and have targeted individuals on the basis of their perceived religious beliefs and physical appearance with no evidence linking them to specific crimes."[258] It is important to point out that Article 24 of the 2014 Tunisian constitution enshrined most of the aforesaid abused rights.[259]

The resurrection of the police security state within a fledgling democratic context cannot be explained only by the rise of insecurity across the country. Rather, it is the mentality of those working within the coercive apparatus that still reflects the authoritarian nature of the fallen regime. This autocratic insularity tends to become corporate behavior within the security sector, one that tries to assert its power as a means of social control. However, this security authoritarian enclave has failed to understand that the Tunisian citizens who tore down the wall of fear are not disposed to turn back the clock of freedom. Indeed, corporate authoritarianism is inherent to the country's intelligence and security apparatus themselves. Their vertical, archaic, bureaucratic, and hierarchical structures are not conducive to the flow of information, nor to transparency, accountability, and oversight. These structural challenges prove that democratic governance of Tunisia's intelligence apparatus is an illusion. Intelligence reform is neither embraced by those from within the intelligence services nor prioritized by the executive who seeks to empower their capacities and grant them immunity from prosecutions related to their security arbitrariness; thus, validating the technicalities discourse comes at the detriment of civil liberties and fundamental freedoms.

These authoritarian trends within the country's intelligence architecture have become more tangible as the executive body has embraced a seemingly controversial approach in tackling the issue of terrorism. In November 2016, the NSC adopted a "National Strategy to Fight Terrorism and Extremism" (NSFTE) that was signed by President Qā'id al-Sabsī and revolved around the four main principles of "prevention, protection, monitoring and response."[260] Although the communiqué from the presidency was very succinct, it did not make any reference to details about the definition of priorities or assessed threats, which are considered critical to achieving the objectives of any strategy. Yet the necessary means by which resources will be used to obtain the anticipated strategic outcomes have not been mentioned. Most importantly, the communiqué was silent about the role of the security sector leadership (i.e., TAF, ISF, and intelligence services) and how other stakeholders would play out in this strategy, as well as on the adherence to human rights and the country's constitutional standards that such a strategy implies.

However, the communiqué pointed out that civil society has been involved in the early stages of discussing the so-called NS-FTE. Given the prolific number of civil society organizations operating in the country, some 19,000 associations,[261] and considering the strong ideological polarization of political and associational life, it is difficult to agree upon a consensual representation of civil society actors. Thus, one can doubt the truthfulness of the presidential communiqué, and one can assume that a limited number of civil society actors would have been associated with the process of drafting such a strategy. Such a process should have entailed at least a minimum level of transparency with regard to public debate on the points of convergence and contention that could have been raised by either side with regard to such a strategy. Furthermore, the media made no mention of discussions, criticisms, and reservations that could have been highlighted by political actors and civil society organizations. Such discrepancies strongly question the credibility and legitimacy of the whole process and reveal its flaws.

In the same way, the refusal of the head of the state to consider submitting this document to the parliament for approval on the pretext that it is a "special reference document for the executive branch"[262] is not a persuasive argument. In fact, this strategy was drafted by the National Counterterrorism Committee (NCTC), which initially was established within the Ministry of Foreign Affairs in February 2015. In August of that year, Article 46 of the Organic Law n° 26-2015 relating to the Fight against Terrorism and Prevention of Money Laundering granted the NCTC legal status. Thus, the NCTC became a permanent committee under the authority of the Head of the Government. Article 47 identifies the NCTC's permanent members who represent the security sector and various governmental departments. The same article enables the NCTC to include a civil society representative to its meetings, as needed for consultation. This consultative rather than compulsory role of civil society explains, in part, the lack of public consultation and dissemination of a pubic version of this document among large segments of political and civil society actors, which could have been used to secure their adherence and support. In addition, the process in which the document's draft has been carried out illustrates the complete marginalization of the legislative body regarding the development, resourcing, oversight, and completion of such a strategy. Interestingly, a senior military officer cogently elucidated the main reasons behind the opacity of the whole process:

> Any official document seeking to address key strategic sensitive threats such as terrorism should have at least two major functions that revolve around deterrence and public information. The function of deterrence should deter any potential attack by powerfully displaying the numerous means and available options at the state's disposal in meeting the threats posed by VNSAs. The function of public information aims at sensitizing the country's public about the negative outcomes that could impact the cohesion of society and the country's stability if such threats are not tackled effectively. Also, it should enlighten the public and private spheres on the challenges of democratic security governance that imply professionalism and strong accountability of the security sector as an ill-conceived and poorly implemented strategy could further complicate the mission of law enforcement and the military who are still lacking appropriate capacity and training to operate in this gray zone within the framework of rule of law and safeguarding of human rights. The function of information should send a clear message to Tunisia's international partners affirming the country's commitment to respect all its international obligations related to democratic universal values. Finally, it should acknowledge that countering terrorism domestically has to start by ad-

dressing the socio-political and economic causes conducive to such a phenomenon. Unfortunately, the non-publication of such a document while undermining these functions could generate public contention if the implementation of such strategy leads to wrongdoing and an abuse of power. However, the secrecy surrounding this document could be explained by the concise presidential communiqué per se. The four key words of prevention, protection, monitoring and response, emphasized in the statement suggest that the document is more a technical operational guideline than a strategy. For instance, prevention, at the operational level, could involve preventive action to respond to an imminent threat from VNSAs while it requires reliable intelligence. However, intelligence in the context of preventive operations is more prone to evaluate the trends and risks than forecast immediate intentions and capabilities of a potential assailant. Thus, employing intelligence to foresee the future as correctly as possible could lead the country's security apparatus to adopt a more coercive posture that could fuel further violence. Monitoring within the context of counterterrorism risks to provide intelligence services with further illegal and ethically questionable practices as they are still operating outside any comprehensive legal framework that should hold them accountable for their activities. In short, this counterterrorism approach may involve unlawful operations that will likely violate basic standards of due process rights. [263]

The above statement illustrates perfectly how Tunisia's counterterrorism approach will likely fail to move the country's intelligence apparatus beyond the technicalities and procedures that have been predominant in the post-authoritarian security sector "reform" discourse. This narrow one-dimensional counterterrorism approach focuses on VNSAs while neglecting foreign actors' illegal activities, such as the involvement of states, private companies or groups engaged in covert actions. These clandestine operations encompass a broad spectrum of actions ranging from internal destabilization to state and non-state-sponsored terrorism, regardless of whether they are planned at home or abroad, and may include espionage, infiltration, penetration, disruption, deception, manipulation, subversion, sabotage, targeted assassinations, and the like. Thwarting such hostile activities entails robust counterintelligence defensive capabilities that Tunisia's intelligence and security services have failed miserably to acquire as a result of the lack of any serious reform since the demise of the autocratic regime in January 2011. The lack of counterintelligence capabilities, including offensive counterespionage functions, have become salient with the assassination of Muhammad al-Zawārī outside his house located near the city of Sfax (170 miles southeast of Tunis) on December 15, 2016. This act of terrorism confirmed yet again the obvious unpreparedness and inefficiency of the country's dysfunctional intelligence architecture in countering foreign threats. A Tunisian citizen and an aviation engineer, al-Zawārī, reportedly had been a member of the Palestinian Ḥamās' military wing Al Qassām Brigades for ten years and "one of the main pioneering leaders in supervising and developing its UAVs program."[264] Two days after al-Zawārī's assassination, Al Qassām had explicitly accused the Israeli Mossad spy agency of being the perpetrator in the attack.[265] The details of this covert operation, provided by the Tunisian Minister of the Interior Hādī Majdūb, seem concurrent with Al Qassām's conclusions, though Majdūb, during his press conference, which lasted more than an hour and a half, acknowledged the involvement of foreign services in the assassination and avoided singling out the Mossad agency on the pretext that his services "did not have enough evidence to openly point the finger at [the Mossad]."[266] Although Israel has neither confirmed nor denied its responsibility in al-Zawārī's killing—as was the case in other assassinations of Palestinian leaders and Iranian scientists targeted by Israel—in al-Zawārī's case the attack carried the hallmarks of the Mossad agency. According to Majdūb, the assassination was planned as early as June 2016 in two European capitals, Vienna and Budapest, through a fictitious media company. This company astutely hired Tunisian personnel, who seemingly were unwarily involved, to provide the operative's hit-team with logistical support by renting cars and safe houses as well as acquiring mobile phones that were used in the assassination. Among the suspects who played a key role in facilitating the assassination was a Tunisian woman who was used, apparently without her knowledge, to collect information on al-Zawārī. She alleged that she was commissioned by a Malaysian TV channel to conduct a video interview with al-Zawārī for a documentary film about the development of the aeronautic industry in many Arab countries, including Tunisia, but that the "interview" was just a rouge for collecting information on the target.[267]

Given the lesser degree of plausible deniability on the part of Israeli officials, the Mossad agency is believed to have been behind al-Zawārī's assassination. Indeed, Israeli Minister of Defense Avigdor Liberman commented on the murder of the Tunisian aviation engineer and pointed out, "If someone was killed in Tunisia, he's not likely to be a peace activist or a Nobel Prize candidate," before adding, "We will continue to do in the best possible way what we know how to do—that is to protect our interests."[268] This ambiguous statement has been corroborated by other Israeli analysts, chief among them Ronen Bergman, the *Yedioth Ahronoth's* senior political and military analyst. Bergman praised the Mossad's "long arm, as an aggressive and merciless organization" in targeting al-Zawārī, whose "ties to Hamas in Gaza and Damascus and to Hezbollah put him in the crosshairs of Israeli intelligence officials, who gradually saw him as an increasingly dangerous element and decided to target him."[269] Bergman also confirmed that Tunisia, from the Mossad agency's perspective, is seen as a "soft target" vulnerable to covert actions and a country where an "operation in such a distant arena … must only be carried out against a principled target—a target whose removal will clearly cause the rival considerable damage."[270] Adding insult to injury, two days after al-Zawārī's assassination, Moav Vardi, an Israeli journalist (who was holding a German passport) for Israel TV Channel 10, entered Tunisia and traveled to Sfax, where he succeeded in accessing the crime scene and reporting from it in Hebrew, and even walked into al-Zawārī's house, where he interviewed some of the deceased's family and neighbors.[271] Majdūb confirmed that Vardi concealed his Israeli professional identity from his interviewees, to whom he introduced himself as a BBC and ZDF (German public-service television) broadcast journalist.[272] Not surprisingly, Tunisia's Interior Minister expressed his deep frustration and disappointment regarding Vardi's freedom of movement across the country and his ability to report from the "14 January 2011 Square" next to the Interior Ministry without worry and promised to investigate these security shortfalls.[273]

Notwithstanding all the aforementioned evidence about the strong presumption of Mossad's involvement in al-Zawārī's assassination, the Interior Ministry and subsequently the Tunisian government continued to be in a state of denial. Seemingly, this reluctance to spare Israel from any responsibility for terrorism is motivated by international considerations, as one senior security official from the Interior Ministry asserts:

> Most of the security personnel within the Interior Ministry like the majority of the Tunisian people believe that the Israeli Mossad is the principal orchestrator of al-Zawārī's assassination while the undercover hit-team is still at large. The *modus operandi* employed reflects the Israeli intelligence tactics of gunning down, blowing up or poisoning individuals without due process under the false pretext that they may pose a "security threat" to Israel. Given that Ḥamās and its military wing are blacklisted by the U.S. State of Department as Foreign Terrorist Organizations, Tunisian government seems exposed to pressure from the United States to abstain from denouncing Israel's responsibility in the Zawārī's assassination with the risk to be considered itself a country providing facilities to what is already labeled by the American government a terrorist organization. Furthermore, the United States is currently actively involved in supporting Tunisia with security and military assistance while the Tunisian government is unwilling to run the risk of jeopardizing such assistance.[274]

The alleged foreign interference seeking to leverage the investigation outcomes of al-Zawārī's assassination is likely aimed at redirecting the country's intelligence and security services national priorities away from countering multidimensional threats that may endanger the country's stability toward narrowly embracing the very controversial U.S. global terror agenda. For Tunisia's intelligence apparatus, this agenda entails a more repressive approach, a lack of democratic control and supervision, greater immunity from public accountability and oversight, and a heightened obsession with secrecy. "Secrecy is the enemy of democracy,"[275] as it undermines accountability, which is the cornerstone of any democratic system. Interestingly, the negative political implications of al-Zawārī's assassination are more obvious at the domestic level, and have led to further public distrust and discrediting of the country's intelligence and security establishment, as one member of the parliament emotionally stated:

> Those people came to Tunisia, stepped on our land and violated our dignity ... About what dignity are we talking? We have to ask ourselves, do we have a state? Do we have intelligence agencies? Do we have borders?[276]

This crisis of confidence will likely escalate and go hand in hand with further politicization of the already highly politicized Tunisian security sector. While intelligence reform is a central factor in the success of the democratization process, the successive governments since 2011 have failed to initiate a road map tackling such reform. Furthermore, the political elite who strongly opposed any transformation of the intelligence services that would expose the country to additional security vulnerabilities has perceived the complex implications of intelligence reform in the transitional process in a negative way. Indeed, the ruling elite failed to realize that the "goals during the transformation process were to limit the decline in efficiency while minimizing the time that it would take for the organization to recover," as both happened in other countries that have experienced a transition from authoritarian regime to democratic rule and successfully operationalized intelligence reform.[277] This misunderstanding of this sacrosanct rule regarding the conception and implementation of intelligence reform during a political transition led to more stagnation and a decline in the country's intelligence and security apparatus—which had failed to comply with the rule of law—and resulted in neither the transformation into a cohesive and efficient community, a redirection of missions, nor an adjustment to meet the new spectrum of threats.

Conclusion

The evolution of Tunisia's post-independence intelligence and security services has undergone different phases of authoritarian institutionalization. Throughout its history, the security complex was at the center of the country's political and security dynamics. It operated as one of the key coercive instruments of the regime's durability and the principal tool of social and political control. Human rights abuses, oppression of dissidents, the policing of society, and the manipulation of information for the purpose of undermining individuals and groups thought to be a threat for the regime's survival were the main functions of Tunisia's intelligence apparatus. This lawlessness would have not been easy for Tunisia's "rogue elephants" to carry out without the salient complicity of the political leadership, the covering-up of the bureaucracy, the acquiescence of many key segments within the society, the pervasive corruption, the thick veil of secrecy governing the intelligence and security apparatus structures, and, most importantly, the feeling of invincibility, impunity, and complete absence of accountability.

The ouster of the autocratic ruler in early 2011, and the subsequent democratic dynamic, has failed to bring about a revolutionary change to the security sector in general, and its intelligence subset in particular. The increase in politicization of the security sector in the post-authoritarian era, the resilient authoritarian legacy within the coercive system, the lack of political vision with regard to reform, the security illiteracy among the legislature about the complexity of intelligence, and the absence of constitutional provisions ensuring democratic control and oversight of the intelligence services all obstructed the reform process. Given the obsession of secrecy entrenched within Tunisia's security sector, intelligence and security services are pursuing their business-as-usual policy, disregarding the post-uprising political context and risking the distortion of the democratic consolidation into an unconsolidated or failed process, leading to "de-democratization" trends that could pave the way for institutional manipulation and subversion.[278]

The authoritarian legacy of Tunisia's intelligence apparatus is obvious. In fact, the intelligence services' monopoly of access to, control, and manipulating sensitive information without any checks and balances further consolidated their autonomous structures while they operated outside the rule of law and without transparency or accountability, which led to the rise of a patronizing fraternity or secret brotherhood. Needless to say, it is difficult to overcome this secret corporatism without authentic reform of the performance of organizations' intelligence and security functions, which are parts of the security problem. Interestingly, Tunisia's process of nurturing new democratic mechanisms of governance overlooked the institutionalization of intelligence reform, while the post-authoritarian political elite has been inclined—under various pretexts that include the "prestige of the state," continuity of government, inclusion, political stability, and consensus—to avoid infuriating intelligence and security apparatus, which was deeply involved in human rights violations and abuses of citizenry and strongly reluctant to change. Such an approach strengthened intelligence organizations' lack of accountability, further tipped the balance between efficiency and transparency, and strongly prevented any democratic control.

Arguably, the political elite is leaning more toward having the country's intelligence and security services function in a "liberal autocracy" mode of operation by instrumentalizing the "fear" of terrorism to circumvent their oversight while enabling them to expand their influence with the risk of subverting the country's democratization process. Taking advantage of the lack of public awareness and the quasi-absence of elite intelligence expertise, Tunisia's intelligence services are not ready to move beyond the secretive realm of abuse and misuse. Likely, these services will reject any measures to make them be fully and rigorously held accountable. Given their historical role in the inception and resilience of authoritarian rule, it is likely that intelligence and security services will emerge among other potential key spoilers in Tunisia's democratization process.

The new post-authoritarian security context enabled Tunisia's intelligence and security services to reposition themselves as seekers of managed rehabilitation with the aim of revamping their operational capabilities. This was empowered by the technicalities discourse. This mending process is considered a substitute to any robust reform that would enshrine a culture of transparency and accountability based on strong legal mechanisms of democratic control and oversight. In all likelihood, ruling elite will use the post-transition uncertainties to further undermine any prospective intelligence reform and justify its postponing *ad Kalendas Graecas* (that is, never). However, democratic control of the state's coercive apparatus cannot be reinvented, as it is necessary to the development of any modern democracy. The ancient Roman adage *"Quid custodit ipsos custodies?,"* meaning, "Who shall guard the guards themselves?" is more than relevant to Tunisia's bourgeoning democratic context. Indeed, "who watches the watchers" in order to ensure the legality and legitimacy of the country's intelligence and security apparatus activities? More than ever before, policies on intelligence are needed to appease the debate, and foster and sustain institutional reform in order to demystify the country's national intelligence in a way that would enable Tunisians to oversee, held accountable, and trust their "invisible [and secret] government."

Appendices

Appendix A

Presidential Decree n° 1763, November 23, 1991 amending and completing Decree n° 453-1991 on the Structural Organization of the Ministry of the Interior, *OJRT*, n° 83, December 6, 1991.

وزارة الداخلية

التنظيم الهيكلي لوزارة الداخلية

أمر عدد 1763 لسنة 1991 مؤرخ في 23 نوفمبر 1991 يتعلق بإتمام الأمر عدد 453 لسنة 1991 المؤرخ في غرة أفريل 1991 المتعلق بالتنظيم الهيكلي لوزارة الداخلية.

إن رئيس الجمهورية،

باقتراح من وزير الدولة وزير الداخلية،

بعد الاطلاع على الأمر عدد 453 المؤرخ في غرة أفريل 1991 المتعلق بالتنظيم الهيكلي لوزارة الداخلية، وخاصة فصليه 11 و 12.

وعلى رأي وزير المالية.

وعلى رأي المحكمة الادارية.

يصدر الأمر الآتي نصه :

الفصل الأول ـ تمم الفصلان 11 و 12 من الأمر المشار اليه أعلاه عدد 453 المؤرخ في غرة افريل 1991 على النحو التالي :

الفصل 11 (جديد) ـ ان الادارة العامة للشؤون الجهوية مكلفة خاصة :

ـ بتنشيط عمل الولاة وتوجيهه ومراقبته في الميادين الادارية والسياسية والاقتصادية والاجتماعية والثقافية والدينية.

ـ بالسهر على التنسيق بين الوزارات والهياكل المعنية الأخرى في كل المسائل الراجعة بالنظر للادارة العامة للشؤون الجهوية.

ـ بمتابعة تنفيذ البرامج الجهوية للتنمية.

ـ بالسهر على التنسيق بين مختلف الولايات وبدراسة المشاكل والاصلاحات المتعلقة بالهياكل الادارية الجهوية.

ـ بجمع كل المعلومات والقيام بتحليلها والسهر على استغلالها.

ـ بتنظيم مختلف الندوات والاجتماعات الدورية لاطارات الادارة الجهوية.

ـ بمتابعة الحياة الادارية للاطارات العليا للادارة الجهوية.

ـ بالتحديد الترابي الاداري للولايات والمعتمديات والعمادات.

ـ بالسهر على تنظيم العمليات الانتخابية وإجرائها ومتابعتها.

ـ بالسهر على احداث لجان الاحياء ومتابعة نشاطها وتنظيم ندواتها الوطنية والجهوية والمحلية.

ـ باعداد الدراسات واقتراح التدابير اللازمة لتطوير عمل لجان الاحياء.

الفصل 12 (جديد) ـ تشتمل الادارة العامة للشؤون الجهوية على :

1) ادارة الدراسات والانتخابات والشؤون الادارية وتشتمل على :

أ ـ الادارة الفرعية للندوات والانتخابات وتتكون من :

ـ مصلحة الدراسات والندوات.

ـ مصلحة الانتخابات.

ب ـ الادارة الفرعية للشؤون الادارية وتتكون من :

ـ مصلحة الاطارات الجهوية.

ـ مصلحة التكوين والندوات.

ـ مصلحة الترتيب.

2) ادارة التنمية الجهوية وتشتمل على :

أ ـ الادارة الفرعية للشؤون الاقتصادية والاجتماعية وتتكون من :

ـ مصلحة الشؤون الاقتصادية.

ـ مصلحة الشؤون الفلاحية.

ـ مصلحة الشؤون الاجتماعية.

ب ـ الادارة الفرعية للتنمية الجهوية وتتكون من :

ـ مصلحة التخطيط والبرامج الجهوية.

ـ مصلحة التقسيم الترابي.

3) وحدة لجان الاحياء

رئيس وحدة لجان الاحياء رتبة وصلاحيات مدير ادارة مركزية وينتفع بنفس المنح والامتيازات المخولة لهذا الاخير.

يمكن ان يلحق بهذه الوحدة رؤساء مكاتب يعهد اليهم بالقيام بالدراسات والاعمال الكفيلة بتطوير نشاط لجان الاحياء ومتابعتها ويمكن ان تسند لهم

خطة وصلاحيات كاملة مدير ادارة مركزية او رئيس مصلحة ادارة مركزية
طبقا للتراتيب الجاري بها العمل.

الفصل 2 ــ وزير الدولة وزير الداخلية ووزير المالية مكلفان كل في ما
يخصه بتنفيذ هذا الامر الذي ينشر بالرائد الرسمي للجمهورية التونسية.

تونس في 23 نوفمبر 1991.

زين العابدين بن علي

Appendix B

Presidential Decree nº 147 on Watchdog Citizen, January 18, 1993, *OJRT*, nº 7, January 26, 1993.

الاوامــر والقــرارات

الوزارة الاولى

أمر عدد 147 لسنة 1993 مؤرخ في 18 جانفي 1993 يتعلق بإحداث فريق «المواطن الرقيب».

إن رئيس الجمهورية.

باقتراح من الوزير الاول.

بعد الاطلاع على القانون عدد 112 لسنة 1983 المؤرخ في 12 ديسمبر 1983 المتعلق بضبط النظام الاساسي العام لاعوان الدولة والجماعات العمومية المحلية والمؤسسات العمومية ذات الصبغة الادارية.

وبعد الاطلاع على الامر عدد 400 لسنة 1969 المؤرخ في 7 نوفمبر 1969 المتعلق بإحداث وزارة اول وضبط مشمولات الوزير الاول.

وعلى الامر عدد 118 لسنة 1970 المؤرخ في 11 أفريل 1970 المتعلق بتنظيم مصالح الوزارة الاول وعلى جميع النصوص التي تممته أو نقحته.

وعلى رأي وزير المالية.

وعلى رأي المحكمة الادارية.

يصدر الامر الآتي نصه

الباب الاول
مقتضيات عامة

الفصل الاول ـ أحدث بالوزارة الاول جهاز لمعاينة نوعية الخدمات العمومية يسمى «فريق المواطن الرقيب».

الباب الثاني
مشمولات المواطن الرقيب

الفصل 2 ـ تتمثل مشمولات المواطن الرقيب في :

ـ القيام بعمليات حقيقية لكبار المواطنين قصد معاينة نوعية الخدمات بالمصالح الادارية وملاحظة أداء العمل من طرف الاعوان العموميين.

في يقوم المواطن الرقيب بمهامه لدى مصالح الدولة والمؤسسات العمومية والجماعات العمومية المحلية وبصفة عامة لدى كافة المؤسسات التي تساهم الدولة أو الجماعات العمومية المحلية في رأس مالها بصفة مباشرة أو غير مباشرة.

الباب الثالث
انتداب المواطن الرقيب

الفصل 4 ـ يعين المواطن الرقيب بقرار من الوزير الاول لمدة سنة قابلة للتجديد مرة واحدة من بين :

ـ الموظفين الرسميين المباشرين الذين ينتمون على الاقل لرتبة من صنف ب

ـ المتقاعدين في إطار الاحكام القانونية والترتيبية الجاري بها العمل.

ـ المتعاقدين مع الوزارة الاول.

ويجب أن تتوفر في المترشح لخطة مواطن رقيب الشروط القانونية المنصوص عليها بالفصل 17 من القانون عدد 112 لسنة 1983 المؤرخ في 12 ديسمبر 1983 المذكور اعلاه وأن يكون قد تحصل على الاقل على رتبة من صنف ب أو على شهادة الباكالوريا أو ما يعادلها.

الفصل 5 ـ يخضع المترشح لخطة مواطن رقيب إلى اختبار لتقييم مؤهلاته والإستعدادات اللازمة لديه للقيام بمهامه على أحسن وجه. ويتم ضبط كيفية تطبيق مقتضيات هذا الفصل بقرار من الوزير الاول.

الفصل 6 ـ يحافظ المواطنون الرقاب المعينون من بين الموظفين الرسميين عن الاجر وكل المنح الراجعة لهم ويتقاضون إضافة إلى ذلك منحة جملية تسمى

منحة المواطن الرقيب لتغطية كل التكاليف اللازمة للقيام بمختلف العمليات لدى المصالح العمومية.

ويتم ضبط مقدار هذه المنحة من 100 الى 150 دينارا شهريا بقرار من الوزير الاول بالنسبة الى كل مواطن رقيب.

ويضبط أجر المواطن الرقيب المتعاقد مع الوزارة الاول على أساس الاحكام القانونية والترتيبية الجاري بها العمل.

الفصل 7 ـ يمنح لكل مواطن رقيب، رقم سري يستعمل للتعريف بجميع الوثائق التي يدلي بها لإدارة نوعية الخدمة العمومية بالوزارة الاول وتوضع قائمة مطابقة بين الاسماء والارقام المناسبة وهذا كوثيقة سرية.

الفصل 8 ـ يقوم المواطن الرقيب بأداء اليمين الآتي نصه أمام الوزير الاول أو من ينوبه :

« أقسم بالله العظيم أن أقوم بمهمتي بكل إخلاص وأمانة وأن ألتزم بعدم إنشاء سر العمليات التي توكل الي سواء كان ذلك أثناء أو بعد القيام بهذه العمليات وأن يكون سلوكي سلوك المواطن الامين الشريف ».

الفصل 9 ـ يمكن للإدارة إنهاء مهام المواطن الرقيب حالا وبدون سابق إعلام.

كما يمكن للإدارة فسخ عقد المواطن الرقيب قبل نهايته شريطة التنبيه على المعني بالامر قبل شهر.

الباب الرابع
كيفية قيام المواطن الرقيب بنشاطه

الفصل 10 ـ يلتزم المواطن الرقيب بالتقيد ببرنامج الزيارات التي تضبطه له إدارة نوعية الخدمة العمومية بالوزارة الاول وهو مطالب بالقيام بمهامه بكامل تراب الجمهورية.

الفصل 11 ـ يحجر على المواطن الرقيب ذكر المهمة الموكولة اليه في وثائقه الشخصية وذلك طيلة مدة قيامه بمهامه وبعد انتهائها.

الفصل 12 ـ يحجر على المواطن الرقيب الكشف عن صفته أو التدخل في سير العمل بالمصالح التي يزورها وهو مطالب كذلك بالمحافظة على السرية التامة عند القيام بمهمته وكذلك الشأن بعد انقضاء المهمة.

الفصل 13 ـ يجب على المواطن الرقيب أن يضع حدا للزيارة التي يقوم بها في إطار البرنامج المعد له كما اتضح له أن أحد الاعوان الاداري الذي هو بصدد زيارته من أقاربه وكذلك الامر كلما تبين له عدم إمكانية القيام بمهمته بصفة موضوعية وفي كلتا الحالتين يتعين عليه إعلام إدارة نوعية الخدمة العمومية بذلك.

الفصل 14 ـ لا يمكن للمواطن الرقيب أن يدون ملاحظات ببطاقة الزيارة في المحلات التابعة للإدارة التي يقوم بزيارتها أو بالاماكن القريبة منها.

الفصل 15 ـ يجب أن تتضمن بطاقة الزيارة خاصة الرقم السري للمواطن الرقيب المعني بالامر واسم الإدارة أو المصلحة أو المؤسسة التي أدى لها الزيارة والتاريخ والساعة ومدة الزيارة ونوع العملية المنجزة والملاحظات المتعلقة بهذه العملية. ولا يمكن أن تتضمن هذه البطاقة اسم العون القائم بالزيارة او كل ما من شأنه أن يساعد على التعرف على هويته.

الفصل 16 ـ على الإدارة أن تحمي المواطن الرقيب من التهديدات والإعتداءات مهما كان نوعها التي قد يتعرض اليها وعند اللزوم يجبر الضرر الذي قد ينتج عن ذلك.

الفصل 17 ـ يرفع الوزير الاول الى رئيس الجمهورية تقريرا سنويا بتضمن نتائج عمل فريق المواطن الرقيب.

الفصل 18 ـ الوزير الاول ووزير المالية مكلفان كل فيما يخصه بتنفيذ هذا الامر الذي ينشر بالرائد الرسمي للجمهورية التونسية.

تونس في 18 جانفي 1993

زين العابدين بن علي

أمر عدد 147 لسنة 1993 مؤرخ في 18 جانفي 1993 يتعلق بإحداث فريق "المواطن الرقيب "

إن رئيس الجمهورية

باقتراح من الوزير الأول

بعد الاطلاع على القانون عدد 112لسنة 1983 المؤرخ في 12 ديسمبر 1983المتعلق بضبط النظام الأساسي العام والجماعات العمومية المحلية والمؤسسات العمومية ذات الصبغة الإدارية.

وبعد الاطلاع على الأمر عدد 400 لسنة 1969 المؤرخ في 7 نوفمبر 1969 المتعلق بإحداث وزارة أولى وضبط مشمولات الوزير الأول.

وعلى الأمر عدد 118 لسنة 1970المؤرخ في 11 أفريل 1970 المتعلق بتنظيم مصالح الوزارة الأولى وعلى جميع النصوص التي تممته أو نقحته.

وعلى رأي المحكمة الإدارية

يصدر الأمر الآتي نصه:

الباب الأول – مقتضيات عامة

الفصل الأول – أحدثت بالوزارة الأولى فريق لمعاينة نوعية الخدمات العمومية يسمى "فريق المواطن الرقيب ".

الباب الثاني – مشمولات المواطن الرقيب

الفصل 2 – تتمثل مشمولات المواطن الرقيب في:

–   القيام بعمليات حقيقية كسائر المواطنين لدى المصالح العمومية قصد معاينة نوعية الخدمات بالمصالح الإدارية وملاحظة كيفية أداء العمل من طرف الأعوان العموميين.

الفصل 3 – يقوم المواطن الرقيب بمهامه لدى مصالح الدولة والمؤسسات العمومية والجماعات العمومية المحلية وبصفة عامة لدى كافة المؤسسات التي تساهم الدولة والجماعات العمومية المحلية في رأس مالها بصفة مباشرة أو غير مباشرة.

الباب الثالث – انتداب المواطن الرقيب

الفصل 4 – يعين المواطن الرقيب بقرار من الوزير الأول لمدة سنة قابلة للتجديد مرة واحدة من بين:

–   الموظفين المرسمين المباشرين الذين ينتمون على الأقل لرتبة من صنف "ب".
–   المتعاقدين في إطار الأحكام القانونية والترتيبية الجاري بها العمل.
–   المتعاقدين مع الوزارة الأولى.

ويجب أن تتوفر في المترشح لخطة مراقب رقيب الشروط القانونية المنصوص عليها الشروط القانونية المنصوص عليها بالفصل 17 من القانون عدد 112 لسنة 1983 المؤرخ في 12 ديسمبر 1983 المؤرخ في 12 ديسمبر 1983 المذكور أعلاه وأن يكون قد تحصل على الأقل على رتبة من صنف "ب" أو على شهادة الباكالوريا أو ما يعادلها.

الفصل 5 – يخضع المترشح لخطة مواطن رقيب إلى اختبار لتقييم مؤهلاته والاستعدادات اللازمة لديه للقيام على أحسن وجه ويتم ضبط كيفية تطبيق مقتضيات هذا الفصل بقرار من الوزير الأول.

الفصل 6 – يحافظ المواطنون الرقباء المعينون من بين الموظفين المرسمين على الأجر وكل المنح الراجعة لهم ويتقاضون إضافة إلى ذلك منحة جملية تسمى منحة المواطن الرقيب لتغطية كل التكاليف اللازمة للقيام بمختلف العمليات لدى المصالح العمومية.

ويتم ضبط مقدار هذه المنحة من 170 إلى 250 دينارا شهريا بقرار من الوزير الأول بالنسبة إلى كل مواطن رقيب **(فقرة ثانية جديدة – نقحت بمقتضى الأمر عدد 1862 لسنة 2006 المؤرخ في 3 جويلية 2006 -).**

ويضبط أجر المواطن الرقيب المتعاقد مع الوزارة الأولى على أساس الأحكام القانونية والترتيبية الجاري بها العمل.

الفصل 7 – يمنح لكل" مواطن رقيب" رقم سري يستعمل للتعريف بجميع الوثائق التي يدلي بها لإدارة نوعية الخدمة العمومية بالوزارة الأولى وتوضع قائمة مطابقة بين الأسماء والأرقام المناسبة ويحتفظ بها كوثيقة سرية.

الفصل 8 – يقوم المواطن الرقيب بأداء اليمين الآتي نصه أمام الوزير الأول أو من ينوبه:

"أقسم بالله العظيم أن أقوم بمهمتي بكل إخلاص وأمانة وأن التزم بعدم إفشاء سر العمليات التي توكل إليّ سواء كان ذلك أثناء أو بعد القيام بهذه العمليات وأن يكون سلوكي سلوك المواطن الأمين الشريف".

الفصل 9 – يمكن للإدارة إنهاء مهام المواطن الرقيب حالا وبدون سابق إعلام.

كما يمكن للإدارة فسخ عقد المواطن الرقيب قبل نهايته شريطة التنبيه على المعني بالأمر قبل شهر.

الباب الرابع – كيفية قيام المواطن القيب بنشاطه

الفصل 10 – يلتزم المواطن الرقيب بالتقيد ببرنامج الزيارات التي تضبطه له إدارة نوعية الخدمة العمومية بالوزارة الأولى وهو مطالب بالقيام بمهامه بكامل تراب الجمهورية.

الفصل 11 – يحجر على المواطن الرقيب ذكر المهمة الموكولة إليه في وثائقه الشخصية وذلك طيلة مدة قيامه بمهامه وبعد انتهائها.

الفصل 12 – يحجر على المواطن الرقيب الكشف عن صفته أو التدخل في سير العمل بالمصلحة التي يزورها. وهو مطالب كذلك بالمحافظة على السرية التامة عند القيام بمهمته وكذلك الشأن بعد انقضاء المهمة.

الفصل 13 – يجب على المواطن الرقيب أن يضع حدا للزيارة التي يقوم بها في إطار البرنامج المعد له كلما اتضح أن العون الإداري الذي هو بصدد زيارته من أقربائه وكذلك الأمر إذا تبين له عدم امكانية القيام بمهمته بصفة موضوعية وفي كلتا الحالتين يتعين عليه إعلام إدارة نوعية الخدمة العمومية بذلك.

الفصل 14 – لا يمكن للمواطن الرقيب أن يدون ملاحظاته ببطاقة الزيارة في المحلات التابعة للإدارة التي يقوم بزيارتها أو بالأماكن القريبة منها.

الفصل 15 – يجب أن تتضمن بطاقة الزيارة خاصة الرقم السري للمواطن الرقيب المعني بالأمر واسم الإدارة أو المؤسسة أو المصلحة التي أدى لها الزيارة والتاريخ والساعة ومدة الزيارة ونوع العملية المنجزة والملاحظات المتعلقة بهذه العملية.

ولا يمكن ان تتضمن هذه البطاقة اسم العون القائم بالزيارة او كل ما من شأنه ان يساعد على التعرف على هويته.

الفصل 16 – على الإدارة التي تحمي المواطن الرقيب من التهديدات والاعتداءات مهما كان نوعها التي قد يتعرض إليها وعند اللزوم يجبر الضرر الذي قد ينتج عن ذلك.

الفصل 17 – يرفع الوزير الأول إلى رئيس الجمهورية تقريرا سنويا يتضمن نتائج عمل فريق المواطن الرقيب.

الفصل 18 – الوزير الأول ووزير المالية مكلفان كل فيما يخصه بتنفيذ هذا الأمر الذي ينشر بالرائد الرسمي للجمهورية التونسية.

تونس في 18 جانفي 1993.

Appendix C

Law n° 2001-1 of January 15, 2001 on the Promulgation of the Tele-communications Code, *OJRT*, n° 5, January 16, 2001.

القوانيـن

قانون عدد 1 لسنة 2001 مؤرخ في 15 جانفي 2001 يتعلق بإصدار مجلة الاتصالات. (1)

باسم الشعب،

بعد موافقة مجلس النواب،

يصدر رئيس الجمهورية القانون الآتي نصه :

الفصل الأول . تصدر بمقتضى هذا القانون مجلة الاتصالات.

الفصل 2 . تدخل أحكام هذه المجلة حيز التطبيق بعد مرور ثلاثة أشهر من تاريخ نشر هذا القانون بالرائد الرسمي للجمهورية التونسية.

الفصل 3 . يمنح متعاطو أنشطة الاتصالات المرخص لهم في تاريخ نشر هذا القانون مهلة لمدة سنتين من تاريخه لتسوية وضعياتهم طبقا لأحكام هذه المجلة.

الفصل 4 . تلغى جميع الأحكام السابقة المخالفة لأحكام هذه المجلة وخاصة مجلة المواصلات السلكية واللاسلكية الصادرة بالقانون عدد 58 لسنة 1977 المؤرخ في 3 أوت 1977 عند دخول هذه المجلة حيز التطبيق.

ينشر هذا القانون بالرائد الرسمي للجمهورية التونسية وينفذ كقانون من قوانين الدولة.

تونس في 15 جانفي 2001.

زين العابدين بن علي

الباب الأول
في الأحكام العامة

الفصل الأول . تهدف هذه المجلة إلى تنظيم مجال الاتصالات، ويشمل هذا التنظيم :

. إقامة وتشغيل شبكات الاتصالات،

. توفير الخدمات الأساسية للاتصالات،

. توفير خدمات الاتصالات،

. توفير خدمات البث الإذاعي والتلفزي،

. التصرف في الموارد النادرة للاتصالات.

القسم الأول
في المصطلحات

الفصل 2 . يقصد بالمصطلحات التالية على معنى هذه المجلة :

. الاتصالات : كل عملية تراسل أو بث أو استقبال لإشارات بواسطة حوامل معدنية أو بصرية أو راديوية.

(1) الأعمال التحضيرية

مداولة مجلس النواب وموافقته بجلسته المنعقدة بتاريخ 18 ديسمبر 2000.

. الترددات الراديوية : الترددات الكهرومغناطيسية المتعلقة بالذبذبات التي تستعمل في الاتصالات حسب القواعد العالمية الجاري بها العمل.

. الموارد النادرة : الترددات الراديوية والترقيم والعنونة.

. شبكة اتصالات : مجموع التجهيزات والأنظمة التي تؤمن الاتصالات.

. شبكة عمومية للاتصالات : شبكة اتصالات مفتوحة للعموم.

. شبكة خاصة للاتصالات : شبكة اتصالات مخصصة للاستعمال الخاص أو للاستعمال بين مجموعة مغلقة من المستعملين لأغراض محددة في إطار المصلحة المشتركة.

. مشغل شبكة اتصالات : كل شخص معنوي متحصل على لزمة لاستغلال شبكة عمومية للاتصالات.

. اللزمة : امتياز يمنح لشخص معنوي بمقتضى اتفاقية لإقامة وتشغيل شبكة عمومية للاتصالات.

. الربط البيني : ربط بين شبكتين عموميتين للاتصالات أو أكثر.

. خدمة اتصالات : كل خدمة تؤمن الاتصالات بين طرفين أو أكثر.

. الخدمات الأساسية للاتصالات : خدمات الاتصالات الدنيا الواجب توفيرها للعموم حسب التطور التكنولوجي في المجال.

. خدمات البث الإذاعي والتلفزي : خدمات الاتصالات التي تؤمن إرسال وبث البرامج الإذاعية والتلفزية عبر الترددات الراديوية.

. الخدمات ذات القيمة المضافة للاتصالات : الخدمات التي توفر للعموم عبر الشبكات العمومية للاتصالات بواسطة منظومات معلوماتية تمكن من النفاذ إلى معطيات تتعلق بميادين محددة قصد الاطلاع عليها أو الاطلاع عليها وتبادلها.

. مزود خدمات الاتصالات : كل شخص طبيعي أو معنوي تتوفر فيه الشروط القانونية والترتيبية ويقوم بإسداء خدمات الاتصالات.

. التشفير : استعمال رموز أو إشارات غير متداولة تصبح بمقتضاها المعلومات المرغوب تمريرها أو إرسالها غير قابلة للفهم من قبل الغير أو استعمال رموز أو إشارات لا يمكن الوصول إلى المعلومة بدونها.

. جهاز طرفي للاتصالات : كل جهاز يمكن ربطه مع طرف شبكة اتصالات قصد توفير خدمات الاتصالات للعموم.

. جهاز راديوي : كل جهاز اتصالات يشتغل باستعمال الترددات الراديوية.

. المصادقة : جميع عمليات الاختبارات والتثبت التي تنجز من قبل هيكل مؤهل ليشهد أن النموذج التمثيلي لأجهزة ومنظومات الاتصالات مطابق للتراتيب والمواصفات التقنية الجاري بها العمل.

القسم الثاني
في حق الاتصال

الفصل 3 . لكل شخص الحق في التمتع بخدمات الاتصالات ويتمثل هذا الحق في :

. الحصول على الخدمات الأساسية للاتصالات على كامل تراب الجمهورية التونسية.

. التمتع بخدمات الاتصالات الأخرى حسب مجال التغطية لكل خدمة.

. حرية اختيار مزود خدمات الاتصالات حسب مجال التغطية لكل خدمة.

. المساواة في الحصول على خدمات الاتصالات.

. الحصول على المعلومات الأساسية المتعلقة بشروط توفير خدمات الاتصالات وتعريفاتها.

الفصل 4 . يتعين على كل شخص يتمتع بخدمات الاتصالات احترام التراتيب الجاري بها العمل والمتعلقة بالربط بالشبكات العمومية للاتصالات.

الباب الثاني
في خدمات الاتصالات

القسم الأول
في توفير خدمات الاتصالات

الفصل 5 . يخضع توفير خدمات الاتصالات إلى ترخيص مسبق من قبل الوزير المكلف بالاتصالات وتضبط شروط وطريقة إسناد هذا الترخيص بمقتضى أمر يتضمن خاصة كيفية إيداع مطلب الترخيص وأجال إجابة الوزارة المكلفة بالاتصالات وتعليل قرار الرفض.

الفصل 6 . توفر خدمات الاتصالات طبقا لكراس شروط تتم المصادقة عليه بقرار من الوزير المكلف بالاتصالات ويتضمن وجوبا الشروط العامة للاستغلال

وتستثنى من أحكام الفصل 5 من هذه المجلة والفقرة الأولى لهذا الفصل الخدمات الأساسية للاتصالات وخدمات البث الإذاعي والتلفزي والخدمات ذات القيمة المضافة للاتصالات وكذلك كل خدمة اتصالات أخرى يتم ضبطها بمقتضى أمر. ويخضع توفير هذه الخدمات إلى الأحكام المنصوص عليها بالفصول 10 و12 و91 من هذه المجلة.

الفصل 7 . يمنح الترخيص إلى مزود خدمات الاتصالات بعنوان شخصي ولا يمكن إحالته إلى الغير إلا بموافقة الوزير المكلف بالاتصالات.

الفصل 8 . مع مراعاة أحكام الفصل 5 من هذه المجلة يجب أن تتوفر في مزود خدمات الاتصالات الشروط التالية :

. بالنسبة إلى الشخص الطبيعي : أن يكون تونسي الجنسية.

. بالنسبة إلى الشخص المعنوي : أن يكون مكونا طبقا للتشريع التونسي.

الفصل 9 . تضبط بمقتضى أمر شروط وإجراءات استعمال وسائل أو خدمات التشفير عبر شبكات الاتصالات وكذلك شروط تعاطي الأنشطة ذات العلاقة.

الفصل 10 . يخضع توفير الخدمات ذات القيمة المضافة للاتصالات وخدمة الاتصالات الأخرى التي يتم ضبطها بمقتضى الأمر المنصوص عليه بالفصل 6 من هذه المجلة لتصريح مسبق يودع لدى الوزارة المكلفة بالاتصالات قبل فتح الخدمة.

ويتضمن هذا التصريح خاصة البيانات التالية :

. نوع الخدمة المقدمة.

. طريقة وشروط الاستفادة من الخدمة.

. التعريفات المزمع تطبيقها على الخدمات.

وتضبط قائمة الخدمات ذات القيمة المضافة للاتصالات وشروط تعاطي نشاط مزودي هذه الخدمات طبقا لكراس شروط تتم المصادقة عليه بقرار من الوزير المكلف بالاتصالات.

القسم الثاني
في توفير الخدمات الأساسية للاتصالات

الفصل 11 . مع مراعاة أحكام الفصل 3 من هذه المجلة يخضع توفير الخدمات الأساسية للاتصالات للشروط التالية :

. توفير نقاط اتصال بكامل تراب الجمهورية التونسية مفتوحة بصفة منتظمة.

. ضمان المساواة في تقديم الخدمات بين كل المستعملين.

. تنمية هذه الخدمات وفقا للتطور التكنولوجي والاقتصادي والاجتماعي وحاجيات المستعملين.

وتضبط قائمة هذه الخدمات بقرار من الوزير المكلف بالاتصالات بعد أخذ رأي الهيئة الوطنية للاتصالات.

وتتضمن هذه القائمة وجوبا الخدمات الهاتفية الدنيا وتمرير نداءات الاستغاثة وتقديم خدمات الإرشادات ودليل المشتركين في شكله المطبوع أو الإلكتروني.

الفصل 12 . يمكن تكليف كل مشغل لشبكة اتصالات بتأمين الخدمات الأساسية للاتصالات، وتضبط شروط توفير هذه الخدمات ضمن الاتفاقية المنصوص عليها بالفصل 19 من هذه المجلة.

الفصل 13 . يتعين على كل مشغل مكلف بتأمين الخدمات الأساسية للاتصالات نقل نداءات الاستغاثة مجانا.

الفصل 14 . يتعين على كل مشغل مكلف بتأمين الخدمات الأساسية للاتصالات أن يضع على ذمة العموم دليلا في شكل مطبوع أو إلكتروني يمكن من الحصول على :

. إرشادات تتعلق بأسماء وأرقام وعناوين كل المشتركين في الخدمات الأساسية للاتصالات التي توفرها الشبكات العمومية للاتصالات باستثناء المشتركين الذين يرفضون صراحة ذلك.

. الأرقام والعناوين المفيدة المتعلقة بالخدمات ذات المصلحة العامة.

الفصل 15 . يتعين على المشغلين المكلفين بتأمين الخدمات الأساسية للاتصالات تبادل قائمات مشتركيهم في هذه الخدمات باستثناء قائمات المشتركين الذين يرفضون صراحة نشر الإرشادات الخاصة بهم.

الفصل 16 . يجب على مشغل شبكات الاتصالات توفير الاشتراك في خدمات الاتصالات لكل شخص يرغب في ذلك. ولا يمكن لمالك العقار أو وكيله الاعتراض على تركيز خطوط الاتصالات وفقا لطلب المتسوغ.

الفصل 17 . تخضع التعريفات القصوى المطبقة على الخدمات الأساسية للاتصالات لمصادقة الوزير المكلف بالاتصالات بمقتضى قرار.

ويمكن للدولة في المقابل إسناد منحة تعويضية للمشغلين المعنيين.

الفصل 26 . يتعين على صاحب اللزمة :

. وضع المعلومات المتعلقة بالمسائل التقنية والعملية والمالية والحسابية لكل شبكة ولكل خدمة على ذمة الوزارة المكلفة بالاتصالات.

. عرض نموذج من عقد الخدمة المزمع إبرامه مع الحرفاء على موافقة الهيئة الوطنية للاتصالات وكذلك الاتفاقيات المبرمة مع مزودي خدمات الاتصالات.

. الالتزام بشروط السرية والحياد تجاه الإشارات المنقولة.

. احترام الاتفاقيات والمعاهدات الدولية المصادق عليها من قبل الدولة التونسية.

. تمرير نداءات الاستغاثة مجانا.

. الالتزام بتطبيق المواصفات التقنية المتعلقة بشبكات الاتصالات وتوفير خدمات الاتصالات.

. المساهمة في برامج التكوين والبحث العلمي المتعلقة بقطاع الاتصالات.

. الاستجابة لمقتضيات الدفاع الوطني والأمن العام.

الفصل 27 . يعفى صاحب اللزمة في حالة تقديم خدمات الاتصالات المرتبطة بالشبكة والمحددة باللزمة من الترخيص المنصوص عليه بالفصل 5 من هذه المجلة.

الفصل 28 . يمكن لصاحب اللزمة عند إقامة الشبكة استعمال البنية الأساسية التابعة لكل مشغل شبكة الاتصالات أو مرفق عمومي.

ولا تعفي اللزمة من اتباع الإجراءات الضرورية لإقامة أجزاء الشبكة وخاصة منها المتعلقة بتمرير الشبكة عبر الطريق العام وبإنجاز البناءات وإدخال التغييرات عليها.

الفصل 29 . يمكن للوزارة المكلفة بالاتصالات تعديل بعض أحكام اللزمة خلال مدة نفاذها إذا أصبح هذا التعديل ضروريا لحماية المصلحة العامة ومقتضيات الدفاع الوطني والأمن العام.

إذا نتج عن تعديل اللزمة تخفيض في الحقوق المتنازل عنها يتحصل صاحب اللزمة على تعويض مناسب للخسارة الحاصلة وتحدد اللزمة شروط وطريقة إسناد هذا التعويض.

الفصل 30 . يتعين على كل مشغل لشبكة عمومية للاتصالات أن يضع على ذمة حرفائه دليلا في شكل مطبوع أو إلكتروني يمكن من توفير :

. إرشادات تتعلق بأسماء وأرقام وعناوين كل المشتركين في الشبكة باستثناء المشتركين الذين يرفضون صراحة ذلك.

. الأرقام والعناوين المفيدة المتعلقة بالخدمات ذات المصلحة العامة.

الفصل 31 . تخضع إقامة واستغلال الشبكات الخاصة للاتصالات إلى ترخيص مسبق من قبل الوزير المكلف بالاتصالات بعد أخذ رأي وزيري الدفاع الوطني والداخلية والهيئة الوطنية للاتصالات.

ولا يعفي هذا الترخيص من اتباع الإجراءات الضرورية لإقامة أجزاء الشبكة وخاصة منها المتعلقة بتمرير الشبكة عبر الطريق العام وبإنجاز البناءات وإدخال التغييرات عليها.

يخضع هذا الترخيص إلى دفع معلوم يضبط بقرار من الوزير المكلف بالاتصالات بعد أخذ رأي الهيئة الوطنية للاتصالات.

تضبط بمقتضى أمر الشروط العامة لإقامة واستغلال الشبكات الخاصة للاتصالات.

الباب الثالث

في شبكات الاتصالات

القسم الأول

في إقامة وتشغيل الشبكات

الفصل 18 . يمكن للدولة إسناد لزمات إقامة وتشغيل الشبكات العمومية للاتصالات إلى مؤسسات عمومية أو خاصة يتم اختيارها طبقا لأحكام الفصل 20 من هذه المجلة.

الفصل 19 . تمنح كل لزمة بمقتضى اتفاقية مبرمة بين الدولة بوصفها مانحة، ممثلة من قبل الوزير المكلف بالاتصالات من جهة ومقيم ومشغل شبكة الاتصالات بوصفه المستفيد من اللزمة من جهة أخرى بعد أخذ رأي الهياكل المعنية.

وتتم المصادقة على اتفاقية اللزمة بأمر.

الفصل 20 . يتم اختيار المترشح بعد الدعوة إلى المنافسة وفق طلب عروض مفتوح أو ضيق يكون مسبوقا بمرحلة انتقاء أولى.

الفصل 21 . يشترط في مقيم ومشغل الشبكات أن يكون شخصا معنويا مكونا طبقا للتشريع التونسي.

الفصل 22 . تمنح اللزمة لمدة لا تتجاوز خمس عشرة سنة مع إمكانية التمديد فيها، ويتم تحديد هذه المدة ضمن الاتفاقية المنصوص عليها بالفصل 19 من هذه المجلة.

الفصل 23 . تمنح اللزمة بصفة شخصية ولا تخول لصاحبها أي حق استئثاري ولا يمكن إحالتها إلى الغير إلا بموافقة الوزير المكلف بالاتصالات بعد أخذ رأي الهياكل المعنية.

تحال اللزمة بمقتضى اتفاقية تتم المصادقة عليها بأمر.

الفصل 24 . يخضع إسناد اللزمة لدفع معلوم وفقا للشروط التي يتم تحديدها في اتفاقية اللزمة.

الفصل 25 . تبين اتفاقية اللزمة خاصة :

. شروط إقامة الشبكة.

. شروط تقديم الخدمات المرتبطة بالشبكة.

. الشروط العامة للربط البيني.

. الإمكانات البشرية والمادية وكذلك الضمانات المالية الواجب توفرها لدى المترشحين.

. قيمة وكيفية دفع المعلوم المشار إليه بالفصل 24 من هذه المجلة.

. قيمة وكيفية دفع المعلوم عن استغلال الموارد النادرة المخصصة.

. طريقة تحديد التعريفات المطبقة على الحرفاء وكيفية تعديلها ومراجعتها.

. كيفية مراقبة الحسابات الخاصة باللزمة.

. شروط وطريقة إسناد التعويض المنصوص عليه بالفصل 29 من هذه المجلة.

. شروط وكيفية ضمان استمرارية توفير الخدمات في حالة إخلال صاحب اللزمة بالتزاماته أو انتهاء مدة صلاحية اللزمة.

. شروط دخول المواقع المرتفعة التابعة للملك العام، عند الاقتضاء.

الفصل 42 . يتعين على مشغلي الشبكات، عند توفر الإمكانات التقنية، تمكين حرفائهم الراغبين في ذلك من المحافظة على أرقامهم وعناوينهم عند تغيير المشغل.

القسم الرابع
في الارتفاقات

الفصل 43 . يتمتع مشغلو الشبكات العمومية للاتصالات بحقوق ارتفاق تنشأ عند الضرورة وبعد التصريح بالمصلحة العمومية للأشغال المقررة حسب التشريع الجاري به العمل وذلك قصد :

. تركيز واستغلال وصيانة خطوط الربط وتجهيزات الشبكات العمومية للاتصالات في ملك الدولة العام وملك الدولة العمومي للطرقات،

. تركيز واستغلال وصيانة خطوط الربط وتجهيزات الشبكات العمومية للاتصالات في الملك الخاص،

. تركيز واستغلال وصيانة التجهيزات الراديوية وحمايتها من العراقيل والاضطرابات الكهرومغناطيسية وغيرها من أشكال التشويش، وتضبط بأمر كيفية تطبيق أحكام هذا الفصل.

الفصل 44 . إذا انجر عن حقوق الارتفاق المشار إليها بالفصل 43 من هذه المجلة إزالة أو تغيير بناءات لم يحصل اتفاق بالتراضي مع أصحابها أو مع أحدهم يمكن انتزاع تلك العقارات طبقا للتشريع الجاري به العمل.

وبعد إعداد تلك العقارات حسبما تقتضيه هذه المجلة والنصوص المتخذة في شأن تطبيقها يمكن لمشغل الشبكة أن يبيع العقارات المنتزعة على أن يحترم المشترون التغييرات المدخلة على أن يحفظوا حقوق الارتفاق المدخلة على العقار.

ولأصحاب العقارات المنتزعة الحق في ممارسة الأولوية في الشراء خلال أجل ثلاثة أشهر من تاريخ إعلامهم برغبة مشغل الشبكة في بيعها بواسطة عدل منفذ على أن يلتزموا باحترام التغييرات المدخلة عليها وبالمحافظة على حقوق الارتفاق المنصوص عليها بالفصل 43 من هذه المجلة.

الفصل 45 . إذا ترتب عن حقوق الارتفاق المشار إليها بالفصل 43 من هذه المجلة ضرر لأصحاب الأملاك أو المنشآت فإنه يدفع لهم أو لمن انجر له حق منهم تعويض عن ذلك الضرر. ويجب أن يبلغ مطلب التعويض بواسطة رسالة مضمونة الوصول أو وثيقة إلكترونية موثوق بها مع الإعلام بالبلوغ إلى مشغل الشبكة الذي يهمه الأمر والوزير المكلف بالاتصالات في ظرف ستة أشهر بداية من تاريخ حصول الضرر وإلا سقط حقهم في التعويض.

في صورة عدم الاتفاق بين الطرفين، ترفع النزاعات المتعلقة بالتعويض لدى المحكمة ذات النظر.

الباب الرابع
في الاتصالات والترددات الراديوية

الفصل 46 . تشكل الترددات الراديوية جزءا من الملك العام للدولة ويخضع استعمالها إلى ترخيص من الوكالة الوطنية للترددات المنصوص

الفصل 32 . تخضع الأجهزة الطرفية للاتصالات المستوردة أو المصنعة بتونس والمعدة للتسويق أو للاستعمال العمومي وكذلك الأجهزة الطرفية الراديوية المخصصة أو غير المخصصة للربط بالشبكة العمومية للاتصالات إلى المصادقة المسبقة. وتضبط شروط وطرق المصادقة بأمر.

الفصل 33 . لا تخضع التجهيزات الراديوية المكونة من أجهزة منخفضة القدرة ومحدودة المدى إلى الترخيص المنصوص عليه بالفصل 31 من هذه المجلة. ويضبط الحد الأقصى لقدرة هذه الأجهزة ومداها بقرار من الوزير المكلف بالاتصالات بعد أخذ رأي الوكالة الوطنية للترددات المنصوص عليها بالفصل 47 من هذه المجلة.

الفصل 34 . تعفى من تطبيق أحكام هذا الباب، شبكات الاتصالات التابعة للدولة المقامة لحاجيات الدفاع الوطني أو الأمن العام.

القسم الثاني
في الربط البيني

الفصل 35 . يتعين على مشغل شبكات عمومية للاتصالات الاستجابة إلى مطالب الربط البيني لأصحاب اللزم المسلمة طبقا لأحكام الفصل 19 من هذه المجلة ولا يمكن للمشغل رفض أي مطلب للربط البيني إن كان ممكنا تقنيا وذلك بالنظر إلى حاجيات الطالب من جهة وقدرة المشغل على تلبيتها من جهة أخرى. وإذا ما تعذر ذلك يتعين على الطالب توفير الحلول البديلة بعد استشارة الهيئة الوطنية للاتصالات.

الفصل 36 . يتم الربط البيني بمقتضى اتفاقية بين الطرفين المتعاقدين تحدد الشروط التقنية والمالية للربط.

الفصل 37 . تضبط الشروط العامة للربط البيني وطريقة تحديد التعريفات بمقتضى أمر.

الفصل 38 . يتعين على مشغل شبكة عمومية للاتصالات نشر العرض التقني للربط البيني وتعريفاته وذلك بعد مصادقة الهيئة الوطنية للاتصالات.

القسم الثالث
في الترقيم والعنونة

الفصل 39 . تتولى الوزارة المكلفة بالاتصالات إعداد المخطط الوطني للترقيم والعنونة ويضبط هذا المخطط شروط إسناد وتوزيع وتخصيص الترقيم والعنونة.

وتتم المصادقة على المخطط الوطني للترقيم والعنونة بقرار من الوزير المكلف بالاتصالات بعد أخذ رأي الهيئة الوطنية للاتصالات.

الفصل 40 . تتولى الهيئة الوطنية للاتصالات التصرف في المخطط الوطني للترقيم والعنونة بشكل يضمن توفير حاجيات مشغلي الشبكات ومزودي الخدمات وكذلك نفاذ المستعملين بصفة مبسطة ومتساوية إلى مختلف الشبكات وخدمات الاتصالات.

الفصل 41 . يخضع إسناد الترقيم والعنونة إلى دفع معلوم يضبط بقرار من الوزير المكلف بالاتصالات بعد أخذ رأي الهيئة الوطنية للاتصالات.

عليها بالفصل 47 من هذه المجلة وفقا لمخطط وطني للترددات الراديوية.

وتتم المصادقة على المخطط الوطني للترددات الراديوية بقرار من الوزير المكلف بالاتصالات.

الفصل 47 . تحدث مؤسسة عمومية لا تكتسي صبغة إدارية تتمتع بالشخصية المعنوية وبالاستقلال المالي يطلق عليها اسم "الوكالة الوطنية للترددات" وتخضع في علاقتها مع الغير إلى التشريع التجاري ومقرها بتونس العاصمة.

الفصل 48 . تتولى الوكالة الوطنية للترددات القيام بالمهام التالية :

. إعداد المخطط الوطني للترددات الراديوية بالتنسيق مع الهياكل المعنية.

. التصرف في الترددات الراديوية بالتنسيق مع الهياكل المعنية.

. مراقبة الشروط التقنية للتجهيزات الراديوية والسهر على حماية استعمال الترددات الراديوية.

. مراقبة استخدام الترددات طبقا للتراخيص المسندة وتسجيلات كراس الترددات.

. السهر على تطبيق الاتفاقات والمعاهدات الدولية في ميدان الاتصالات الراديوية.

. تسجيل الترددات الراديوية لدى الهيئات الدولية المختصة.

. السهر على حماية المصالح الوطنية في ميدان استعمال الترددات الراديوية المسجلة والمواضع المدارية المخصصة للبلاد التونسية.

. المساهمة في أنشطة البحث والتكوين والدراسات ذات العلاقة بالاتصالات الراديوية، وبصفة عامة كل نشاط آخر يقع تكليفها به من قبل سلطة الإشراف وله علاقة بميدان تدخلها.

وهي تخضع لإشراف الوزارة المكلفة بالاتصالات.

الفصل 49 . يمكن أن تسند إلى الوكالة الوطنية للترددات عن طريق التخصيص ممتلكات الدولة المنقولة وغير المنقولة الضرورية للقيام بمهامها. وفي صورة حل الوكالة ترجع ممتلكاتها إلى الدولة التي تتولى تنفيذ التزاماتها وتعهداتها طبقا للتشريع الجاري به العمل.

الفصل 50 . يتم إسناد الترددات الراديوية من قبل الوكالة الوطنية للترددات طبقا للمخطط الوطني للترددات الراديوية بعد أخذ رأي الوزيرين المكلفين بالدفاع الوطني وبالداخلية.

على أنه يجوز للوزيرين المكلفين بالدفاع الوطني وبالداخلية إقامة واستعمال تجهيزات راديوية طبقا للمخطط الوطني للترددات بشرط أن يعلما بذلك في أقرب وقت ممكن الوكالة الوطنية للترددات وذلك قصد التنسيق في مادة الترددات.

الفصل 51 . يخضع إسناد الترددات الراديوية لدفع معلوم يضبط بقرار من الوزير المكلف بالاتصالات.

الفصل 52 . بقطع النظر عن التجهيزات الراديوية المخصصة للربط بالشبكات العمومية للاتصالات والتجهيزات المنصوص عليها بالفصل 33 من هذه المجلة يخضع صنع وتوريد وتركيز واستغلال أجهزة الاتصالات والبث المستعملة للترددات الراديوية لموافقة الوكالة الوطنية للترددات بعد أخذ رأي الوزيرين المكلفين بالدفاع الوطني وبالداخلية. وتحدد الموافقة الذبذبات المستعملة وقدرة الأجهزة ومجال تغطيتها.

كما يخضع لنفس الإجراءات كل تحويل لهذه التجهيزات من مكان إلى آخر وكل تغيير يدخل على جزء من أجزائها وكل إتلاف لها.

الفصل 53 . في نطاق ضمان حسن انتشار الترددات الراديوية يتم عند الضرورة، تحديد محيط معين ضمن الملك العام أو الخاص في أمثلة التهيئة العمرانية، قصد تحديد ضوابط العلو للبناءات والغراسات المقامة داخل هذا المحيط والتي تقتضيها مواصفات انتشار الترددات.

الفصل 54 . كل مالك أو مستعمل لجهاز راديوي مركز بأية نقطة كانت بالبلاد التونسية يحدث أو ينشر اضطرابات تعرقل استغلال مراكز شبكات الاتصالات ملزم بالامتثال إلى التدابير الصادرة إليه عن الوزير المكلف بالاتصالات قصد وضع حد للتشويش وفي كل الحالات يجب عليه أن يمتثل لأبحاث الموظفين المحلفين المكلفين بالمراقبة.

الفصل 55 . يجب أن لا يضايق استغلال التجهيزات الراديوية الخاصة سير التجهيزات الراديوية الأخرى. وفي صورة حصول مضايقة، على الوزير المكلف بالاتصالات أن يتخذ جميع التدابير التقنية التي يراها صالحة.

الفصل 56 . لا يمكن لمستغل تجهيزات راديوية خاصة أن يتعامل في مادة الاتصالات مع الأجانب، دولا أو مؤسسات أو أفرادا إلا تحت مراقبة الوزارة المكلفة بالاتصالات وبعد موافقتها وبعد أخذ رأي الوزيرين المكلفين بالدفاع الوطني وبالداخلية.

الفصل 57 . يمكن حجز التجهيزات الراديوية مهما كان نوعها مؤقتا إلى أن يتم رفع أسباب بدون تعويض بقرار من الوزير المكلف بالاتصالات بناء على اقتراح من وزير الدفاع الوطني أو وزير الداخلية كلما كان استعمال هذه التجهيزات من شأنه أن يخل بمقتضيات الدفاع الوطني والأمن العام، وذلك بعد سماع صاحب التجهيزات.

ويمكن اتخاذ نفس الإجراءات في كل الحالات التي ينجر فيها عن استعمال هذه التجهيزات تشويش على الاتصالات الراديوية أو عندما يكون هذا الاستعمال غير مطابق للشروط المنصوص عليها بالرخصة.

وتتولى وزارتا الدفاع الوطني والداخلية كل فيما يخصها البحث عن المحطات الخفية ومراقبة فحواها.

الفصل 58 . في الحالات الاستثنائية، يمكن تسخير التجهيزات الراديوية مهما كان نوعها للمصلحة العامة بمقتضى أمر، باقتراح من الوزير المعني كلما حتمت استعمالها أسباب لها صلة بالدفاع الوطني والأمن العام.

وفي جميع الحالات التي يكون فيها استعمال تلك التجهيزات من شأنه أن يخل بمقتضيات الدفاع الوطني أو الأمن العام يكون التسخير بدون تعويض.

الفصل 59 . يتعين إعلام الوزير المكلف بالاتصالات حالا بالكف عن استغلال تجهيزات راديوية أو جزء من أجزائها ويمكن للوزير المكلف بالاتصالات أن يأمر بوضع الأختام على التجهيزات أو على جزئها الذي كف المستغل عن استعماله.

الفصل 60 . بقطع النظر عن التحديدات التي قد تقرر بموجب النصوص المتخذة لتطبيق هذه المجلة فيما يتعلق باقتناء واستغلال تجهيزات الاتصالات الراديوية على متن الطائرات أو السفن القائمة بالملاحة في الفضاء الجوي أو المياه الإقليمية للجمهورية التونسية. لا يرخص للطائرات والسفن الأجنبية باستعمال تجهيزاتها للاتصالات الراديوية إلا لحاجيات الملاحة أو لحاجيات استغلال تلك الطائرات أو السفن وذلك فقط إن لم تتوفر لهذه الطائرات أو السفن أية إمكانية أخرى للاتصال بالأرض وهي ملزمة في كل الحالات بالامتثال لكل أمر بالسكوت قد تصدره السلط المدنية أو العسكرية التونسية.

الفصل 67 . تعرض الدعاوى على الهيئة الوطنية للاتصالات من قبل الوزير المكلف بالاتصالات أو من مقيمي ومشغلي الشبكات في النزاعات المتعلقة :

. بالربط البيني والنفاذ إلى الشبكات،

. بشروط الاستعمال المشترك بين مستعملي الشبكات للبنية الأساسية المتوفرة،

وترفع العرائض مباشرة أو عن طريق محام باسم رئيس الهيئة الوطنية للاتصالات بواسطة رسالة مضمونة الوصول أو وثيقة إلكترونية موثوق بها مع الإعلام بالبلوغ أو بالإيداع لدى الهيئة مقابل وصل إيداع وتقدم العريضة التي يجب أن تتضمن وسائل الإثبات الأولية في أربعة نظائر.

ويتولى رئيس الهيئة إرسال نسخة إلى الوزير المكلف بالاتصالات عن كل العرائض التي يتلقاها عدا تلك الصادرة عن الوزير.

الفصل 68 . عند انتهاء البحث يحرر المقرر بالنسبة إلى كل نزاع تقريرا يقدم فيه ملاحظاته ويحيله رئيس الهيئة بواسطة رسالة مضمونة الوصول أو وثيقة إلكترونية موثوق بها مع الإعلام بالبلوغ إلى الأطراف المعنية الذين يتعين عليهم الرد عليه في أجل مدته خمسة عشر يوما ابتداء من تاريخ بلوغ الإعلام سواء بأنفسهم أو عن طريق محام وذلك بواسطة مذكرة تتضمن مستندات الدفاع التي يرونها صالحة.

مع مراعاة أحكام الفقرة الثانية من الفصل 72 من هذه المجلة يحق للأطراف الإطلاع على الوثائق المدرجة بالملف.

الفصل 69 . تكون جلسات الهيئة الوطنية للاتصالات سرية وتتولى الهيئة النظر في الملفات حسب الترتيب الذي يقرره رئيس الهيئة.

تتولى الهيئة سماع أطراف النزاع الذين لهم الحق في إنابة محام والاستعانة بغير وكذلك سماع الأطراف المعنية التي تمت دعوتها بصفة قانونية للمثول أمامها وإلى أي شخص ترى أنه من الممكن أن يساهم في إفادتها في حل النزاع.

تتخذ الهيئة قراراتها بأغلبية الأصوات وتصدرها بصفة حضورية.

لكل عضو من أعضاء الهيئة صوت واحد وفي حالة تعادل الأصوات يرجح صوت الرئيس.

ويمكن لرئيس الهيئة طلب تعويض كل عضو يتغيب بدون عذر ثلاث مرات من جلسات الهيئة.

الفصل 70 . تتعارض وظيفة عضو في الهيئة الوطنية للاتصالات مع كل امتلاك مباشر أو غير مباشر لمصالح في مؤسسة تمارس نشاطها في مجال الاتصالات.

ويمكن لكل من يهمه الأمر التجريح في أي عضو من أعضاء الهيئة بواسطة مطلب كتابي يعرف صاحبه بإمضاء صاحبه أو مطلب إلكتروني مدعم بإمضاء صاحبه يعرض على رئيس الهيئة الذي يبت فيه في أجل خمسة أيام بعد سماع الطرفين. ويقوم نائب الرئيس مقام رئيس الهيئة إذا كان هذا الأخير محل التجريح.

الفصل 71 . لا يمكن للهيئة أن تجري مفاوضاتها بصورة قانونية إلا بحضور ثلثي أعضائها على الأقل ومن بينهم رئيسها ونائبه.

ولا يمكن لأي عضو من أعضاء الهيئة المشاركة في المفاوضات التي تتعلق بالنزاع إذا كانت له مصلحة مباشرة أو غير مباشرة فيها أو كان مثل أو هو يمثل فيها أحد الأطراف المعنية.

وكل مخالفة لأحكام هذا الفصل ينجر عنها علاوة عن العقوبات التي نصت عليها هذه المجلة غلق التجهيزات ووضع الأختام عليها وذلك إلى أن تغادر الطائرة أو السفينة المرتكبة للمخالفة الفضاء الجوي أو المياه الإقليمية للجمهورية التونسية.

الفصل 61 . يمكن إعفاء البعثات الديبلوماسية والقنصلية المعتمدة بالجمهورية التونسية من دفع المعلوم المنصوص عليه بالفصل 51 من هذه المجلة إذا طلبت ذلك وبشرط أن تعامل بلادها البعثات التونسية بالمثل.

الفصل 62 . لا تنطبق أحكام الفصول 51 و52 و53 و54 و59 من هذه المجلة على تجهيزات وزارتي الدفاع الوطني والداخلية.

الباب الخامس

في الهيئة الوطنية للاتصالات

الفصل 63 . تحدث هيئة مختصة تسمى الهيئة الوطنية للاتصالات يكون مقرها بتونس العاصمة العاصمة تكلف بـ :

. إبداء الرأي حول طريقة تحديد تعريفات الشبكات والخدمات،

. التصرف في المخططات الوطنية المتعلقة بالترقيم والعنونة،

. مراقبة احترام الالتزامات الناتجة عن الأحكام التشريعية والترتيبية في ميدان الاتصالات.

. النظر في النزاعات المتعلقة بإقامة وتشغيل واستغلال الشبكات،

. إبداء الرأي في أي موضوع يطرح عليها ويدخل في إطار مشمولاتها من قبل الوزير المكلف بالاتصالات.

الفصل 64 . تتركب الهيئة الوطنية للاتصالات من :

. رئيس مباشر كامل الوقت،

. نائب رئيس، مستشار لدى محكمة التعقيب مباشر كامل الوقت،

. عضو مستشار بإحدى الفرقتين المكلفتين بمراقبة المنشآت العمومية بدائرة المحاسبات مباشر كامل الوقت.

. أربعة أعضاء يتم اختيارهم من الشخصيات ذات الكفاءة في الميدان التقني أو الاقتصادي أو القانوني ذي العلاقة بالاتصالات.

يتم تعيين رئيس الهيئة ونائبه وأعضائها بأمر.

الفصل 65 . يعين رئيس الهيئة الوطنية للاتصالات مقررا من بين أعضاء الهيئة.

ويمكن لرئيس الهيئة تعيين خبراء متعاقدين باعتبار تجربتهم وكفاءتهم في ميدان الاتصالات للمساعدة على القيام بالأبحاث والتحريات التي يكلفون بها من قبل رئيس الهيئة في نطاق مشمولاته.

الفصل 66 . يمكن لرئيس الهيئة، عند الاقتضاء أن يستعين بأعوان الوزارة المكلفة بالاتصالات لإجراء أبحاث واختبارات خاصة.

ويمكن لأعضاء الهيئة، بتكليف من رئيسها، القيام بجميع الأبحاث والتدقيقات على عين المكان حسب الشروط القانونية. كما يمكن لهم أن يطالبوا بالحصول على جميع الوثائق التي يرونها ضرورية للبحث في القضية.

ويتعين على مقيمي ومشغلي الشبكات إمداد رئيس الهيئة بالوثائق والبيانات الضرورية لإنجاز الأبحاث والتحريات التي يقوم بها في إطار مشمولاته.

الفصل 72 . يتعين على أعضاء الهيئة وأعوانها المحافظة على السر المهني المتعلق بالأعمال والمعلومات التي اطلعوا عليها عند القيام بمهامهم.

ويمكن لرئيس الهيئة رفض تسليم الوثائق المخلة بسرية النزاع الا في الحالات التي يكون فيها تسليم هذه الوثائق أو الاطلاع عليها ضروريا للقيام بالإجراءات أو لممارسة الأطراف لحقوقهم.

الفصل 73 . تتضمن القرارات الصادرة عن الهيئة الوطنية، عند البت في الأصل، وجوبا حلا للنزاع.

الفصل 74 . يمكن للهيئة الوطنية للاتصالات اتخاذ إجراء أو أكثر من الإجراءات التالية :

ـ توجيه أوامر للأطراف المعنية بانهاء الممارسات المخلة بمقتضيات هذه المجلة ونصوصها التطبيقية في أجل معين أو فرض شروط خاصة عليهم لممارسة نشاطهم.

ـ ايقاف النشاط المتصل بهذا المجال لمدة لا تزيد عن 3 أشهر ولا يمكن إعادة تعاطي النشاط إلا بعد أن يوضع حد للمخالفات موضوع النزاع.

ـ إحالة الملف على وكيل الجمهورية المختص ترابيا قصد القيام بالتتبعات الجزائية عند الاقتضاء.

الفصل 75 . تكون قرارات الهيئة معللة ويضفي عليها رئيس الهيئة وعند الاقتضاء نائبه الصبغة التنفيذية.

وتبلغ قرارات الهيئة إلى المعنيين بواسطة عدل منفذ.

ويمكن الطعن في قرارات الهيئة بالاستئناف أمام محكمة الاستئناف بتونس.

الفصل 76 . يمكن للهيئة الوطنية للاتصالات إحداث لجان فنية تكلف بالقيام بدراسات تقنية في ميدان الاتصالات يترأسها أحد أعضاء الهيئة وتتكون من خبراء وفنيين في ميدان الاتصالات وتكنولوجيا المعلومات.

ويمكن لهذه اللجان الاستعانة بخبراء تونسيين أو أجانب باعتبار كفاءتهم في الميدان بواسطة عقود تخضع إلى مصادقة الوزير المكلف بالاتصالات.

الفصل 77 . تمد الهيئة الوطنية للاتصالات مجلس النواب والوزارة المكلفة بالاتصالات بتقرير سنوي حول نشاطها.

الباب السادس

في المخالفات والعقوبات

القسم الأول

في معاينة المخالفات

الفصل 78 . تتم معاينة المخالفات لأحكام هذه المجلة والنصوص المتخذة لتطبيقها بمحاضر يحررها اثنان من الأعوان المشار إليهم بالفصل 79 من هذه المجلة طبقا للتشريع الجاري به العمل.

الفصل 79 . يتولى معاينة المخالفات لأحكام هذه المجلة :

ـ مأمورو الضابطة العدلية المشار إليهم بالعددين 3 و4 من الفصل 10 من مجلة الإجراءات الجزائية.

ـ الأعوان المحلفون للوزارة المكلفة بالاتصالات.

ـ الأعوان المحلفون لوزارة الداخلية.

ـ أعوان المصلحة الوطنية لحراسة السواحل وضباط وأمرو الوحدات البحرية الوطنية.

الفصل 80 . تحال المحاضر إلى الوزير المكلف بالاتصالات الذي يحيلها إلى وكيل الجمهورية المختص ترابيا للتتبع مع مراعاة أحكام الفصل 89 من هذه المجلة.

القسم الثاني

في العقوبات الجزائية

الفصل 81 . يعاقب بخطية من ألف إلى خمسة آلاف دينار كل من قام عن غير عمد بإتلاف أو إفساد خطوط أو أجهزة الاتصالات بأية طريقة كانت.

الفصل 82 . يعاقب بالسجن لمدة تتراوح بين ستة أشهر وخمس سنوات وبخطية من ألف إلى عشرين ألف دينار أو بإحدى هاتين العقوبتين :

ـ كل من أقام أو شغل شبكة عمومية للاتصالات دون الحصول على اللزمة المنصوص عليها بالفصل 19 من هذه المجلة.

ـ كل من قام بتوفير خدمات الاتصالات للعموم دون الحصول على الترخيص المنصوص عليه بالفصل 5 من هذه المجلة أو استمر في توفير هذه الخدمات بعد سحب الترخيص.

ـ كل من استعمل ترددات راديوية بدون الحصول على موافقة الوكالة الوطنية للترددات.

ـ كل من أقام أو استغل شبكة خاصة للاتصالات دون الحصول على الترخيص المنصوص عليه بالفصل 31 من هذه المجلة أو استمر في تشغيلها بعد سحب الترخيص.

ـ كل من تسبب عمدا في تعطيل الاتصالات بقطع خطوط الربط أو إفساد أو إتلاف التجهيزات بأية طريقة كانت.

الفصل 83 . يعاقب بالسجن لمدة تتراوح بين شهر واحد وستة أشهر وبخطية من ألف إلى عشرة آلاف دينار أو بإحدى هاتين العقوبتين، كل من صنع للسوق الداخلية أو استورد أو حاز لأجل البيع أو التوزيع مجانا أو بمقابل أو عرض للبيع أو باع الأجهزة الطرفية أو الأجهزة الراديوية المنصوص عليها بالفصل 32 من هذه المجلة أو ربطها بشبكة عمومية للاتصالات دون الحصول على المصادقة.

ويعاقب بنفس العقوبة كل من قام بالإشهار لصالح بيع التجهيزات غير المصادق عليها.

الفصل 84 . يعاقب طبقا لأحكام الفصل 264 من المجلة الجنائية كل :

ـ من يختلس خطوط الاتصالات أو يستعمل عمدا خطوط اتصالات مختلسة.

ـ من يستعمل عمدا بيان نداء من السلسلة الدولية وقع إسناده إلى محطة تابعة لشبكة اتصالات.

الفصل 85 . يعاقب طبقا لأحكام الفصل 253 من المجلة الجنائية كل من يفشي أو يحث أو يشارك في إفشاء محتوى المكالمات

والمبادلات المرسلة عبر شبكات الاتصالات، في غير الحالات التي يجيز فيها القانون ذلك.

الفصل 86 . يعاقب بالسجن لمدة تتراوح بين سنة واحدة وسنتين وبخطية من مائة إلى ألف دينار كل من يتعمد الإساءة إلى الغير أو إزعاج راحتهم عبر الشبكات العمومية للاتصالات.

الفصل 87 . يعاقب بالسجن لمدة تتراوح بين ستة أشهر وخمس سنوات وبخطية من ألف إلى خمسة الاف دينار أو بإحدى هاتين العقوبتين، كل من استعمل أو صنع أو استورد أو صدر أو حاز لأجل البيع أو التوزيع مجانا أو بمقابل أو عرض للبيع أو باع وسائل أو خدمات التشفير أو أدخل تغييرا عليها أو أتلفها دون مراعاة أحكام الأمر المنصوص عليه بالفصل 9 من هذه المجلة.

القسم الثالث

في العقوبات الإدارية

الفصل 88 . بقطع النظر عن العقوبات الجزائية التي نصت عليها هذه المجلة يمكن للوزير المكلف بالاتصالات أن يسلط على المخالفين لأحكام هذه المجلة ونصوصها التطبيقية إحدى العقوبات الإدارية التالية بعد سماع المخالف :

. تحديد الترخيص وشروط استغلاله بصفة مؤقتة أو نهائية.

. سحب الترخيص بصفة مؤقتة.

. سحب الترخيص نهائيا مع وضع الأختام.

الفصل 89 . مع حفظ الحقوق المدنية للمتضررين، يمكن للوزير المكلف بالاتصالات إجراء الصلح في المخالفات المنصوص عليها بالفصل 81 من هذه المجلة والتي تتم معاينتها وتتبعها وفقا لأحكام هذا القانون.

وتنقرض الدعوى العمومية وتتبعات الإدارة بدفع المبلغ المعين في عقد الصلح.

الباب السابع

في الأحكام المختلفة

الفصل 90 . تمنح قانونا إلى الديوان الوطني للاتصالات لزمة لاستغلال شبكات وخدمات الاتصالات الموكولة إليه في تاريخ نشر هذه المجلة.

وتتضمن هذه اللزمة توفير الخدمات الأساسية للاتصالات.

الفصل 91 . تمنح قانونا إلى الديوان الوطني للإرسال الإذاعي والتلفزي لزمة لاستغلال شبكات وخدمات الاتصالات الموكولة إليه في تاريخ نشر هذه المجلة.

وتتضمن هذه اللزمة توفير خدمات البث الإذاعي والتلفزي على كامل تراب الجمهورية.

الفصل 92 . مع مراعاة أحكام الفصلين 90 و91 من هذه المجلة تخضع إقامة وتشغيل شبكات الاتصالات وتوفير خدمات جديدة للاتصالات والموارد النادرة الضرورية لتشغيل الشبكات من قبل الديوان الوطني للاتصالات والديوان الوطني للإرسال الإذاعي والتلفزي إلى أحكام هذه المجلة.

Appendix D

Ministerial Decision nº 562 of March 11, 2002 on the Creation of the Permanent Committee for Monitoring Armament. Committee's names members detracted.

الجمهــوريـة التونسيــة

وزارة الدفاع الوطني

18 مارس 2002

مقـــــرر

من وزير الدفاع الوطني عـــدد 562 /2002 مؤرخ في 11 مارس 2002

يتعلق ببعث لجنة قارة لمتابعة التسلح

إن وزير الدفاع الوطني،

بعـد إطلاعـه علـى الأمر عدد 671 لسنة 1975 المؤرخ في 25 سبتمبر 1975 والمتعلق بضبط مشمولات وزير الدفاع الوطني،

وعلـى الأمــر عدد 735 لسنة 1979 المؤرخ في 22 أوت 1979 والمتعلق بتنظيم وزارة الدفاع الوطني وعلى جميع النصوص التي نقحته وتممته،

وعلى القرار عدد 560 لسنة 2002 المؤرخ في 11 مارس 2002 والمتعلق بإحداث دائرة متابعة التسلح،

وعلـى القرار عدد 561 لسنة 2002 المؤرخ في 11 مارس 2002 والمتعلق بتعيين العقـيد رئيس دائـرة متابعة التسلح بالإدارة العـامـة للأمن العسكـري ابتداء من 11 مارس 2002،

قـــــرر ما يلي

الفصل الأول : تبعـث لجنة قارة لمتابعة التسلح يترأسها العقيد رئيس دائرة متابعة التسلح بالإدارة العامة للأمن العسكري بداية من 11 مارس 2002.

الفصل الثاني : في إطار المهـام الموكولـة إلى دائرة متـابعة التسلح تعقد اللجنة القارة لمتابعة التسلح إجتماعات شهرية وكلما دعت الحاجة لذلك بدعوة من رئيسها.

الفصل الثالث : تتركــب اللجنــة القارة لمتابعة التسلح من الأعضاء الآتي ذكرهم ويمكن لرئيس
اللجنة الاستعانة بكل من يراه صالحا في نطاق قيام اللجنة بأعمالها :

– × – المقدم	: ممثل أركان جيــش البــر
– المقدم	: ممثل أركان جيــش الطيران
– المقدم بالبحرية	: ممثل أركان جيــش البحــر
– السيد	: من هيئة التعليم العالي العسكري
– × – السيد	: من هيئة التعليم العالي العسكري
– العقيد	: من هيئة التعليم العالي العسكري
– المقدم طبيب	: ممثل إدارة الصحة العسكرية
– الرائد صيدلي	: ممثل إدارة الصحة العسكرية
– الرائد صيدلي	: ممثل إدارة الصحة العسكرية
– المقدم	: ممثل إدارة الأسلحة والذخيرة

الفصل الرابع : تقــدم اللجنــة القــارة لمتــابعة التسلح حصيلة أعمالها إلى وزير الدفاع الوطني
في بداية كل شهر .

وزير الدفاع الوطني

الــدالــي الجـــازي

المرسل إليهم :
ـ نشرة عدد 1 و 2

Appendix E

Memorandum of Understanding between the Republic of Tunisia and the United States of America, May 20, 2015.

Memorandum of Understanding
Between the Republic of Tunisia and the United States of America

Reaffirming the common bonds of long-standing friendship between the Republic of Tunisia and the United States of America and recognizing that Tunisia's historic democratic transition offers an unprecedented opportunity to forge a durable strategic partnership based on shared values and interests, the Governments of the Republic of Tunisia and the United States of America underscore the importance of continuing cooperation in a way that strengthens the bilateral relationship between the two countries and supports Tunisia in undertaking necessary reforms, strengthening its security and stability, ensuring a more prosperous future for its citizens, and serving as a force of strength and progress in its region.

As friends and partners, Tunisia and the United States share a commitment to the promotion of regional security and economic development, as well as social, political and economic reform.

Security Cooperation

Tunisia and the United States affirm their common will to work for the preservation of the security of the two countries. Both countries intend to enhance the ongoing strategic dialogue and increase military cooperation through programs aimed at reinforcing Tunisia's security and developing its capacities to face major regional security challenges and advancing shared interests in a secure, stable, and prosperous Maghreb, Africa and Middle East.

Both countries note the vital importance of supporting Tunisia's security needs, counterterrorism efforts, and stability. They condemn attacks on Tunisian civilians and security forces and are committed to continuing their cooperation to combat terrorism and violent extremism. Both governments underscore the value of foreign military assistance in enabling the purchase of U.S. military goods and services. Both nations are committed to the most efficient and most effective use of assistance funds of all kinds.

Economic Progress

A newly created Joint Economic Commission (JEC) between Tunisia and the United States is to serve as a forum for discussing key economic issues on a recurring basis. The JEC would initially focus on advancing Tunisia's reform agenda and expanding private sector ties between our two countries for the benefit of our two peoples.

Tunisia and the United States share the belief that bilateral investment, trade, and private sector engagement could significantly expand through the implementation of policy reforms. Tunisia is working with international financial institutions on achieving economic reform goals. In order to increase bilateral coordination on achieving these reform goals, the United States intends to work with the Tunisian government to develop a Country Development Cooperation Strategy. Both countries also intend to continue to work together to promote advances in scientific and educational achievement that will spur job opportunities and contribute to Tunisia's continued economic growth.

Consolidating Democratic Gains

Tunisia and the United States remain committed to continuing to work together to reinforce Tunisia's important and remarkable democratic progress, respect for the rule of law, and commitment to human rights and social and political inclusion. Both countries also recognize the importance of a vibrant civil society to a functioning democracy and underscore Tunisia's commitment to the protection of the freedoms enshrined in Tunisia's constitution as well as respect for universal human rights. Tunisia and the United States highlight the key role these democratic norms play in the Tunisia-U.S. strategic partnership and their commitment to promoting these shared values. Both nations recognize the importance of education to unlocking the potential of its people and intend to work toward greater exchanges and linkages between Tunisian and U.S. educational institutions.

Tunisian-U.S. Strategic Cooperation

Tunisia and the United States share the understanding that the political and security interests of both countries are fundamentally enhanced by increased regional economic integration and cooperation in the Maghreb region and the Middle East. Both countries intend to continue their active dialogue through regular consultations, the Strategic Dialogue, Joint Economic Commission, the Trade and Investment Framework Agreement, and the Joint Military Committee, in order to coordinate on a range of issues of mutual concern and to identify areas for future collaboration.

Signed at Washington, this 20th day of May, 2015, in duplicate.

Mohsen Marzouk
Minister Advisor in Charge Political Affairs
of the Republic of Tunisia

John F. Kerry
Secretary of State
of the United States of America

Notes

Introduction

1 William Easterly, *The Tyranny of Experts: Economists, Dictators, and the Forgotten Rights of the Poor* (New York: Basic Book, 2013).

2 Moncef Kartas, "Foreign Aid and Security Sector Reform in Tunisia: Resistance and Autonomy of the Security Forces," *Mediterranean Politics* 19(3) (2014): 373–391.

3 Kathryn Olmsted, *Challenging the Secret Government: The Post-Watergate Investigations of the CIA and FBI* (Chapel Hill: University of North Carolina Press, 1996), 96.

4 This book draws on interviews conducted by the author with more than 40 security officials from the Ministry of the Interior and military officers from the Ministry of National Defense in active duty and retired. All interviewees were mid and high-ranking officers at the time of the interviews (inspector, chief inspector, superintendent, principal superintendent, director, general director and high-ranking uniformed police officers, Colonel from the National Guard; Major, Lieutenant-Colonel, Senior Colonel, Brigadier General, Lieutenant General from the Tunisian Armed Forces). Because of the sensitivity of the topic most of the interviewees requested anonymity to speak candidly. The interviews were carried out in Tunis during the author's numerous visits from April 2011 to May 2015. Only, two interviews were conducted by phone, respectively in late 2016 and early 2017 to inquire about different security developments that the country experienced. Furthermore, the author used some of the information he gathered during informal discussions with Tunisian security and military officials when he served within the Tunisian Ministry of National Defense (1998–2004) as a professor at the National War College, Command and Staff College, and National Defense Institute, as well as a senior lecturer at the High Institute of Internal Security Forces

(2000–2004) within the Ministry of the Interior. The author also inter-
acted with Tunisian military officials in Rome during his sojourn at
the NATO Defense College (2001) and met many Tunisian military
as well as a Tunisian Minister of Defense in Washington, D.C. during
their multiple visits in the post-uprising.

5   Derek Lutterbeck, "Tool of Rule: The Tunisian Police under Ben Ali,"
      The Journal of North African Studies 20(5) (2015): 813–831.

Chapter One

6   Among many other works see Panayiotis Vatikiotis, *The Egyptian Army
      in Politics: Pattern for New Nation?* (Bloomington: Indiana University
      Press, 1961); Anouar Abdel Malek, *Egypt: Military Society* (New York:
      Random House, 1968); George Haddad, *Revolutions and Military Rule
      in the Middle East* (New York: Speller, 1973); Fuad Khuri and Gerald
      Obermeyer, "The Social Bases for Military Intervention in the Middle
      East," in *Political Military Systems*, ed. Catherine McArdle Kelleher
      (Beverly Hills: Sage, 1974), 55–85.

7   Among many other works see Noureddine Jebnoun, "In the Shad-
      ow of Power: Civil-Military Relations and the Tunisian Popular
      Uprising," *The Journal of North African Studies* 19(3) (2014): 296–316;
      Holger Albrecht and Dina Bishara, "Back on Horseback: The Mili-
      tary and Regime Change in Egypt," *Middle East Law and Governance*
      3(1–2) (2011): 13–23; Holger Albrecht, "Does Coup-Proofing Work?
      Political-Military Relations in Authoritarian Regimes amid the Arab
      Uprisings," *Mediterranean Politics* 20(1) (2015): 36–54; Yezid Sayigh,
      Above the State: The Officers' Republic in Egypt, *The Carnegie Papers*,
      Beirut, Lebanon: Carnegie Middle East Center, August 2012; Derek
      Lutterbeck, Arab Uprisings and Armed Forces: Between Openness
      and Resistance, *SSR Paper*, No. 2, Geneva: The Geneva Centre for the
      Democratic Control of Armed Forces (DCAF), 2011; "Arab Uprisings,
      Armed Forces, and Civil-Military Relations," *Armed Forces & Society*
      39(1) (2012): 28–52; Zoltan Barany, "Comparing the Arab revolts: The
      Role of the Military," *Journal of Democracy* 22(4) (October 2011): 28–39;
      Michael Makara, "Coup-Proofing, Military Defection, and the Arab
      Spring," *Democracy and Security* 9(4) (2013): 334–359; Shana Marshall,
      The Egyptian Armed Forces and the Remaking of Economic Empire,
      The Carnegie Papers, Beirut, Lebanon: Carnegie Middle East Center,
      April 2015; DCAF International Expert Conference, Conference Re-
      port, *Security Sector Reform in Egypt: Civil-Military Relations in Focus*,
      Montreux, Switzerland, 2-4 April 2014.

8   Further scholarly inquiries are needed to assess the potential impact of

the professional intelligence background of the former military leaders on their political ascension. Had Sīsī not been the former head of Egypt's Military Intelligence and Reconnaissance Administration, he likely would not have been able to stage his coup.

9   For instance see Derek Lutterbeck, "After the Fall: Security Sector in Post-Ben Ali Tunisia," *Arab Reform Initiative Project* (September 2012): 1–29; Yezid Sayigh, Dilemmas of Reforming Policing in Arab Transitions, *The Carnegie Papers*, Beirut, Lebanon: Carnegie Middle East Center, March 2016; Missed Opportunities: The Politics of Police Reform in Egypt and Tunisia, *The Carnegie Papers*, Beirut, Lebanon: Carnegie Middle East Center, March 2015; Daniel Brumberg and Hesham Sallam, "The Politics of Security Sector Reform in Egypt," *USIP-Special Report* 318 (October 2012):1–16; Omar Ashour, From Bad Cop to Good Cop: The Challenges of Security Sector Reform in Egypt, *Paper Series* No. 3, Brookings Doha Center-Stanford Project on Arab Transitions, November 2012; Haykel Ben Mahfoudh, "Security Sector Reform in Tunisia: Three Years into the Democratic Transition," *Arab Reform Initiative Project* (July 2014): 1–16.

10 Thomas C. Bruneau and Steven C. Boraz, "Intelligence Reform: Balancing Democracy and Effectiveness," in *Reforming Intelligence: Obstacles to Democratic Control and Effectiveness*, ed. Thomas C. Bruneau and Steven C. Boraz (Austin: University of Texas Press, 2007), 4–6.

11 Florina Cristina Matei and Thomas Bruneau, "Intelligence Reform in New Democracies: Factors Supporting or Arresting Progress," *Democratization* 18(3) (2011): 603.

12 Bruneau and Boraz, "Intelligence Reform: Balancing Democracy and Effectiveness," 2.

13 Yezid Sayigh, "Civil-Military Relations in the Middle East: Patterns and Implications," *SEDMED-CIDOB* (June 2011): 2.

14 Joseph Sassoon, *Anatomy of Authoritarianism in the Arab Republics* (New York: Cambridge University Press, 2016).

15 For instance see Ṣalāḥ Naṣr, *Mudhakkirāt Ṣalāḥ Naṣr: Aṣuʿūd* (Vol. I), *Al-Intilāq* (Vol. II), *Al-ʿĀm al-Ḥazīn* (Vol. III) [The Memoirs of Ṣalāḥ Naṣr: The Ascension (Vol. 1), The Takeoff (Vol. 2), The Sad Year (Vol. 3)] (Cairo: Dār al-Khayyāl, 1999); Amīn Huwaydī, *Maʿa ʿAbd al-Nāṣir* [With ʿAbd al-Nasser] (Cairo: Dār al-Mustaqbal al-ʿArabī, 1985); Kamāl Ḥasan ʿAlī, *Mashāwīr al-ʿUmr: Asrār wa-khafāyā 70 ʿĀman min ʿUmr Miṣr fī al-Ḥarb wa-al-Mukhābarāt wa-al-Siyāsah* [Life Journeys: Secrets and Inside Stories of Seventy Years of Egypt's Life in War, Intelligence, and Politics] (Cairo: Dār al-Shurūq, 1994). This sample of memoirs, though not representative of all the memoirs written by Arab intelligence chiefs, is problematic in the way their authors tack-

led the intelligence issue. Naṣr, who built and ran the General Intelligence Directorate (GID) (1957–1967) and under whose tenure the service was accused of abuses and irregularities, devoted less than 15 pages out of 1166 of his memoirs to the intelligence, while the service under his tenure was a major actor in shaping the events that Egypt and the Middle East experienced during this period. In the same vein, Huwaydī, who served as a Minister of War, then GID chief, dedicated a chapter of 14 pages out of 257 to "President Nasser's Back Channel" with the United States in the aftermath of the Six-Day War. As for General ʿAlī, he wrote only 11 pages out 551 on the evolution of intelligence under his leadership.

16 Owen L. Sirrs, *A History of the Egyptian Intelligence Service. A History of the Mukhabarat, 1910–2009* (London; New York: Routledge, 2010), 1.

17 James T. Quinlivan, "Coup-proofing: Its Practice and Consequences in the Middle East," *International Security* 24(2) (Fall 1999): 149.

18 For instance see Niqūlā Nāsīf, *Sirr al-Dawlah: Fosūl fī Tārīkh al-Amni al-ʿĀm 1945–1977* [Secret of the State: Chapters in the History of Public Security 1945–1977] (Beirut: al-Mūdiriyyat al-ʿĀmah lil-Amni al-ʿĀm, 2013). Despite its journalistic style, by all counts this book could be considered a pioneer investigation in the field of Arab intelligence apparatus, by the way it digs deeply into the intrusive role played by the Lebanese intelligence services in the country's domestic and regional politics through surveillance of political parties, state bureaucracy, media, and foreigners living in Lebanon. The author desiccates the leadership profile, priorities and *modus operandi* of the intelligence directorate under-five of its chief spies and debunks the concealed and unlawful side of the apparatus. He redraws the evolution of the Lebanese internal intelligence service since its inception, from an obscure service within the Ministry of the Interior to an omnipotent general directorate in gathering information on people's private and public lives and acting as a main kingmaker of politicians.

19 Lyes Laribi, *Dans les geôles de Nezzar* (Paris: Paris-Méditerranée, 2002), 10–11.

20 Mohammed Samraoui, *Chronique des années de sang. Algérie: comment les services secrets ont manipulé les groupes islamistes* (Paris: Editions Denoël, 2003).

21 Lyes Laribi, *L'Algérie des généraux* (Paris: Milo, 2007), 22.

22 Hazem Kandil, *Soldiers, Spies, and Statesmen: Egypt's Road to Revolt* (London; New York: Verso, 2012), 43.

23 Tawfīq al-Madīnī, *al-Dawlah al-Būlīsīyah fī Tūnis al-Muʿāsirah* [The Police State in Contemporary Tunisia] (Beirut: al-Markaz al-ʿArabī al-Jadīd lil-Tibāʿah wa-al-Nashr, 2001); Amīr Sālim, *al-Dawlah al-*

Būlīsīyah fī Misr: al-Thawrah wa-al-Thawrah al-Mudāddah [The Police State in Egypt: The Revolution and the Counter-Revolution] (Cairo: Dār ʿAyn lil-Nashr, 2013).

24   Kieran Williams, "The StB in Czechoslovakia, 1945–89," in *Security Intelligence Services in New Democracies: The Czech Republic, Slovakia and Romania*, ed. Kieran Williams and Dennis Deletant (New York: Palgrave in association with School of Slavonic and East European Studies, University College, London, 2001), 24.

25   Among many other works see Jonathan R. Adelman, ed. *Terror and Communist Politics: The Role of the Secret Police in Communist States* (Boulder: Westview Press, 1984); Dennis Deletant, *Ceausescu and the Securitate. Coercion and Dissent in Romania, 1965–1989* (London: Hurst, 1995); Alexander Dallin and George W. Breslauer, *Political Terror in Communist Systems* (Stanford: Stanford University Press, 1970); David Childs and Richard Popplewell, *The Stasi: The East German Intelligence and Security Service* (New York: New York University Press, 1996); John O. Koehler, *Stasi: The Untold Story of the East German Secret Police* (Boulder: Westview Press, 1999); Mike Dennis, *Stasi: Myth and Reality* (Harlow: Pearson/Longman, 2003); Gary Bruce, *The Firm: The Inside Story of Stasi* (Oxford; New York: Oxford University Press, 2010); Barry McLoughlin and Kevin McDermott, ed. *Stalin's Terror: High Politics and Mass Repression in the Soviet Union* (Houndmills, Basingstoke, Hampshire; New York: Palgrave Macmillan, 2003).

26   Istvan Szikinger, "National Security in Hungary," in *Democracy, Law and Security: Internal Security Services in Contemporary Europe*, ed. Jean-Paul Brodeur, Peter Gill, Dennis Töllborg (Aldershot; Burlington, VT, USA: Ashgate, 2003), 81.

27   J. A. Tapia-Valdes, "A Typology of National Security Policies," *Yale Journal of World Public Order* 9(10) (1982): 28.

28   See J. Patrice McSherry, *Predatory States: Operation Condor and Covert War in Latin America* (Lanham, Md.: Rowman & Littlefield Publishers, 2005); Daniel Feierstein, "National Security Doctrine in Latin America: The Genocide Question," in *The Oxford Handbook of Genocide Studies*, ed. Donald Bloxham and A. Dirk Moses (Oxford; New York: Oxford University Press, 2010), 489–508; Marcia Esparza, Henry R. Huttenbach, and Daniel Feierstein, ed. *State Violence and Genocide in Latin America: the Cold War Years* (London; New York: Routledge, 2010).

29   David R. Mares, "The National Security State," in *A Companion to Latin American History*, ed. Thomas H. Holloway (Oxford: Blackwell Publishing Ltd, 2011), 396–397.

30   Marco Cepik, "Structural Change and Democratic Control of Intelligence in Brazil," in *Reforming Intelligence: Obstacles to Democratic*

Control and Effectiveness, 149–169; Priscila Carlos Brandão Antunes, "Establishing Democratic Control of Intelligence in Argentina," in *Reforming Intelligence: Obstacles to Democratic Control and Effectiveness*, 195–218; Eduardo Estévez, "Intelligence Community Reforms: The Case of Argentina," in *Intelligence Elsewhere: Spies and Espionage outside the Anglosphere*, ed. Philip H. J. Davies and Kristian C. Gustafson (Washington, DC: Georgetown University Press, 2013), 219–237.

31   Dustin Dehéz, "Intelligence Services in Sub-Saharan African," *ASPJ Africa & Francophonie* (3rd Quarter 2010): 57–63.

32   Carlson Anyangwe, *Revolutionary Overthrow of Constitutional Orders in Africa* (Mankon, Bamenda: Labngaa Research & Publishing CIG; Distributed by African Books Collective, 2012).

33   Emmanuel Kwesi Aning, Ema Birikorang, and Ernest Lartey, "The Process and Mechanisms of Developing a Democratic Intelligence Culture in Africa," in *Intelligence Elsewhere: Spies and Espionage outside the Anglosphere*, 199–217; Johnny Kwadjo, "Changing the Intelligence Dynamics in Africa: The Ghana Experience," in *Changing Intelligence Dynamics in Africa*, ed. Sandy Africa and Johnny Kwadjo (Birmingham: GFN-SSR Publications, 2009), 95–123.

34   Sandy Africa, "The South African Intelligence Services: A Historical Perspective," in *Changing Intelligence Dynamics in Africa*, 61–94; Kenneth R. Dombroski, "Transforming Intelligence in South Africa," *Reforming Intelligence: Obstacles to Democratic Control and Effectiveness*, 241–268; "Reforming Intelligence After Apartheid," *Journal of Democracy* 17(3) (July 2006): 43–57.

35   Sandy Africa, "The Restructuring of Intelligence Services in South Africa: An Assessment of the Transformation Process," in *Providing Security for People: Enhancing Security through People, Justice, and Intelligence Reform in Africa*, ed. Chris Ferguson and Jeffrey O. Isima (Shrivenham: Cranfield University, 2004), 37.

36   U.S. Senate Select Committee on Intelligence, *Report on the U.S. Intelligence Community's Prewar Intelligence Assessment on Iraq's War*, July 7, 2004. Accessed April 25, 2016. https://fas.org/irp/congress/2004_rpt/ssci_iraq.pdf.

37   For instance see Open Society Justice Initiative, *Globalizing Torture. CIA Secret Detention and Extraordinary Detention* (New York: Open Society Foundations, 2013). Accessed April 25, 2016. https://www.opensocietyfoundations.org/sites/default/files/globalizing-torture-20120205.pdf.

38   U.S. Senate Select Committee on Intelligence, *Committee Study of the Central Intelligence Agency's Detention and Interrogation Program*, December 3, 2014. Accessed April 25, 2016. https://upload.wikimedia.

org/wikipedia/commons/a/a2/US_Senate_Report_on_CIA_Deten-tion_Interrogation_Program.pdf.

39 Edward Snowden's revelations have exposed the extensive global surveillance system and spy programs run by the National Security Agency targeting Internet and phone records of millions Americans. This mass surveillance system has illegally broken into hundreds of thousands of computers in the United States and across the world. Snowden's leaks proved that information privacy is not only breached by intelligence under authoritarian rule but also in democracy.

40 Robert Jervis, "Intelligence, Civil-Intelligence Relations, and Democracy," in *Reforming Intelligence: Obstacles to Democratic Control and Effectiveness*, viii.

41 OECD, *OECD DAC Handbook on Security System Reform: Supporting Security and Justice* (Paris: OECD 2007 Edition), 22.

Chapter Two

42 Al-Sāfī Saʿīd, *Būrqībah: Sīrah Shubh Muḥarramah* [Bourguiba: A Quasi-Prohibited Biography] (Beirut: Riyāḍ al-Rayyis lil-Kutub wa-al-Nashr, 2000), 191–207.

43 Royal Decision of March 31, 1956 on the Creation of the Vigilance Councils, *al-Rāʿid al-Rasmī al-Tūnisī* [*The Official Journal of Tunisia (OJT)*], nᵒ 34, April 27, 1956, 781.

44 Royal Decree of April 19, 1956 on the Payment of Financial Compensation to the Members of Vigilance Councils, *OJT*, nᵒ 34, April 27, 1956, 781.

45 *Shahādat al-Ṭāhir Balkhūjah al-Siyasīyah* [al-Ṭāhir Balkhūjah's Testimonies] (Zaghwān: Muʿassasat al-Tamīmī lil-Bahth al-ʿBaht wa-al-Maʿlūmāt, 2002), 26.

46 Roger Faligot and Pascal Krop, *La Piscine. The French Secret Service since 1944*, trans. W. D. Halls (Oxford, UK; New York: B. Blackwell, 1989), 168–170.

47 Decree nᵒ 373, November 19, 1962, *al-Rāʿid al-Rasmī lil-Jumhūrīyah al-Tūnisīyyah* [*The Official Journal of the Republic of Tunisia (OJRT)*], nᵒ 58, November 16-20, 1962, 1678; Decree nᵒ 374, November 19, 1962, *OJRT*, nᵒ 58, November 16-20, 1962, 1678–1679; Decree nᵒ 375, November 19, 1962, *OJRT*, nᵒ 58, November 16-20, 1962, 1679–1681. These decrees were strengthened by Decree nᵒ 12, January 8, 1973, *OJRT*, nᵒ 2, January 16, 1973, 96–99. The latter added some restrictive clauses with regard to the SIGINT operators. Indeed, Article 11 pointed out that these operators "are not allowed to travel abroad without the authorization of the Minister of the Interior." Article 12 stated: "The SIGINT

operators are required to obtain the authorization of the Minister of the Interior before signing their marriage contract. In order to obtain the minister's authorization, they must provide the Minister of the Interior with all information regarding the identity of the fiancée, her profession, incomes and all changes in the social status that could occur in the aftermath of the marriage." As for Article 13, it "prohibits SIGINT operators from publishing, giving public lectures or making any statement to the media, unless they obtain an express authorization from the Minister of the Interior."

48   Azzedine Azzouz, *L'histoire ne pardonne pas: Tunisie, 1938–1969* (Paris: L'Harmattan; Tunis: Dar Ashraf, 1988), 224.

49   Souhayr Blehassen, "Les legs bourguibiens de la représsion," in *Habib Bourguiba, la trace et l'héritage*, ed. Michel Camau and Vincent Geisser (Paris: Karthala; Aix-en-Provence: Institut d'etudes politiques, 2004), 396.

50   Al-Ṭāhir Balkhūjah, *al-Ḥabīb Būrqībah: Sīrat Za ʿīm, Shahādah ʿalá ʿAṣr* [Ḥabīb Bourguiba: Biography of a Leader, Witness of His Age] (Cairo: al-Dār al-Thaqāfīyah, 1999), 110–111.

51   Ibid., 112–113.

52   American Embassy in Tunisia to State Department, "Sayah Calls on Party To Face Up To Achour," January 13, 1976, US Cable 1976TUNIS00209_b. Accessed May 5, 2016. https://www.wikileaks.org/plusd/cables/1976TUNIS00209_b.html.

53   Al-Ṭāhir Bilkhūjah, *al-Ḥabīb Būrqībah: Sīrat Za ʿīm, Shahādah ʿalá ʿAṣr*, 171–195.

54   Jebnoun, "In the Shadow of Power: Civil-Military Relations and the Tunisian Popular Uprising," 301.

55   Decree nº 1244, October 20, 1984 on the Organization of the Ministry of the Interior, *OJRT*, nº 62, October 26, 1984, 2624–2631.

56   In 2006, these missions were quoted verbatim in the Article 2 of the Presidential Decree nº 1160 of April 13, 2006 on the Status of National Security and National Police Officers, *OJRT*, nº 34, April 28, 2006, 1475–1489.

57   Royal Decree of May 6, 1956 on the Creation of the National Guard, *OJT*, nº 72, September 7, 1956, 1694.

58   In Tunisia, arm-bearing forces are classified into three categories regarding the range of their intervention required in times of emergency: 1st category: police forces, 2nd category: National Guard, and 3rd category: armed forces.

59   Decree nº 1244, October 20, 1984.

60   Eric Rouleau, "Onde de choc dans le monde arabe; Souvenirs d'un diplomate," *Le Monde Diplomatique* (February 2011).

61 Royal Decree of January 19, 1956 on the Installation of Military Intelligence Device, *OJT*, nº 7, January 24, 1956, 137–138.

62 Ibid.

63 Royal Decree of May 3, 1956 on the Organization of the Ministry of Defense, *OJT*, nº 36, May 4, 1956, 823–824.

64 Royal Decree of June 30, 1956 on the Creation of the Tunisian Armed Forces, *OJT*, nº 52, June 29-30, 1956, 1173–1174.

65 Royal Decree of January 19, 1956.

66 Royal Decree of May 3, 1956.

67 Figure 1: A 1956-NDC organizational charter drawn by the author based on the Royal Decree of May 3, 1956, *OJT*, nº 36, May 4, 1956, 823–824.

68 Figure 2: A 1970-NDC organizational charter drawn by the author based on the decree nº 61, February 21, 1970, *OJRT*, nº 10, February 24, 1970, 218.

69 Military Security (French acronym SM) also known as General Directorate of Military Security (French acronym DGSM) is used interchangeably in this book.

70 The attachment of the SM to the Office of the Minister of Defense was operated in 1974. See Article 9 of the Decree nº 7 of January 5, 1974 on the Organization of the Ministry of National Defense, *OJRT*, nº 2, January 11, 1974, 63.

71 In 1974, Bin ʿAlī was assigned as a defense attaché to Rabat consequently to the failure of the aborted union between Tunisia and Libya. Qadhdhāfī, who signed with Bourguiba the Jerba declaration on January 12, 1974, incautiously recommended the name of Bin ʿAlī for chief of the Military Intelligence Department in the new union government of the Arab Islamic Republic that lasted only one day. Bourguiba, who had never heard of Bin ʿAlī would have had doubts about him and suspected Bin ʿAlī of maintaining dangerous connections with Qadhdhāfī. Thus, he ordered to remove him from his position.

72 Jebnoun, "In the Shadow of Power: Civil-Military Relations and the Tunisian Popular Uprising," 301.

73 Figure 3: Table established by the author on the Tenure of Military Intelligence Chiefs (1964–1987).

74 Decree nº 735 of August 22, 1979 on the Organization of the Ministry of National Defense, *OJRT*, nº 50, August 28-31, 1979, 2263–2267.

75 Ibid.

76 American Embassy in Tunisia to State Department, "Annual Integrated Assessment of Security Assistance to Tunisia," July 21, 1978, US Cable 1978TUNIS05209_d. Accessed May 20, 2016. https://wikileaks.org/plusd/cables/1978TUNIS05209_d.html.

77 See, United Nations, "Mapping, Charting and Geodesy Cooperative and Exchange Agreement (with annexes). Signed at Tunis on 8 December 1980," in *Treaties Series: Treaties and international agreements registered or filed and recorded with the Secretariat of the United Nations* (New York, 2001), 97–107. Accessed May 20, 2016. https://treaties.un.org/doc/Publication/UNTS/Volume%202005/v2005.pdf.

78 Intelligence blindness was used several times by a retired colonel and artillery officer Nūr al-Dīn Laʿrībī during my numerous discussions with him of the topic.

79 Author interview, Tunis, December 23, 2013.

80 Jebnoun, "In the Shadow of Power: Civil-Military Relations and the Tunisian Popular Uprising," 300.

Chapter Three

81 Decree n° 1297 of November 27, 1987 on the Creation of National Security Council, *OJRT*, n° 84, December 1-4, 1987, 1478.

82 Decree n° 252, February 26, 1988 on the Establishment of National Security Council, *OJRT*, n° 15, March 1, 1988, 325–326.

83 Figure 4: NSC's organizational charter drawn by the author based on the Decree n° 1195, July 6, 1990, *OJRT*, n° 48, July 20, 1990, 965–966.

84 Decree n° 250, February 26, 1988 on the Organization of the Presidency's Services, *OJRT*, n° 15, March 1, 1988, 327–328.

85 Figure 5: PSSDI's organizational charter drawn by the author based on fieldwork interviews.

86 Noureddine Jebnoun, "Ben Ali's Tunisia: The Authoritarian Path of a Dystopian State," in *Modern Middle East Authoritarianism: Roots, Ramifications, and Crisis*, ed. Noureddine Jebnoun, Mehrdad Kia, and Mimi Kirk (Abingdon, Oxon: Routledge, 2013), 110. On Neighborhood Watch Committees, see, Decree n° 1763, November 23, 1991 amending and completing Decree n° 453-1991 on the Structural Organization of the Ministry of the Interior, *OJRT*, n° 83, December 6, 1991, 1645–1646. A copy of this decree is available in Appendix A.

87 Decree n° 147 on Watchdog Citizen, January 18, 1993, *OJRT*, n° 7, January 26, 1993, 139. A copy of this decree is available in Appendix B.

88 See public testimony of Sāmī Barāhim on torture in the public hearing sessions before the Tunisian Truth and Dignity Commission (TDC), mainly the segment from 24:00" to 28:53". Accessed November 20, 2016. https://www.youtube.com/watch?v=rbfBKKjoER4.

89 Nicolas Beau and Jean-Pierre Tuquoi, *Notre ami Ben Ali: l'envers du miracle tunisien* 2nd Ed. (Tunis, Paris, Med Ali Editions, R.M.R. Editions, Découverte, 2011), 183–198.

90 Clement Henry, "Tunisia 'Sweet Little' Regime," in *Worst of the Worst: Dealing with Repressive and Rogue Nations*, ed. Robert I. Rotberg (Cambridge, Mass.: World Peace Foundation; Washington, D.C.: Brookings Institution Press, 2007), 302.

91 In 1990, Bin ʿAlī purged the Interior Ministry from the last relics of Bourguiba's security system by dismissing Shādly Ḥāmmī alias Muhammad ʿAlī Maḥjūbī, the then State Secretary for National Security. Ḥāmmī was a Bourguiba's ruthless security henchman involved in the suppression of the Yūsufists. Bin ʿAlī falsely accused Maḥjūbī of facilitating the assassination in Tunis of the Palestinian leader Khalīl al-Wazīr also known as Abū Jihād (April 16, 1988). Maḥjūbī was sentenced to four years. He was released after spending two years in jail. In 1992, Bin ʿAlī dropped his concocted accusations on Maḥjūbī and apologized to him by saying "they misled me." Maḥjūbī was loyal to Bourguiba and did not show any zeal for Bin ʿAlī's coup. Thus, he became Bin ʿAlī's perfect scapegoat in the murder of Abū Jihād. Later, the French intelligence exonerated Maḥjūbī from these accusations. However, David Yallop, the British investigative journalist, highlighted the complicity of the U.S. and Tunisian governments in the assassination of Abū Jihād. See, David Yallop, *To the End of the Earth: Hunt for the Jackal* 1st Ed. (London: Hachette, 1993), 224–226. Furthermore, Ahmad Binnūr—the former head of the GDNS, former State Secretary in Charge of National Security, former State Secretary in Charge of National Defense, and former ambassador of Tunis to Rome—in his testimony on the Bourguiba era that was aired on Al Jazeera in late 2012 and early 2013 openly accused Bin ʿAlī of enabling Abū Jihād's liquidation. He raised many questions about the puzzle of this assassination, as well as the alleged relations between Bin ʿAlī and the Israeli Mossad agency. For further information on this issue, see the following link: https://www.youtube.com/watch?v=J-i5Yd1rlzA. Accessed May 25, 2016.

92 Figure 6: GDSS's organizational charter drawn by the author based on fieldwork interviews.

93 Figure 7: DII's organizational charter drawn by the author based on fieldwork interviews. The DII is based in al-Aouina NG headquarters in Tunis.

94 Barraket al-Sahel is a southern suburb of the city of Hammamet where officers allegedly met in the early 1991 to stage a coup against the regime. For further information on this affair see Sami Koudra, *Le "complot" de Barraket Essahel. Chronique d'un Calvaire* (Tunis: Sud Editions, 2012); "Les témoignages des officiers de l'armée nationale tunisi-

enne dans l'affaire de Barakat Essahel [vidéo]," *Nawaat.org*, 8 August 2011. Accessed May 25, 2016. http://nawaat.org/portail/2011/08/08/les-temoignages-des-officiers-de-larmee-nationale-tunisienne-dans-laffaire-de-barakat-essahel-video/; Wafa Sdiri, "Vidéo: Le complot de Barraket Essahel": Nos militaires réclament justice," *tunisienumerique. com*, June 21, 2011. Accessed May 25, 2016. https://www.tunisienu-merique.com/video-«le-complot-de-barraket-essahel»-nos-militaires-reclament-justice/47745.

95 Habib Boularès, "Réponse de Habib Boularès au colonel Zoghlami et au lieutenant-colonel Mohamed Ahmed," *Réalités*, May 26-June 1, 2011.

96 Derek Lutterbeck, "Tool of Rule: The Tunisian Police under Ben Ali," 4.

97 Among many other reports see Amnesty International, *In the Name of Security: Routine Abuses in Tunisia*, June 23, 2008; *Tunisia: Continuing Abuses in the Name of Security*, August 20, 2009; *Independent Voices Stifled in Tunisia*, July 13, 2010; Human Rights Watch, *Tunisia: Repression and Harassment of Human Rights Defenders and Organizations*, February 14, 2004; *Tunisia: Crushing the Person, Crushing a Movement*, April 19, 2005; *A Larger Prison: Repression of Former Political Prisoners in Tunisia*, March 24, 2010; Jean-François Julliard, "Tunisia: 'You have no rights here but welcome to Tunisia!'" *Reporters Without Borders*, July 7, 2005.

98 Decree n° 91-704, May 3, 1991 on the Structures of the ISF within the Ministry of the Interior; Decree n° 96-92, September 9, 1996 on the Organization and Missions of the Institute of National Security of Manouba (Tunis); Decree n° 97-139, November 3, 1997 on the Composition of the High Council of the ISF; Decree n° 2001-201, October 22, 2001 on the Structures of the ISF within the Ministry of the Interior; Decree n° 2003-61, April 7, 2003 on the Structures of the ISF within the Ministry of the Interior and Local Development; Decree n° 2003-97, May 22, 2003, amending and completing Decree n° 2003-61, April 7, 2003 on the Structures of the ISF within the Ministry of the Interior and Local Development; Decree n° 2004-64, April 24, 2004, amending and completing Decree n° 2003-61, April 7, 2003 on the Structures of the ISF within the Ministry of the Interior and Local Development; Decree n° 2004-82, June 5, 2004, amending and completing Decree n° 2003-61, April 7, 2003 on the Structures of the ISF within the Ministry of the Interior and Local Development; Decree n° 2007-246, August 15, 2007 on the Structures of the ISF within the Ministry of the Interior and Local Development; Decree n° 2009-161, June 10, 2009, amending Decree n° 91-543, April 1, 1991 on the Organization of the Ministry of the Interior.

99   Author interview, Tunis, April 12, 2015.

100   Yves Aubin de La Messuzière, *Mes années de Ben Ali. Un ambassadeur de France en Tunisie* (Tunis, Cérès éditions, 2011), 124–125.

101   On the eve of the World Summit on the Information Society that was held in Tunis in November 2005, Christophe Boltanski, a French journalist, was tasked by *Libération* newspaper to cover the summit. He published an article in the same newspaper entitled "Demonstrators beaten by the police." As a result, he was stabbed and beaten by four unidentified thugs. The assault occurred next to his hotel in a busy street of Tunis where police officers witnessed the aggression but did not intervene to protect him. The Tunisian government denied any responsibility in this assault and decided to conduct its own investigation. It was only in 2012 when the Interior Ministry opened a new investigation and concluded that Bin ʿAlī himself ordered the assault and tasked the DSS with the mission to punish Boltanski for his criticism of the regime.

102   Reporters Without Borders, "Intelligence services go to great lengths to prevent visiting Algerian journalist from working," November 9, 2006 (Updated on January 20, 2016). Accessed January 25, 2016. https://rsf.org/en/news/intelligence-services-go-great-lengths-prevent-visiting-algerian-journalist-working.

103   Yves Aubin de La Messuzière, Chapter VI: "Diplomates sous la préssion du régime," 121–142.

104   American Embassy in Tunisia to State Department, "Tunis Security Environment Profile Questionnaire (SEPQ) Spring 2009," March 6, 2009, US Cable 09TUNIS129_a. Accessed June 10, 2016. https://wikileaks.org/plusd/cables/09TUNIS129_a.html.

105   Author interview, Tunis, March 27, 2014.

106   See for instance, Reporters Without Borders, "List of 13 Internet enemies," November 7, 2006 (Updated on January 25, 2016). Accessed January 25, 2016. https://rsf.org/en/news/list-13-internet-enemies.

107   Tom Stevenson, "NSA-Style: Tunisia Setting Up Counterterrorism Unit That Will Also Spy On Citizens," *International Business Times*, February 26, 2014. Accessed January 25, 2016.
Online at: http://www.ibtimes.com/nsa-style-tunisia-setting-counterterrorism-unit-will-also-spy-citizens-1558013.

108   Reporters Without Borders, "Cyber-dissident arrested and his on-line newspaper censored," June 5, 2002 (Updated on January 20, 2016). Accessed January 25, 2016. https://rsf.org/en/news/cyber-dissident-arrested-and-his-online-newspaper-censored.

109   Jebnoun, "Ben Ali's Tunisia: The Authoritarian Path of a Dystopian State," 112.

110   Ibid., 112.

111   Eric Gobe, "The Tunisian Bar to the Test of Authoritarianism: Professional and Political Movements in Ben Ali's Tunisia (1990–2007)," *The Journal of North African Studies* 15(3) (2010): 340.

112   Open Net Initiative, *Internet Filtering in Tunisia in 2005: A Country Study* (Citizen Lab, Munk School of Global Affairs, University of Toronto; Berkman Center for Internet & Society, Harvard University; SecDev Group, Ottawa, 2005), 9.

113   International League of Human Rights, "Tunisie: Condamnation des 'internautes de Zarzis' à de lourdes peines au terme d'un procès entaché d'irrégularités," July 7, 2004. Accessed January 25, 2016. https://www.fidh.org/spip.php?page=article&id_article=1558.

114   Reporters Without Borders, "The country where Internet users are tortured," December 14, 2004 (Updated on January 20, 2016). Accessed January 25, 2016. https://rsf.org/en/news/country-where-internet-users-are-tortured.

115   Reporters Without Borders, "Appeal court upholds unjustified sentences against Zarzis Internet-users," July 7, 2004 (Updated January 20, 2016). Accessed January 25, 2016. https://rsf.org/en/news/appeal-court-upholds-unjustified-sentences-against-zarzis-internet-users. See also, Florence Beaugé, "Six jeunes internautes devant la cour d'appel de Tunis," *Le Monde*, July 6, 2004; José Garçon, "Six internautes tunisiens dans la toile de Ben Ali," *Libération*, July 7, 2004.

116   Presidential Decree n° 501, March 14, 1997, *OJRT*, n° 24, March 25, 1997, 497–498.

117   Ibid.

118   Ibid.

119   Ministerial Decision of September 9, 1997, *OJRT*, n° 76, September 23, 1997, 1885.

120   Ibid.

121   Law n° 2001-1 of January 15, 2001 on the Promulgation of the Telecommunications Code, *OJRT*, n° 5, January 16, 2001, 123–130. A copy of this law is available in Appendix C.

122   Ibid.

123   Ibid.

124   Law n° 2004-5 of February 3, 2004 on the Creation of the National Agency for Information Security, *OJRT*, n° 10, February 3, 2004, 251.

125   Elvira Diana, "'Literary Spring' in Libyan Literature: Contributions of Writers to the Country's Emancipation," *Middle East Critique* 23(4) (2014): 449.

126   It was commonly known that airline pilots flying Tunisair abstained from talking politics as they suspected that operatives from the Interior Ministry had installed listening devices in jet cockpits.

127   Clement M. Henry, "Reverberations in the Central Maghreb of the 'Global War in Terror,'" in *North Africa: Politics, Region, and the Limits of Transformation*, ed. Yahia H. Zoubir and Haizam Amirah-Fernández (London; New York: Routledge, 2008), 304.

128   Christophe Boltanski, "Un commando islamiste algérien frappe en Tunisie," *Libération*, February 15, 1995.

129   In 1990, the ATCE was created and provided with an autonomous budget. Its main objective was to embellish the image of the regime abroad and control the media inside the country. It played a critical role in corrupting many foreign media outlets, mainly in France, Lebanon, and the United States in order to promote the regime's propaganda in these countries. However, the ATCE also served as a tool of intelligence spying on dissents overseas. The author during his forced exile in the Unites States experienced surveillance activities performed by a network of Tunisian informants working for ʿAzzadīn Hammādī, a former Army Corporal appointed as a Tourist office's manager and the ATCE bureau's representative within the Tunisian embassy in Washington, D.C. Hammādī's diplomatic status enabled him to develop a network of Tunisian informants in North America (i.e., Canada and the United States). Given Hammādī's close relationship with Bin ʿAlī and his wife, Tunisian ambassadors and the defense attachés avoided any interaction with him that could have shortened their sojourns in D.C. and eventually jeopardized their careers.

130   "Mali: Libération de deux otages autrichiens enlevés en Tunisie en février," *Le Monde*, November 2, 2008.

131   Colonel ʿEmād Makkī from the USGN.

132   Mounia Daoudi, "La thèse de l'attentat évoquée par Tunis," *Radio France International*, April 14, 2002. Accessed June 15, 2016. http://www.rfi.fr/actufr/articles/028/article_14858.asp.

133   Before entering any military school as cadets, the newly selected candidates were subjected to *al-Baḥith al-Amnī* (security investigation). In the 1970s, this security investigation was a routine background check. However, with the emergence of Islamism as one of the main challenges to Bourguiba's regime, the investigation became a more thorough security clearance conducted by the services of the Interior Ministry at the request of the Defense Ministry. The investigation was not limited to the profile of the candidate but it was extended to his/her inner family and relatives. In the post-uprising, the investigation continues to be performed by the Interior Ministry. However, the Defense Ministry conducts its own investigation seeking to validate or reject the Interior Ministry's investigation.

134   Figure 8: Table established by the author on the Tenure of Military Intelligence Chiefs (1987–2011).

135   The author who taught at the Tunisian National War College noticed that most of the artillery officers praised the artillery weapon as the "God of War" in reference to Napoleon's nickname. Such a sarcastic name was given to Napoleon from Clausewitz for his military achievements rather than for his artillery officer's background.

136   Besides the role played by the DGSM in monitoring the activities of the Tunisian defense attachés abroad, it should be noted that the directorate had full power and authority to supervise and authorize any contact between senior military officers and foreign diplomats based in Tunis within the remits of the official duties. Distrusting Tunisian military personnel to report on the contacts and activities when they were invited to foreign diplomatic facilities, the DGSM always assigned an intelligence officer to the receptions and dinners organized by foreign diplomats to keep the directorate informed about suspicious interaction between the Tunisian military and their foreign counterparts.

137   The article was written by Guilain Denoeux, "La face cachée du miracle tunisien," *Politique internationale* 89 (Fall 2000): 395–420.

138   Author interview, Tunis, May 3, 2015.

139   Khaled Nezzar, *Mémoires du general* 2nd Ed. (Algiers: Chihab, 2000), 75–77.

140   Ibid.

141   Dālī al-Jāzī was reported to have said to Bin ʿAlī "Mr. president, I can no longer work with a person who spends his time and energy spying on the highest authority within the Ministry of Defense. You have a choice to keep General Farza or me. If him, then I must leave, because what is at stake are the credibility of the military institution that I am committed to serving with loyalty and my own credibility too." Senior Colonel Ḥassān Kaʿnīsh, a close friend of the late Dālī al-Jāzī, quoted these words to me, verbatim. Kaʿnīsh served as a defense attaché in Italy (2000–2003) while I was a Mediterranean Dialogue Fellowship at the NATO Defense College in Rome (2001). Given the strong personality of the late al-Jāzī, with whom I worked on several occasions, I trust the report from Kaʿnīsh.

142   Ministerial Decision 562 of March 11, 2002 on the Creation of the Permanent Committee for Monitoring Armament is available in Appendix D.

143   Often, officers from the Army, Air Force, and the Navy involved in different capacities with the DGSM followed some unwritten rules by reporting on their activities to their military hierarchy, especially

to their respective chief of staff, in order to keep them informed. Such practices further widened the mistrust between the DGSM and the three components of the TAF.

Chapter Four

144 Jebnoun, "In the Shadow of Power: Civil-Military Relations and the Tunisian Popular Uprising," 306.
145 Figure 9: Post-2011 GDNS's unofficial organizational charter drawn by the author based on fieldwork interviews.
146 On March 7, 2011, the then Minister of the Interior Farḥāt al-Rājḥī announced the disbanding of the DSS and the political police. The latter did not exist as an autonomous organization. Rather, it was made-up of operatives dispatched to different services within the Interior Ministry tasked with the mission of surveillance and oppression of political activists, human rights militants, students, Islamists, bloggers, labor union members, journalists, civil society activists, etc. The abolition of these entities did not affect those who served within these bodies or were in charge of them. Some of these security officials were forced to retire with full benefits and others have been moved to other services within the ministry. However, none of these security officials have been held accountable for the crimes and abuses committed during their tenure.
147 Decree n° 2011-166, July 8, 2011 on the Size of the National Guard; Decree n° 2012-35, June 2, 2012, amending and completing Decree n° 2007-246, August 15, 2007 on the Structures of the ISF within the Ministry of the Interior and Local Development; Decree n° 2012-35, September 5, 2012, amending and completing Decree n° 2007-246, August 15, 2007 on the Structures of the ISF within the Ministry of the Interior and Local Development; Circular of the Minister of the Interior n° 85, January 23, 2014 on the Statements about the Ongoing Operations; Decree n° 2014-45, April 21, 2014, amending and completing Decree n° 2007-246, August 15, 2007 on the Structures of the ISF within the Ministry of the Interior and Local Development; Governmental Decree n° 2015-31, January 19, 2015, amending and completing Decree n° 2007-246, August 15, 2007 on the Structures of the ISF within the Ministry of the Interior and Local Development.
148 United Nations General Assembly, Human Rights Council, Twentieth session, A/HRC/20/14/Add.1, Martin Scheinin, *Report of the Special Rapporteur on the promotion and protection of human rights and fundamental freedoms while countering terrorism*, March 14, 2012, 12–13.
149 United Nations General Assembly, Human Rights Council, Twen-

tieth-fourth session, A/HRC/24/42/Add.1, Pablo de Greiff, *Report of the Special Rapporteur on the promotion of truth, justice, reparation and guarantees of non-recurrence*, July 30, 2013, 17.

150   Security Assistance Monitor, *Country Profile: U.S. Security Assistance to Tunisia*, Center for International Policy, (April 2015).

151   The author met Hādī Majdūb, then Chief of Staff of the Minister of the Interior in Algiers at "North Africa Strategic Forum: Transnational Threats," organized by the Algerian Ministry of Foreign Affairs and the Near East South Asia-Center for Strategic Studies (June 2-5, 2014) and in which the author participated as a panelist. Majdūb raised his concerns to the author about the negative role played by the ISF unions in the process of security reform.

152   Author interview with Sihām Bin Sadrīn, President of the Truth and Dignity Commission, Tunis, May 3, 2015.

153   Walid Mejri, "Investigation: Carthage Airport... A 'Barrack' for Parallel Security," *nawaat.org*, March 26, 2013 (In Arabic). Accessed June 25, 2016. http://nawaat.org/portail/2013/03/26/%D8%AA%D8%AD%D9%82 %D9%8A%D9%82-%D8%A7%D8%B3%D8%AA%D9%82%D8%B5 %D8%A7%D8%A6%D9%8A-%D9%85%D8%B7%D8%A7%D8%B1- %D8%AA%D9%88%D9%86%D8%B3- %D9%82%D8%B1%D8%B7%D8%A7%D8%AC- %D8%AB%D9%83%D9%86%D8%A9-%D8%A7/.

154   Rafīq Shallī who served as a Secretary of State to the Minister of the Interior in Charge of National Security (January-December 2015) depicted the disbanding decision of the DSS as "criminal and impulsive." See *al-Ṣarīḥ*, April 21, 2015, 3.

155   The DES is one of GDSS components, worked closely with the DSS under Bin 'Alī's rule. Author interview, Tunis, April 21, 2015.

156   Joseph Fitsanakis, "CIA warned Tunisian officials about murder of opposition politician," *intelNews.org*, September 23, 2013. Accessed June 25, 2016. https://intelnews.org/2013/09/23/01-1345/.

157   Author interview, Tunis, 21 April 2015.

158   *Al-Amn wa al-Tanmiyah: Naḥwa Amnin fī Khidmati al-Dīmukrātiyyah* [Security and Development: Toward Security in the Service of Democracy], (Tunis: Ministry of the Interior, 2011).

159   Noureddine Jebnoun, "Tunisia's Security Syndrome," *IPRIS Viewpoints*, No. 123 (May 2013): 4. Accessed June 25, 2016. http://www.ipris.org/php/download.php?fid=765.

160   Ibid., 4–5.

161   Noureddine Jebnoun, "Security & the Tunisian Constitution," *Middle East Institute Transitions Project*, February 18, 2014. Accessed June 25, 2016. http://www.mei.edu/content/security-tunisian-constitution.

162 David Wise and Thomas Ross, *The Invisible Government* (London: Mayflower, 1968).

163 Amel Boubekeur, "Islamists, Secularists and Old Regime Elites in Tunisia: Bargained Competition," *Mediterranean Politics* 21(1) (2016): 107–127.

164 The 143 pages of the Interior Ministry's budget for the 2016 fiscal year are devoid of any figure on the funding allocated to its intelligence services. Interestingly, the ministry published on page 43 the amounts of its membership contributions to some regional security organizations such as the Arab League Interior Ministers Council (TND 0.1 million), Nayef Arab University for Security Sciences (TND 0.32 million), and the Committee of Intelligence and Security Services of Africa (TND 0.21 million). See Republic of Tunisia, Ministry of Finance, *Ministry of the Interior's 2016 Budget Bill*. Accessed June 25, 2016.
http://www.finances.gov.tn/index.php?option=com_jdownloads&Itemid=715&view=finish&cid=1014&catid=28&lang=ar-AA.

165 See for example Amnesty International, *Tunisia: Evidence of Torture and Deaths in Custody Suggest Gains of the Uprising Sliding into Reverse Gear*, January 14, 2016; Henda Chennaoui, "Tunisie: Vers la normalisation de la torture au nom de la lutte-antiterroriste,"
nawaat.org, August 15, 2015. Accessed June 25, 2016. https://nawaat.org/portail/2015/08/15/tunisie-vers-la-normalisation-de-la-torture-au-nom-de-la-lutte-antiterroriste/.

166 Amnesty International, *Tunisia: Severe Restrictions on Liberty and Movement Latest Symptoms of Repressive Emergency*, March 17, 2016. From January 15, 2011 to September 19, 2016, more than 20 presidential decisions and decrees were issued declaring and extending the state of emergency that enables the government to hand the army and the ISF more power in terms of search and arrest and to restrict certain rights, chief among them the right to assembly. In nearly six years, the heads of the executive body abused their rights in declaring a state of emergency. President Fuʾād al-Mubazzaʿ did it for three times, President al-Marzūqī eleven times, and President Qāʾid al-Sabsī nine times so far.

167 Figure 10: Sample of Reactive Security Meetings to Terror Attacks.

168 "'Cowardly' Tunisian police condemned by UK inquest into 2015 Sousse attacks," *Middleeasteye.net*, February 28, 2017. Accessed February 28, 2017. http://www.middleeasteye.net/news/verdict-expected-uk-inquest-2015-sousse-attack-deaths-443227424.

169 Ibid.

170 Ibid.

171 Ibid.

172 European Parliament, *European Parliament Resolution of 14 September 2016 on the EU Relations with Tunisia in the Current Regional Context 2015/2273 (INI)*. Accessed September 18, 2016. http://www.europarl. europa.eu/sides/getDoc.do?pubRef=-//EP//TEXT+TA+P8-TA-2016-0345+0+DOC+XML+V0//EN.

173 See the statement of the Head of the Government, Tunis, March 29, 2015. Accessed June 28, 2016. https://www.youtube.com/ watch?v=XVSqIH9zoso.

174 Souad Mekhennet and Missy Ryan, "Outside the wire: How U.S. Special Operations troops secretly help foreign forces target terrorists," *Washington Post*, April 16, 2016. Accessed June 28, 2016. https://www.washingtonpost.com/world/national-security/out-side-the-wire-how-us-special-operations-troops-secretly-help-for-eign-forces-target-terrorists/2016/04/16/a9c1a7d0-0327-11e6-b823-707c79ce3504_story.html. A well-informed Tunisian senior military officer confirmed to the author that American Special forces teams who provide Tunisian military with "intelligence and technical assistance" supervise most of the military operations conducted in the Mount Ash-Sha'nabī area.

175 Ibid.

176 See Appendix E: "Memorandum of Understanding between the Republic of Tunisia and the United States of America signed on May 20, 2015."

177 Corinna Mullin, "Tunisia's 'transition': Between revolution and globalized national security," *Pambazuka News*, October 12, 2012. Accessed June 28, 2016. http://www.pambazuka.org/global-south/ tunisia's-"transition"-between-revolution-and-globalized-national-security.

178 Gayatri Oruganti and Todd Ruffner, "U.S.-Tunisia Security Cooperation: What It Mean to be a Major Non-NATO Ally," *Security Assistance Monitor*, July 14, 2015. Accessed July 15, 2016.
     http://securityassistance.org/blog/us-tunisia-security-cooperation-what-it-means-be-major-non-nato-ally.

179 Ibid.

180 Ibid.

181 Presidency of the Republic of Tunisia, Diplomatic Section, *Memorandum on the Main Points discussed between the President of the Republic and the U.S. Secretary John Kerry*, Friday, November 13, 2015. Accessed July 15, 2016. https://docs.google.com/viewerng/viewer?url=http:// nawaat.org/portail/wp-content/uploads/2016/03/essebsi-john-kerry3.pdf&hl=en_US.

182   American Embassy in Tunisia to State Department, "COM USAFE and Minister of Defense Discuss SOFA, Afghan PRTS and Tip," June 27, 2006, US Cable 06TUNIS1603_a. Accessed July 15, 2016. https://wikileaks.org/plusd/cables/06TUNIS1603_a.html.

183   Adam Entous and Gordon Lubold, "U.S. Wants Drones in North Africa to Combat Islamic State in Libya," *The Wall Street Journal*, August 11, 2015.

184   Mark Hosenball and Andrea Shalal, "U.S. using Tunisia to conduct drone operations in Libya: U.S. sources," *Reuters*, October 26, 2016. Accessed October 28, 2016. http://www.reuters.com/article/us-usa-drones-tunisia-idUSKCN12Q2PW.

185   Martin Berger, "Tunisia Denies Harboring US Drones," *New Eastern Outlook*, November 1, 2016. Accessed November 2, 2016. http://journal-neo.org/2016/11/01/tunisia-denies-harboring-us-drones/.

186   U.S. Department of State, *Remarks With Tunisian President Beji Caid Essebsi at the U.S. Africa Business Forum and Remarks John Kerry Secretary of State*, The Palace Hotel New York City, September 21, 2016. Accessed November 2, 2016. https://2009-2017.state.gov/secretary/remarks/2016/09/262325.htm.

187   Adam Entous and Missy Ryan, "U.S. has secretly expanded its global network of drone bases to North Africa," *The Washington Post*, October 26, 2016. Accessed November 2, 2016. https://www.washingtonpost.com/world/national-security/us-has-secretly-expanded-its-global-network-of-drone-bases-to-north-africa/2016/10/26/ff19633c-9b7d-11e6-9980-50913d68eacb_story.html?utm_term=.b04a568710f7.

188   Ibid.

189   Nick Turse, "Tomgram: Nick Turse, The U.S. Military Moves Deeper into Africa," *TomDispatch.com*, April 27, 2017. Accessed April 28, 2017. http://www.tomdispatch.com/blog/176272/.

190   The White House, *Fact Sheet: Enduring U.S.-Tunisian Relations* (Washington, D.C.: Office of the Press Secretary, May 21, 2015). Accessed November 4, 2016. https://www.whitehouse.gov/the-press-office/2015/05/21/fact-sheet-enduring-us-tunisian-relations.

191   Author phone discussion with a Tunisian senior military officer based in Tunis, October 30, 2016.

192   U.S. Joint Chiefs of Staff, *Joint Publication 1, Doctrine for the Armed Forces of the United States* (Washington, D.C.: Joint Staff, March 25, 2013), V-6.

193   Curtis E. Lemay Center for Doctrine Development and Education, *Annex 3-30 Command and Control. Operational Control*, (Last updated: November 7, 2014). Accessed November 4, 2016. https://doctrine.af.mil/download.jsp?filename=3-30-D62-C2-OPCON.pdf.

194 Author phone discussion with a Tunisian senior military officer based in Tunis, October 30, 2016.

195 "Tunisia, sovereign country, it is not home to any foreign military base," *TAP*, October 27, 2016. Accessed November 4, 2016. http://www.tap.info.tn/en/Portal-Politics/8365234-tunisia-sovereign-country-it-is-not.

196 Wajīh al-Wāfī, "The vagueness of the official statement embarrasses Tunisia vis-à-vis Algeria: What is the reality about the American presence on Tunisian soil?" *al-Ṣabāḥ* (Tunis), October 28, 2016. Accessed November 5, 2016.

http://www.assabah.com.tn/article/126548/تحرج-الرسمي-الموقف-ضبابية ‏الأراضي-على-الأمريكي-التواجد-حقيقة-ما-الجزائر-مع-تونس.

197 Chaabane Bensaci, "Le Washington Post révèle l'existence d'une base de drones en Tunisie: Le coup de poignard de Carthage," *L'Expression-Le Quotidien*, October 29, 2016. Accessed November 5, 2016. http://www.lexpressiondz.com/actualite/252946-le-coup-de-poignard-de-carthage.html.

198 Akram Kharief, "ANALYSIS: Just where are the US drone bases in North Africa?" *Middleeasteye.net*, October 28, 2016. Accessed November 5, 2016. http://www.middleeasteye.net/news/drones-just-where-are-us-bases-northern-africa-2142422444.

199 See President Qā'id al-Sabsī's interview on *al-Ḥiwār al-Tūnisī TV*, November 22, 2016, mainly the segment from 42:50" to 48:54". Accessed November 23, 2016. https://www.youtube.com/watch?v=a-ipZ_jTSnw.

200 Mullin, "Tunisia's 'transition': Between revolution and globalized national security."

201 Jameel Jaffer, *The Drone Memos: Targeted Killing, Secrecy, and the Law* (New York: The New Press, 2016).

202 Turse, "Tomgram: Nick Turse, The U.S. Military Moves Deeper into Africa."

203 Ibid.

204 Ibid.

205 Joe Sterling and Richard Roth, "Tunisia joins International Criminal Court," *CNN*, June 24, 2011. Accessed 25 June 2016. http://www.cnn.com/2011/WORLD/africa/06/24/tunisia.icc/; "Jhinaoui: Tunisia will not withdraw from International Criminal Court," *TAP*, July 28, 2016. Accessed November 5, 2016. http://www.tap.info.tn/en/Portal-Politics/8091439-jhinaoui-tunisia-will-not-withdraw.

206 Thomas Escrit, "Hague prosecutors say U.S. forces may have committed war crimes," *Reuters*, November 14, 2016. Accessed November 15, 2016. http://www.reuters.com/article/us-warcrimes-usa-idUSKBN1392OI.

207 Author meeting with the then Chief of Staff of the Tunisian Armed Forces General Rashīd ʿAmmār in his office at the Tunisia's Ministry of National Defense on March 13, 2012. General ʿAmmār told the author that he requested from the French Chief of the Defense Staff to keep him informed "about the evolving situation inside Libya in a range of 500 km beyond Tunisia's south-eastern border." Later General ʿAmmār confirmed this information by using the same quote during his long broadcast interview on *al-Tūnisiyyah TV*, June 24, 2013 (Part 3). Accessed November 15, 2016. https://www.youtube.com/watch?v=lEnesSvsz2Y.

208 See General Rashīd ʿAmmār's interview on *al-Tūnisiyyah TV*, June 24, 2013 (Part 2). Accessed November 15, 2016. https://www.youtube.com/watch?v=Oa1uFL7aNPU.

209 Some of the interviewees affirmed to the author that the delivery of weapons to the Libyan rebels was only the tip of the iceberg in escalating the crisis that opposed General ʿAmmār to his former protégé General Shābīr. Allegedly, the arm wrestling between the two men started once Shābīr tried to take over a wire-tapping system that was ordered at the end of Bin ʿAlī's rule, likely from France, for the Interior Ministry. ʿAmmār opposed Shābīr's willingness to transfer this system to the Defense Ministry, as it could strengthen the DGSM's capabilities at the detriment of the armed forces.

210 Figure 11: Table established by the author on the Tenure of Military Intelligence Chiefs (2011 to present).

211 Khalil Abdelmoumen, "Putsch, un coup banal dans la République des bananes," *webdo.tn*, February 24, 2014. Accessed November 15, 2016. http://www.webdo.tn/2014/02/24/putsch-coup-banal-dans-la-republique-des-bananes/; Maher Chaabane, "Adnan Manser: 'Il y a eu deux tentatives de coup d'Etat en Tunisie, le 8 février et le 6 août 2013,'" *webdo.tn*, September 23, 2014. Accessed November 15, 2016. http://www.webdo.tn/2014/09/23/tunisie-adnene-mancer-il-y-a-bien-eu-tentative-de-coup-detat-en-ete-2013/.

212 All military officers interviewed whether retired or on active duty expressed unanimity in condemning Manṣar's allegations that reminded them "Bin ʿAlī unfounded accusations of a coup" and called "the judiciary to investigate Manṣar's grave assertions that sought to tarnish the TAF, the only institution that preserved the country's unity and security in the post-uprising volatile era."

213 "Aziz Krichen: Le coup d'Etat est une invention de Adnen Manser pour aider Marzouki," *tuniscope.com*, April 3, 2016. Accessed November 16, 2016. http://www.tuniscope.com/article/92471.

214 Author interview with a senior military officer from the DGSM, Tunis, January 4, 2014.

215   Rori Donaghy and Linah Alsaafin, "UAE conspiring to end Tunisia's fledgling democracy: Source," *Middleeasteye.net*, December 7, 2015. Accessed November 20, 2016. http://www.middleeasteye.net/news/details-emerge-uae-desire-end-tunisias-democracy-1134923414.

216   Figure 11.

217   Jebnoun, "Security & the Tunisian Constitution."

218   See Presidential Decree n° 230, August 29, 2013 on the Declaration of a Border Buffer Zone, *OJRT*, n° 71, September 3, 2013, 2851; Presidential Decree n° 70, April 11, 2014, *OJRT*, n° 31, April 18, 2014, 908–909.

219   Meeting with the Minister of National Defense Ghāzī Jarībī during his visit to Washington, D.C., October 28-November 2, 2014.

220   Under al-Ṣīd's government the Crisis Cell was relabeled Security Coordination and Monitoring Unit further emphasizing the coordination between the TAF and the ISF.

221   Figure 11.

222   Governmental Decree n° 4208, November 20, 2014 on the Creation of Public Institution of Administrative Character subjected to the Authority of the Ministry of National Defense (Defense Intelligence and Security Agency), *OJRT*, n° 94, November 21, 2014, 3296.

223   Ibid.

224   Ibid.

225   Ibid.

226   The Governmental Decree n° 4208 established the DISA prior to the adoption of the controversial counterterrorism law by Tunisia's Assembly of Representatives on July 24, 2015. The counterterrorism bill was signed by the president and issued as Organic Law n° 26-2015 relating to the Fight against Terrorism and Prevention of Money Laundering, *OJRT*, n° 63, August 7, 2015, 2163–2184. This new law that replaced the 2003 anti-terrorism law is flawed, as the definition of terrorism is too broad and ambiguous. The law could be used to squash social movements and to infringe on fundamental freedoms. For further comments on this law, see Human Rights Watch, *Tunisia: Counterterror Law Endangers Rights*, July 31, 2015; Amnesty International, *Tunisia: Letter to the Tunisian Parliament: Concerning Draft Organic Law n° 22/2015 Relating to the Fight against Terrorism and Prevention of Money Laundering*, July 7, 2015.

227   Governmental Decree n° 4208, November 20, 2014.

228   It is the first time since 1956 that the budget of an intelligence apparatus has been rendered public. In fact, the rules were that the budget of intelligence services within the Interior and Defense Ministries are kept secret, which continue to be the case within the Interior Ministry. This relative transparency was recently praised in a report au-

thored by Tehmina Abbas et al., *Regional Results Africa: Government Defence Anti-Corruption Index* (London: Transparency International Defence & Security, 2015), and in which the authors state: "The only countries that provide any useful spending information are Benin, South Africa, Tunisia, Ghana, Tanzania, and Liberia. In those countries, the Ministry of Defence's budget provides information on spending for training, construction, personnel, acquisitions, salaries, and maintenance, though the level of detail varies" (p. 2). The report adds: "In Tunisia, South Africa, and Benin chains of command are separated from chains of payment, and this is a published policy" (p. 11). The DISA budget is listed on page 45 of the 2016-Defense Ministry budget. See, Republic of Tunisia, Ministry of Finance, *Ministry of the National Defense's 2016 Budget Bill*. Accessed November 20, 2016. http://www.finances.gov.tn/index.php?option=com_jdownloads&view=finish&cid=1007&catid=1&lang=fr.

229   Presidential Decree n° 42, February 20, 2015, *OJRT*, n° 17, February 27, 2015, 522.

230   Figure 12: DISA's unofficial organizational charter drawn by the author based on fieldwork interviews.

231   "Beji Caid Essebsi announces set of measures on 60th anniversary of Army creation," *TAP*, June 24, 2016. Accessed November 20, 2016. http://www.tap.info.tn/en/Portal-Politics/8001976-beji-caid-essebsi-announces-set-of.

232   Author phone discussion with a Tunisian senior military officer based in Tunis, November 13, 2016.

233   Ibid.

234   Meeting-discussion with General Tawfīq Raḥmūnī, head of the DISA, during his visit to Washington, D.C., May 23-28, 2015.

235   Ibid.

236   Ibid.

237   Figure 13: IFC's unofficial structure drawn by the author based on fieldwork interviews.

238   North Atlantic Treaty Organization, *NATO steps up efforts to project stability and strengthen partners*, July 9, 2016. Accessed November 20, 2016. http://www.nato.int/cps/on/natohq/news_133804.htm.

239   The White House, Office of the Press Secretary, *FACT SHEET: U.S. and NATO Efforts in Support of NATO Partners, including Georgia, Ukraine, and Moldova*, Washington, D.C., July 9, 2016. Accessed November 20, 2016. https://www.whitehouse.gov/the-press-office/2016/07/09/fact-sheet-us-and-nato-efforts-support-nato-partners-including-georgia.

240   "Defence Ministry denies information on the establishment by NATO of a merger of Intelligence Fusion Centre in Tunisia," *TAP*,

July 11, 2016. Accessed July 12, 2016. http://www.tap.info.tn/en/
Portal-Politics/8044702-defence-denies-information-on.

241   Ibid.

242   "NATO confirms and Tunisian Ministry of Foreign Affairs denies,"
Tunisie Telegraph, July 14, 2016. Accessed November 20, 2016.

http://tunisie-telegraph.com/2016/07/14/الحلف-الأأطلسي-يؤكد-الخارجية-و
29711-التونس.

243   Author meeting-discussion with the U.S. military adviser, Arlington,
March 17, 2016. A senior Tunisian active duty military personnel confirmed to the author the role played by this U.S. military adviser in
setting the IFC structure during a meeting-discussion in Washington,
D.C. on May 5, 2016. Although the Tunisian officer from the Army
G-3 Operations portrayed the American role as "critical" in conceiv-
ing the IFC, he stressed that the development and operationalization
of the structure were exclusively Tunisian-based resources.

244   In August 2014, the then U.S. ambassador to Tunis, Jacob Walles, in a
ceremony for delivery of security equipment to the Tunisian Interior
Ministry pointed out that his country was "please[d] to be supporting the initiative" of the Tunisian government "to establish a 'Pole
Securitaire'—or 'Fusion Center' as we say in English— to bring together the different parts of the Ministries of Interior, Defense and
Justice to coordinate their efforts more closely in the fight against terror." See *Remarks by Ambassador Walles at the Ceremony for the Donation
of Equipment to the Ministry of Interior*, U.S. Embassy in Tunisia, August 14, 2014. Funded by the United States, France, and Qatar, the Security Pole for Counterterrorism and Organized Crime (SPCOC) and
the Judicial Counterterrorism Pole (JCTP) were inaugurated with
great fanfare by the then Head of Government Mahdī Jumʿā and the
ambassadors of the above-mentioned countries in December 2014.
The creation of these two structures raised some valid concerns with
regard to their conformity with the 2014 constitution and to their respect for human rights standards. First, an unpublished administrative decision rather than a law created these two organizations. Such
procedure questioned their constitutionality and underlined the lack
of transparency and accountability in the divisive field of counterterrorism. Although the JCTP's status was later legalized under Article
40 of the controversial Organic Law n° 26-2015 relating to the Fight
against Terrorism and Prevention of Money Laundering (August 7,
2015), the existence of the JCTP itself seems in contradiction with
the spirit of Article 110 of the 2014 constitution, which stipulates:
"The different categories of courts are established by law. No special courts may be established, nor any special procedures that may

prejudice the principles of fair trial." Second, the physical presence in the same building of security officials allegedly in charge of collecting and analyzing information on terrorism and organized crime and judges in charge of investigating such crimes could strongly question the independence of the judiciary as there could be a risk of interference between the two entities. Finally, the SPCOC initially aims at developing a "comprehensive security" approach through a horizontal structure involving officials from the Ministries of the Interior, Defense, Foreign Affairs as well as customs and the penitentiary. Its ultimate goal is to develop an interagency cooperation through centralizing and sharing information processes related to the fight against terrorism between the aforementioned departments. Given the mistrust and the lack of inter and intra-coordination between the intelligence services within the Interior and Defense Ministries, the "SPCOC has come forth stillborn," to use the words of a senior security official from the Interior Ministry interviewed in Tunis on April 21, 2015.

245 U.S. Joint Chiefs of Staff, *Joint Publication 2-0, Joint Intelligence* (Washington, D.C.: Joint Staff, October 22, 2013), GL-9.

246 U.S. Congress, *Public Law 110–53: Implementing Recommendations of the 9/11 Commission Act of 2007* (Washington, D.C.: GPO, August 3, 2007), 121 STAT., 322.

247 Tehmina Abbas et al., *Regional Results Middle East and North Africa: Government Defence Anti-Corruption Index* (London: Transparency International Defence & Security, 2015), 13.

248 The White House, *Fact Sheet: Security Governance Initiative* (Washington, D.C.: Office of the Press Secretary, 6 August 2014). Accessed November 21, 2016. https://obamawhitehouse.archives.gov/the-press-office/2014/08/06/fact-sheet-security-governance-initiative.

249 Figure 14: Tunisia's National Intelligence Architecture in Post-Popular Uprising drawn by the author based on filed research.

250 Jeffrey A. Friedman & Richard Zeckhauser, "Assessing Uncertainty in Intelligence," *Intelligence and National Security* 27(6) (December 2012): 829.

251 George Parker, "Exporting Jihad: The Arab Spring has given Tunisians the freedom to act on their unhappiness," *The New Yorker*, March 21, 2016.

252 Amnesty International, *"We Want an End to the Fear." Abuses under Tunisia's State of Emergency*, February 13, 2017, 11

253 Ibid.,11.

254 Ibid., 15, 18.

255   Ibid., 27.

256   Ibid., 17, 35.

257   Ibid., 41.

258   Ibid., 41.

259   Article 24 states: "The state protects the right to privacy and the inviolability of the home, and the confidentiality of correspondence, communications, and personal information. Every citizen has the right to choose their place of residence, to free movement within the country, and the right to leave the country." See, IEDA (International Institute for Democracy and Electoral Assistance), *Tunisia's Constitution of 2014*. Accessed February 20, 2017. https://www.constituteproject.org/constitution/Tunisia_2014.pdf.

260   "National Security Council discusses national strategy of fight against terrorism and extremism," *TAP*, November 7, 2016. Accessed November 21, 2016. http://www.tap.info.tn/en/Portal-Top-News-EN/8409120-national-security-council-discusses.

261   "Mehdi Ben Gharbia: Tunisia has no means to control 19,000 associations (Interview)," *TAP*, October 27, 2016. Accessed November 21, 2016. http://www.tap.info.tn/en/Portal-Politics/8364981-mehdi-ben-gharbia-tunisia-has-no-means.

262   "Tunisia signs a strategy against terrorism and extremism," *alarab. co.uk*, November 8, 2016. Accessed November 21, 2016.

ضد-استراتيجية-توقع-تونس/ 94248 /اخبار/ http://www.alarab.co.uk/article
.والإرهاب-التطرف

263   Author phone discussion with a Tunisian senior military officer based in Tunis, November 13, 2016.

264   See Al Qassam's mourning statement posted on the group's website. Accessed on December 20, 2016. http://www.alqassam.ps/arabic/specialfiles/details/11.

265   Ibid.

266   See Press Conference of Hādī Majdūb, Tunis, December 19, 2016. Accessed December 20, 2016. https://www.youtube.com/watch?v=TlXw1tsbFFI&t=10s.

267   Ibid.

268   "Liberman: Hamas man killed in Tunisia 'was no Nobel Prize candidate'," *The Times of Israel*, December 21, 2016. Accessed December 22, 2016. http://www.timesofisrael.com/liberman-hamas-man-killed-in-tunisia-was-no-nobel-prize-candidate/.

269   Ronen Bergman, "Tunisia assassination: Yossi Cohen's baptism of fire," *Yedioth Ahronoth*, December 19, 2016. Accessed December 20, 2016. http://www.ynetnews.com/articles/0,7340,L-4895030,00.html.

270   Ibid.

271   See Moav Vardi's reportage from Sfax aired on *Al Mayadeen News*, December 19, 2016. Accessed December 20, 2016. https://www. youtube.com/watch?v=mNVp3hHbbYo.

272   See Press Conference of Hādī Majdūb, mainly the segment from 35:50" to 41:23".

273   Ibid.

274   Author phone discussion with a Tunisian senior security official based in Tunis, January 2, 2017.

275   Pat M. Holt, *Secret Intelligence and Public Policy: A Dilemma of Democracy* (Washington: CQ Press, 1995), 3.

276   Stephen Quillen, "Killing of Hamas-linked drone expert in Tunisia draws public anger," *Middleeasteye.net*, December 30, 2016. Accessed December 31, 2016. http://www.middleeasteye.net/news/ killing-hamas-linked-drone-expert-tunisia-draws-public-condemnation-1495969978.

277   Kenneth R. Dombroski, "Reforming Intelligence After Apartheid," 54.

Conclusion

278   Charles Tilly, "Inequality, Democratization, and De-Democratization," *Sociological Theory* 21(1) (March 2003): 54.

Bibliography

I- Key References

Abbas, Tehmina, and Eva Anderson, Katherine Dixon, Emily Knowles, Gavin Raymond, Leah Wawro. *Regional Results Middle East and North Africa: Government Defence Anti-Corruption Index*. London: Transparency International Defence & Security, 2015.

_____. *Regional Results Africa: Government Defence Anti-Corruption Index*. London: Transparency International Defence & Security, 2015.

Abdel Malek, Anouar. *Egypt: Military Society*. New York: Random House, 1968.

Adelman, Jonathan R., ed. *Terror and Communist Politics: The Role of the Secret Police in Communist States*. Boulder: Westview Press, 1984.

Africa, Sandy. "The Restructuring of Intelligence Services in South Africa: An Assessment of the Transformation Process." In *Providing Security for People: Enhancing Security through People, Justice, and Intelligence Reform in Africa*, edited by Chris Ferguson and Jeffrey O. Isima, 27–39. Shrivenham: Cranfield University, 2004.

_____. "The South African Intelligence Services: A Historical Perspective." In *Changing Intelligence Dynamics in Africa*, edited by Sandy Africa and Johnny Kwadjo, 61–94. Birmingham: GFN-SSR Publications, 2009.

Al-Amn wa al-Tanmiyah: Naḥwa Amnin fī Khidmati al-Dīmukrāṭiyyah [Security and Development: Toward Security in the Service of Democracy]. Tunis: Ministry of the Interior, 2011.

ʿAlī, Kamāl Ḥasan. *Mashāwīr al-ʿUmr: Asrār wa-khafāyā 70 ʿĀman min ʿUmr Miṣr fī al-Ḥarb wa-al-Mukhābarāt wa-al-Siyāsah* [Life Journeys: Secrets and Inside Stories of Seventy Years of Egypt's Life in War, Intelligence, and Politics]. Cairo: Dār al-Shurūq, 1994.

Al-Madīnī, Tawfīq. *Al-Dawlah al-Būlīsīyah fī Tūnis al-Muʿāṣirah* [The Police State in Contemporary Tunisia]. Beirut: al-Markaz al-ʿArabī al-Jadīd lil-Ṭibāʿah wa-al-Nashr, 2001.

Albrecht, Holger, and Dina Bishara. "Back on Horseback: The Military and Regime Change in Egypt." *Middle East Law and Governance* 3(1-2) (2011): 13–23.

Albrecht, Holger. "Does Coup-Proofing Work? Political-Military Relations in Authoritarian Regimes amid the Arab Uprisings." *Mediterranean Politics* 20(1) (2015): 36–54.

American Embassy in Tunisia to State Department. "Annual Integrated Assessment of Security Assistance to Tunisia," July 21, 1978, US Cable 1978TUNIS05209_d.

_____. "COM USAFE and Minister of Defense Discuss SOFA, Afghan PRTS and Tip," June 27, 2006, US Cable 06TUNIS1603_a.

_____."Sayah Calls on Party To Face Up To Achour," January 13, 1976, US Cable 1976TUNIS00209_b.

_____. "Tunis Security Environment Profile Questionnaire (SEPQ) Spring 2009," March 6, 2009, US Cable 09TUNIS129_a.

Amnesty International. *In the Name of Security: Routine Abuses in Tunisia.* June 23, 2008.

_____.*Independent Voices Stifled in Tunisia.* July 13, 2010.

_____.*Tunisia: Continuing Abuses in the Name of Security.* August 20, 2009.

_____.*Tunisia: Evidence of Torture and Deaths in Custody Suggest Gains of the Uprising Sliding into Reverse Gear.* January 14, 2016.

_____.*Tunisia: Letter to the Tunisian Parliament: Concerning Draft Organic Law n° 22/2015 Relating to the Fight against Terrorism and Prevention of money Laundering.* July 7, 2015.

_____.*Tunisia: Severe Restrictions on Liberty and Movement Latest Symptoms of Repressive Emergency.* March 17, 2016.

_____. "We Want an End to the Fear." *Abuses under Tunisia's State of Emergency.* February 13, 2017.

Antunes, Priscila Carlos Brandão. "Establishing Democratic Control of Intelligence in Argentina." In *Reforming Intelligence: Obstacles to Democratic Control and Effectiveness,* edited by Thomas C. Bruneau and Steven C. Boraz, 195–218. Austin: University of Texas Press, 2007.

Anyangwe, Carlson. *Revolutionary Overthrow of Constitutional Orders in Africa.* Mankon, Bamenda: Labngaa Research & Publishing CIG, 2012. Distributed by African Books Collective.

Ashour, Omar. From Bad Cop to Good Cop: The Challenges of Security Sector Reform in Egypt, *Paper Series* No. 3, Brookings Doha Center-Stanford Project on Arab Transitions, November 2012.

Aubin de La Messuzière, Yves. *Mes années de Ben Ali. Un ambassadeur de France en Tunisie.* Tunis: Cérès éditions, 2011.

Azzouz, Azzedine. *L'histoire ne pardonne pas: Tunisie, 1938–1969.* Paris: L'Harmattan; Tunis: Dar Ashraf, 1988.

Balkhūjah, al-Ṭāhir. *Al-Ḥabīb Būrqībah: Sīrat Zaʿīm, Shahādah ʿalá ʿAṣr* [Ḥabīb Bourguiba: Biography of a Leader, Witness of His Age]. Cairo: al-Dār al-Thaqāfīyah, 1999.

Barany, Zoltan. "Comparing the Arab revolts: The Role of the Military." *Journal of Democracy* 22(4) (October 2011): 28–39.

Beau, Nicolas, and Jean-Pierre Turquoi. *Notre ami Ben Ali: l'envers du miracle tunisien* 2nd Ed. Tunis, Paris, Med Ali Editions, R.M.R. Editions, Découverte, 2011.

Ben Mahfoudh, Haykel. "Security Sector Reform in Tunisia: Three Years into the Democratic Transition." *Arab Reform Initiative Project* (July 2014): 1–16.

Blehassen, Souhayr. "Les legs bourguibiens de la représsion." In *Habib Bourguiba, la trace et l'héritage*, edited by Michel Camau and Vincent Geisser, 391–408. Paris: Karthala; Aix-en-Provence: Institut d'etudes politiques, 2004.

Boubekeur, Amel. "Islamists, Secularists and Old Regime Elites in Tunisia: Bargained Competition." *Mediterranean Politics* 21(1) (2016): 107–127.

Bruce, Gary. *The Firm: The Inside Story of Stasi.* Oxford; New York: Oxford University Press, 2010.

Brumberg, Daniel, and Hesham Sallam. "The Politics of Security Sector Reform in Egypt." *USIP-Special Report* 318 (October 2012): 1–16.

Bruneau, Thomas C., and Steven C. Boraz. "Intelligence Reform: Balancing Democracy and Effectiveness." In *Reforming Intelligence: Obstacles to Democratic Control and Effectiveness*, edited by Thomas C. Bruneau and Steven C. Boraz, 1–24. Austin: University of Texas Press, 2007.

Cepik, Marco. "Structural Change and Democratic Control of Intelligence in Brazil." In *Reforming Intelligence: Obstacles to Democratic Control and Effectiveness*, edited by Thomas C. Bruneau and Steven C. Boraz, 149–169. Austin: University of Texas Press, 2007.

Childs, David, and Richard Popplewell. *The Stasi: The East German Intelligence and Security Service.* New York: New York University Press, 1996.

Circular of the Minister of the Interior nº 85, January 23, 2014 (unpublished).

Curtis E. Lemay Center for Doctrine Development and Education, *Annex 3-30 Command and Control. Operational Control.* November 7, 2014.

Dallin, Alexander, and George W. Breslauer. *Political Terror in Communist Systems.* Stanford: Stanford University Press, 1970.

DCAF International Expert Conference, Conference Report. *Security Sector Reform in Egypt: Civil-Military Relations in Focus.* Montreux, Switzerland, April 2-4, 2014.

Decree nº 1160, April 13, 2006, *al-Rāʾid al-Rasmī lil-Jumhūrīyah al-Tūnisīyyah* [*The Official Journal of the Republic of Tunisia (OJRT)*] OJRT, nº 34, April 28, 2006, 1475–1489.

_____ nº 1195, July 6, 1990, *OJRT*, nº 48, July 20, 1990, 965–966.

_____ nº 12, January 8, 1973, *OJRT*, nº 2, January 16, 1973, 96–99.

_____ nº 1244, October 20, 1984, *OJRT*, nº 62, October 26, 1984, 2624–2631.

_____ nº 1297, November 27, 1987, *OJRT*, nº 84, December 1-4, 1987, 1478.

_____ nº 147, January 18, 1993, *OJRT*, nº 7, January 26, 1993, 139.

_____ nº 2001-201, October 22, 2001 (unpublished).

_____ nº 2003-61, April 7, 2003 (unpublished).

_____ nº 2003-97, May 22, 2003, amending and completing Decree nº 2003-61, April 7, 2003 (unpublished).

_____ nº 2004-64, April 24, 2004, amending and completing Decree nº 2003-61, April 7, 2003 (unpublished).

_____ nº 2004-82, June 5, 2004, amending and completing Decree nº 2003-61, April 7, 2003 (unpublished).

_____ nº 2007-246, August 15, 2007.

_____ nº 2009-161, June 10, 2009, amending Decree nº 91-543, April 1, 1991 (unpublished).

_____ nº 2011-166, July 8, 2011(unpublished).

_____ nº 2012-35, June 2, 2012, amending and completing Decree nº 2007-246, August 15, 2007 (unpublished).

_____ nº 2012-35, September 5, 2012, amending and completing Decree nº 2007-246, August 15, 2007 (unpublished).

_____ nº 2014-45, April 21, 2014, amending and completing Decree nº 2007-246, August 15, 2007 (unpublished).

_____ nº 501, March 14, 1997, *OJRT*, nº 24, March 25, 1997, 497–498.

_____ nº 250, February 26, 1988, *OJRT*, nº 15, March 1, 1988, 327–328.

_____ nº 252, February 26, 1988, *OJRT*, nº 15, March 1, 1988, 325–326.

_____ nº 373, November 19, 1962, *OJRT* nº 58, November 16-20, 1962, 1678.

_____ nº 374, November 19, 1962, *OJRT*, nº 58, November 16-20, 1962, 1678–1679.

_____ nº 375, November 19, 1962, *OJRT*, nº 58, November 16-20, 1962, 1679–1681.

_____ nº 61, February 21, 1970, *OJRT*, nº 10, February 24, 1970, 218.

_____ nº 7, January 5, 1974, *OJRT*, nº 2, 11 January 1974, 63.

_____ nº 735, August 22, 1979, *OJRT*, nº 50, August 28-31, 1979, 2263–2267.

_____ nº 91-704, May 3, 1991 (unpublished).

_____ nº 96-92, September 9, 1996 (unpublished).

_____ nº 97-139, November 3, 1997 (unpublished).

Dehéz, Dustin. "Intelligence Services in Sub-Saharan African." *ASPJ Africa & Francophonie* (3rd Quarter 2010): 57–63.

Deletant, Dennis. *Ceausescu and the Securitate. Coercion and Dissent in Romania, 1965–1989.* London: Hurst, 1995.

Dennis, Mike. *Stasi: Myth and Reality.* Harlow: Pearson/Longman, 2003.

Denoeux, Guilain. "La face cachée du miracle tunisien." *Politique internationale* 89 (Fall 2000): 395–420.

Diana, Elvira. "'Literary Spring' in Libyan Literature: Contributions of Writers to the Country's Emancipation." *Middle East Critique* 23(4) (2014): 439–451.

Dombroski, Kenneth R. "Reforming Intelligence After Apartheid." *Journal of Democracy* 17(3) (July 2006): 43–57.

_____. "Transforming Intelligence in South Africa." In *Reforming Intelligence: Obstacles to Democratic Control and Effectiveness*, edited by Thomas C. Bruneau and Steven C. Boraz, 241–268. Austin: University of Texas Press, 2007.

Easterly, William. *The Tyranny of Experts: Economists, Dictators, and the Forgotten Rights of the Poor*. New York: Basic Book, 2013.

Esparza, Marcia, Henry R. Huttenbach, and Daniel Feierstein, eds. *State Violence and Genocide in Latin America: the Cold War Years*. London; New York: Routledge, 2010.

Estévez, Eduardo. "Intelligence Community Reforms: The Case of Argentina." In *Intelligence Elsewhere: Spies and Espionage outside the Anglosphere*, edited by Philip H. J. Davies and Kristian C. Gustafson, 219–237. Washington, DC: Georgetown University Press, 2013.

European Parliament. *European Parliament Resolution of 14 September 2016 on the EU Relations with Tunisia in the Current Regional Context 2015/2273(INI)*.

Faligot, Roger, and Pascal Krop. *La Piscine. The French Secret Service since 1944*. Translated by W. D. Halls. Oxford; New York: B. Blackwell, 1989.

Feierstein, Daniel. "National Security Doctrine in Latin America: The Genocide Question." In *The Oxford Handbook of Genocide Studies*, edited by Donald Bloxham and Dirk A. Moses, 489–508. Oxford; New York: Oxford University Press, 2010.

Gobe, Eric. "The Tunisian Bar to the Test of Authoritarianism: Professional and Political Movements in Ben Ali's Tunisia (1990–2007)." *The Journal of North African Studies* 15(3) (2010): 333–347.

Friedman, Jeffrey A., and Richard Zeckhauser. "Assessing Uncertainty in Intelligence." *Intelligence and National Security* 27(6) (December 2012): 824–847.

Governmental Decree n° 2015-31, January 19, 2015, amending and completing Decree n° 2007-246, August 15, 2007 (unpublished).

_____ n° 4208, November 20, 2014, *OJRT*, n° 94, November 21, 2014, 3296.

Haddad, George. *Revolutions and Military Rule in the Middle East*. New York: Speller, 1973.

Henry, Clement M. "Reverberations in the Central Maghreb of the 'Global

War in Terror.'" In *North Africa: Politics, Region, and the Limits of Transformation*, edited by Yahia H. Zoubir and Haizam Amirah-Fernández, 294–310. London; New York: Routledge, 2008.

Henry, Clement. "Tunisia 'Sweet Little' Regime." In *Worst of the Worst: Dealing with Repressive and Rogue Nations*, edited by Robert I. Rotberg, 300–323. Cambridge, Mass.: World Peace Foundation; Washington, DC: Brookings Institution Press, 2007.

Holt, Pat M. *Secret Intelligence and Public Policy: A Dilemma of Democracy*. Washington: CQ Press, 1995.

Human Rights Watch. *A Larger Prison: Repression of Former Political Prisoners in Tunisia*. March 24, 2010.

_____. *Tunisia: Counterterror Law Endangers Rights*. July 31, 2015.

_____. *Tunisia: Crushing the Person, Crushing a Movement*. April 19, 2005.

_____. *Tunisia: Repression and Harassment of Human Rights Defenders and Organizations*. February 14, 2004.

Huwaydī, Amīn. *Maʿa ʿAbd al-Nāṣir* [With ʿAbd al-Nasser]. Cairo: Dār al-Mustaqbal al-ʿArabī, 1985.

IEDA (International Institute for Democracy and Electoral Assistance). *Tunisia's Constitution of 2014*. Stockholm.

Jaffer, Jameel. *The Drone Memos: Targeted Killing, Secrecy, and the Law*. New York: The New Press, 2016.

Jebnoun, Noureddine. "Ben Ali's Tunisia: The Authoritarian Path of a Dystopian State." In *Modern Middle East Authoritarianism: Roots, Ramifications, and Crisis*, edited by Noureddine Jebnoun, Mehrdad Kia, and Mimi Kirk, 101–122. Abingdon, Oxon: Routledge, 2013.

_____. "In the Shadow of Power: Civil-Military Relations and the Tunisian Popular Uprising." *The Journal of North African Studies* 19(3) (2014): 296–316.

_____. "Tunisia's Security Syndrome." *IPRIS Viewpoints* No. 123 (May 2013): 1–5.

Jervis, Robert. "Intelligence, Civil-Intelligence Relations, and Democracy." In *Reforming Intelligence: Obstacles to Democratic Control and Effectiveness*, edited by Thomas C. Bruneau and Steven C. Boraz, vii–xix. Austin: University of Texas Press, 2007.

Julliard, Jean-François. "Tunisia: 'You have no rights here but welcome to Tunisia!'" *Reporters Without Borders*. July 7, 2005.

Kandil, Hazem. *Soldiers, Spies, and Statesmen: Egypt's Road to Revolt*. London; New York: Verso, 2012.

Kartas, Moncef. "Foreign Aid and Security Sector Reform in Tunisia: Resistance and Autonomy of the Security Forces." *Mediterranean Politics* 19(3) (2014): 373–391.

Khuri, Fuad, and Gerald Obermeyer. "The Social Bases for Military Intervention in the Middle East." In *Political Military Systems*, edited by Catherine McArdle Kelleher, 55–85. Beverly Hills: Sage, 1974.

Koehler, John O. *Stasi: The Untold Story of the East German Secret Police.* Boulder: Westview Press, 1999.

Koudra, Sami. *Le "complot" de Barraket Essahel. Chronique d'un Calvaire.* Tunis: Sud Editions, 2012.

Kwadjo, Johnny. "Changing the Intelligence Dynamics in Africa: The Ghana Experience." In *Changing Intelligence Dynamics in Africa*, edited by Sandy Africa and Johnny Kwadjo, 95–123. Birmingham: GFN-SSR Publications, 2009.

Kwesi Aning, Emmanuel, Ema Birikorang, and Ernest Lartey. "The Process and Mechanisms of Developing a Democratic Intelligence Culture in Africa." In *Intelligence Elsewhere: Spies and Espionage outside the Anglosphere*, edited by Phillip H. J. Davies and Kristian C. Gustafson, 199–217. Washington, DC: Georgetown University Press, 2013.

Laribi, Lyes. *Dans les geôles de Nezzar.* Paris: Paris-Méditerranée, 2002.

_____. *L'Algérie des généraux.* Paris: Milo, 2007.

Law n° 2001-1 of January 15, 2001, *OJRT*, n° 5, January 16, 2001, 123–130.

___ n° 2004-5 of February 3, 2004, *OJRT*, n° 10, February 3, 2004, 251.

Lutterbeck, Derek. "After the Fall: Security Sector in Post-Ben Ali Tunisia." *Arab Reform Initiative Project* (September 2012): 1–29.

Lutterbeck, Derek. "Arab Uprisings and Armed Forces: Between Openness and Resistance." *SSR Paper* No. 2, Geneva: The Geneva Centre for the Democratic Control of Armed Forces (DCAF), 2011.

_____. "Arab Uprisings, Armed Forces, and Civil-Military Relations." *Armed Forces & Society* 39(1) (2012): 28–52.

_____. "Tool of Rule: The Tunisian Police under Ben Ali." *The Journal of North African Studies* 20(5) (2015): 813–831.

Makara, Michael. "Coup-Proofing, Military Defection, and the Arab Spring." *Democracy and Security* 9(4) (2013): 334–359.

Mares, David R. "The National Security State." In *A Companion to Latin American History*, edited by Thomas H. Holloway, 386–405. Oxford: Blackwell Publishing Ltd, 2011.

Marshall, Shana. The Egyptian Armed Forces and the Remaking of Economic Empire. *The Carnegie Papers.* Beirut, Lebanon: Carnegie Middle East Center, April 2015.

Matei, Florina Cristina, and Thomas Bruneau. "Intelligence Reform in New Democracies: Factors Supporting or Arresting Progress." *Democratization* 18(3) (2011): 602–630.

McLoughlin, Barry, and Kevin McDermott, ed. *Stalin's Terror: High Politics and Mass Repression in the Soviet Union.* Houndmills, Basingstoke,

Hampshire; New York: Palgrave Macmillan, 2003.

McSherry, J. Patrice. *Predatory States: Operation Condor and Covert War in Latin America.* Lanham, MD: Rowman & Littlefield Publishers, 2005.

Memorandum of Understanding between the Republic of Tunisia and the United States of America signed on May 20, 2015.

Nāṣīf, Niqūlā. *Sirr al-Dawlah: Foṣūl fī Tārīkh al-Amni al-ʿĀm 1945–1977* [Secret of the State: Chapters in the History of Public Security 1945–1977]. Beirut: al-Mūdiriyyat al-ʿĀmah lil-Amni al-ʿĀm, 2013.

Naṣr, Ṣalāḥ. *Mudhakkirāt Ṣalāḥ Naṣr: Aṣuʿūd* (Vol. 1), *Al-Intilāq* (Vol. 2), *Al-ʿĀm al-Ḥazīn* (Vol. 3) [The Memoirs of Ṣalāḥ Naṣr: The Ascension (Vol. 1), The Takeoff (Vol. 2), The Sad Year (Vol. 3)]. Cairo: Dār al-Khayyāl, 1999.

Nezzar, Khaled. *Mémoires du general.* 2nd ed. Algiers: Chihab, 2000.

North Atlantic Treaty Organization, *NATO steps up efforts to project stability and strengthen partners.* July 9, 2016.

OECD. *OECD DAC Handbook on Security System Reform: Supporting Security and Justice.* Paris: OECD Publishing, 2008.

Olmsted, Kathryn. *Challenging the Secret Government: The Post-Watergate Investigations of the CIA and FBI.* Chapel Hill: University of North Carolina Press, 1996.

Open Society Justice Initiative. *Globalizing Torture. CIA Secret Detention and Extraordinary Detention.* New York: Open Society Foundations, 2013.

Organic Law nº 26, *OJRT*, nº 63, August 7, 2015, 2163–2184.

Presidency of the Republic of Tunisia, Diplomatic Section. *Memorandum on the Main Points discussed between the President of the Republic and the U.S. Secretary John Kerry.* Friday, November 13, 2015.

Presidential Decree nº 230, August 29, 2013, *OJRT*, nº 71, September 3, 2013, 2851.

_____ nº 42, February 20, 2015, *OJRT*, nº 17, February 27, 2015, 522.

_____ nº 70, April 11, 2014, *OJRT*, nº 31, April 18, 2014, 908–909.

Quinlivan, James T. "Coup-proofing: Its Practice and Consequences in the Middle East." *International Security* 24(2) (Fall 1999): 131–165.

Republic of Tunisia, Ministry of Finance. *Ministry of the Interior's 2016 Budget Bill.*

Royal Decision of March 31, 1956, *al-Rāʾid al-Rasmī al-Tūnisī* [*The Official Journal of Tunisia (OJT)*], nº 34, April 27, 1956, 781.

Royal Decree of January 19, 1956, *OJT*, nº 7, January 24, 1956, 137–138.

_____ April 19, 1956, *OJT*, nº 34, April 27, 1956, 781.

_____ May 3, 1956, *OJT*, nº 36, May 4, 1956, 823–824.

_____ June 30, 1956, *OJT*, n° 52, June 29-30, 1956, 1173–1174.

_____ May 6, 1956, *OJT*, n° 72, September 7, 1956, 1694.

Sālim, Amīr. *Al-Dawlah al-Būlīsīyah fī Miṣr: al-Thawrah wa-al-Thawrah al-Muḍāddah* [The Police State in Egypt: The Revolution and the Counter-Revolution]. Cairo: Dār ʿAyn lil-Nashr, 2013.

Samraoui, Mohammed. *Chronique des années de sang. Algérie: comment les services secrets ont manipulé les groupes islamistes.* Paris: Editions Denoël, 2003.

Sassoon, Joseph. *Anatomy of Authoritarianism in the Arab Republics.* New York: Cambridge University Press, 2016.

Saʿīd, al-Ṣāfī. *Būrqībah: Sīrah Shubh Muḥarramah* [Bourguiba: A Quasi-Prohibited Biography]. Beirut: Riyāḍ al-Rayyis lil-Kutub wa-al-Nashr, 2000.

Sayigh, Yezid. Above the State: The Officers' Republic in Egypt. *The Carnegie Papers.* Beirut, Lebanon: Carnegie Middle East Center, August 2012.

_____. "Civil-Military Relations in the Middle East: Patterns and Implications." *SEDMED-CIDOB* (June 2011): 1–6.

_____. Dilemmas of Reforming Policing in Arab Transitions. *The Carnegie Papers.* Beirut, Lebanon: Carnegie Middle East Center, March 2016.

_____. Missed Opportunities: The Politics of Police Reform in Egypt and Tunisia. *The Carnegie Papers.* Beirut, Lebanon: Carnegie Middle East Center, March 2015.

Security Assistance Monitor. *Country Profile: U.S. Security Assistance to Tunisia.* Center for International Policy, April 2015.

Shahādat al-Ṭāhir Balkhūjah al-Siyasīyah [al-Ṭāhir Balkhūjah's Testimonies]. Zaghwān: Muʾassasat al-Tamīmī lil-Baḥth al-ʿIlmī wa-al-Maʿlūmāt, 2002.

Sirrs, Owen L. *A History of the Egyptian Intelligence Service. A History of the Mukhabarat, 1910–2009.* London; New York: Routledge, 2010.

Szikinger, Istvan. "National Security in Hungary." In *Democracy, Law and Security: Internal Security Services in Contemporary Europe*, edited by Jean-Paul Brodeur, Peter Gill, and Dennis Töllborg, 81–109. Aldershot; Burlington, VT, USA: Ashgate, 2003.

Tapia-Valdes, J. A. "A Typology of National Security Policies." *Yale Journal of World Public Order* 9(10) (1982): 10–39.

The White House. *Fact Sheet: Enduring U.S.-Tunisian Relations.* Washington, D.C.: Office of the Press Secretary, May 21, 2015.

_____. *Fact Sheet: Security Governance Initiative.* Washington, D.C.: Office of the Press Secretary, August 6, 2014.

_____. *FACT SHEET: U.S. and NATO Efforts in Support of NATO*

Partners, including Georgia, Ukraine, and Moldova. Washington, D.C. July 9, 2016.

Tilly, Charles. "Inequality, Democratization, and De-Democratization." *Sociological Theory* 21(1) (March 2003): 37–43.

U.S. Congress. *Public Law 110-53: Implementing Recommendations of the 9/11 Commission Act of 2007.* Washington, D.C.: GPO, 2007.

U.S. Department of State. *Remarks With Tunisian President Beji Caid Essebsi at the U.S. Africa Business Forum and Remarks John Kerry Secretary of State.* The Palace Hotel New York City. September 21, 2016.

U.S. Embassy in Tunisia. *Remarks by Ambassador Walles at the Ceremony for the Donation of Equipment to the Ministry of Interior.* August 14, 2014.

U.S. Joint Chiefs of Staff. *Joint Publication 1, Doctrine for the Armed Forces of the United States.* Washington, D.C.: Joint Staff, March 25, 2013.

_____. *Joint Publication 2-0, Joint Intelligence.* Washington, D.C.: Joint Staff, October 22, 2013.

U.S. Senate Select Committee on Intelligence. *Committee Study of the Central Intelligence Agency's Detention and Interrogation Program.* December 3, 2014.

_____. *Report on the U.S. Intelligence Community's Prewar Intelligence Assessment on Iraq's War.* July 7, 2004.

United Nations General Assembly, Human Rights Council. Twentieth session, A/HRC/20/14/Add.1, Martin Scheinin. *Report of the Special Rapporteur on the promotion and protection of human rights and fundamental freedoms while countering terrorism.* March 14, 2012, 1–16.

_____.Twentieth-fourth session, A/HRC/24/42/Add.1, Pablo de Greiff. *Report of the Special Rapporteur on the promotion of truth, justice, reparation and guarantees of non-recurrence.* July 30, 2013, 1–22.

United Nations. "Mapping, Charting and Geodesy Cooperative and Exchange Agreement (with annexes). Signed at Tunis on 8 December 1980." In *Treaties Series: Treaties and international agreements registered or filed and recorded with the Secretariat of the United Nations.* New York, 2001, 97–107.

Vatikiotis, Panayiotis. *The Egyptian Army in Politics: Patterns for New Nations?.* Bloomington: Indiana University Press, 1961.

Williams, Kieran. "The StB in Czechoslovakia, 1945–89," In *Security Intelligence Services in New Democracies: The Czech Republic, Slovakia and Romania,* edited by Kieran Williams and Deletant, Dennis, 24–54. New York: Palgrave in association with School of Slavonic and East European Studies, University College, London, 2001.

Wise, David, and Thomas Ross. *The Invisible Government.* London: Mayflower, 1968.

Yallop, David. *To the End of the Earth: Hunt for the Jackal*. 1st ed. London: Hachette, 1993.

II- Newspaper Articles and Blogs

"'Cowardly' Tunisian police condemned by UK inquest into 2015 Sousse attacks." *Middleeasteye.net*. February 28, 2017.

"Aziz Krichen: Le coup d'Etat est une invention de Adnen Manser pour aider Marzouki." Last modified April 3, 2016. *tuniscope.com*.

"Beji Caid Essebsi announces set of measures on 60th anniversary of Army creation." *TAP*. June 24, 2016.

"Defence Ministry denies information on the establishment by NATO of a merger of Intelligence Fusion Centre in Tunisia." *TAP*. July 11, 2016.

"Jhinaoui: Tunisia will not withdraw from International Criminal Court." *TAP*. July 28, 2016.

"Les témoignages des officiers de l'armée nationale tunisienne dans l'affaire de Barakat Essahel [vidéo]." Last modified August 8, 2011. *Nawaat.org*.

"Liberman: Hamas man killed in Tunisia 'was no Nobel Prize candidate.'" *The Times of Israel*. December 21, 2016.

"Mali: Libération de deux otages autrichiens enlevés en Tunisie en février." *Le Monde*. November 2, 2008.

"Mehdi Ben Gharbia: Tunisia has no means to control 19,000 associations (Interview)." *TAP*. October 27, 2016.

"National Security Council discusses national strategy of fight against terrorism and extremism." *TAP*. November 7, 2016.

"NATO confirms and Tunisian Ministry of Foreign Affairs denies." July 14, 2016. *Tunisie Telegraph*.

"Tunisia signs a strategy against terrorism and extremism," *alarab.co.uk*. November 8, 2016.

"Tunisia, sovereign country, it is not home to any foreign military base." *TAP*. October 27, 2016.

Abdelmoumen, Khalil. "Putsch, un coup banal dans la République des bananes." Last modified February 24, 2014. *webdo.tn*.

Al-Wāfī, Wajīh. "The vagueness of the official statement embarrasses Tunisia vis-à-vis Algeria: What is the reality about the American presence on Tunisian soil?" *al-Ṣabāḥ*. October 28, 2016.

Beaugé, Florence. "Six jeunes internautes devant la cour d'appel de Tunis," *Le Monde*. July 6, 2004.

Bensaci, Chaabane. "Le Washington Post révèle l'existence d'une base de drones en Tunisie: Le coup de poignard de Carthage." *L'Expression-Le Quotidien*. October 29, 2016.

Berger, Martin. "Tunisia Denies Harboring US Drones." *New Eastern Outlook*. November 1, 2016.

Bergman, Ronen. "Tunisia assassination: Yossi Cohen's baptism of fire." *Yedioth Ahronoth*. December 19, 2016.

Boularès, Habib. "Réponse de Habib Boularès au colonel Zoghlami et au lieutenant-colonel Mohamed Ahmed." Réalités. May 26-June 1, 2011.

Chaabane, Maher. "Adnan Manser: 'Il y a eu deux tentatives de coup d'Etat en Tunisie, le 8 février et le 6 août 2013.'" Last modified September 23, 2014. *webdo.tn*.

Chennaoui, Henda. "Tunisie: Vers la normalisation de la torture au nom de la lutte-antiterroriste." *nawaat.org*. August 15, 2015.

Daoudi, Mounia. "La thèse de l'attentat évoquée par Tunis." *Radio France International*. April 14, 2002.

Donaghy, Rori, and Linah Alsaafin. "UAE conspiring to end Tunisia's fledgling democracy: Source." Last modified December 7, 2015. *Middleeasteye.net*.

Entous, Adam, and Gordon Lubold. "U.S. Wants Drones in North Africa to Combat Islamic State in Libya." *The Wall Street Journal*. August 11, 2015.

Entous, Adam, and Missy Ryan. "U.S. has secretly expanded its global network of drone bases to North Africa." *The Washington Post*. October 26, 2016.

Escrit, Thomas. "Hague prosecutors say U.S. forces may have committed war crimes." *Reuters*. November 14, 2016.

Fitsanakis, Joseph. "CIA warned Tunisian officials about murder of opposition politician." Last modified September 23, 2013. *intelNews.org*.

Garçon, José. "Six internautes tunisiens dans la toile de Ben Ali." *Libération*, July 7, 2004.

Hosenball, Mark, and Andrea Shalal. "U.S. using Tunisia to conduct drone operations in Libya: U.S. sources." *Reuters*. October 26, 2016.

International League of Human Rights. "Tunisie: Condamnation des 'internautes de Zarzis' à de lourdes peines au terme d'un procès entaché d'irrégularités." July 7, 2004.

Jebnoun, Noureddine. "Security & the Tunisian Constitution." *Middle East Institute Transitions Project*. February 18, 2014.

Kharief, Akram. "ANALYSIS: Just where are the US drone bases in North Africa?" Last modified October 29, 2016. *Middleeasteye.net*.

Mejri, Walid. "Investigation: Carthage Airport… A 'Barrack' for Parallel Security." Last modified March 26, 2013. *nawaat.org* (In Arabic).

Mekhennet, Souad, and Missy Ryan. "Outside the wire: How U.S. Special Operations troops secretly help foreign forces target terrorists." *Washington Post*. April 16, 2016.

Mullin, Corinna. "Tunisia's 'transition': Between revolution and globalized national security." *Pambazuka News*. October 12, 2012.

Oruganti, Gayatri, and Todd Ruffner. "U.S.-Tunisia Security Cooperation: What It Mean to be a Major Non-NATO Ally." *Security Assistance Monitor*. July 14, 2015.

Parker, George. "Exporting Jihad: The Arab Spring has given Tunisians the freedom to act on their unhappiness." *The New Yorker*. March 21, 2016.

Quillen, Stephen. "Killing of Hamas-linked drone expert in Tunisia draws public anger." Last modified December 31, 2016. *Middleeasteye.net*.

Reporters Without Borders. "Appeal court upholds unjustified sentences against Zarzis Internet-users." July 7, 2004.

_____. "Cyber-dissident arrested and his online newspaper censored." June 5, 2002.

_____. "Intelligence services go to great lengths to prevent visiting Algerian journalist from working." November 9, 2006.

_____. "List of 13 Internet enemies." November 7, 2006.

_____. "The country where Internet users are tortured." December 14, 2004.

Rouleau, Eric. "Onde de choc dans le monde arabe; Souvenirs d'un diplomate." *Le Monde Diplomatique*. February 2011.

Sdiri, Wafa. "Vidéo: Le complot de Barraket Essahel: Nos militaires réclament justice." Last modified June 21, 2011. *tunisienumerique.com*.

Sterling, Joe, and Richard Roth. "Tunisia joins International Criminal Court." *CNN*. June 24, 2011.

Stevenson, Tom. "NSA-Style: Tunisia Setting Up Counterterrorism Unit That Will Also Spy On Citizens." *International Business Times*. February 26, 2014.

Turse, Nick. "Tomgram: Nick Turse, The U.S. Military Moves Deeper into Africa." *TomDispatch.com*. April 27, 2017.

About the Author

NOUREDDINE JEBNOUN teaches at Georgetown University's Center for Contemporary Arab Studies in the Edmund A. Walsh School of Foreign Service. Previously, in Tunisia, he served as professor of strategy and geopolitics at the National War College, the Command and Staff College, and the National Defense Institute (1998–2004), as well as a senior lecturer at the High Institute of Internal Security Forces (2000–2004). He is co-editor of and contributor to *Modern Middle East Authoritarianism: Roots, Ramifications, and Crisis* (Routledge, 2013 & 2015) and author of *L'espace méditerranéen: les enjeux de la coopération et de la sécurité entre les rives nord et sud à l'aube du XXIème siècle* [*The Mediterranean Region: Implications of Security and Cooperation between the Northern and Southern Shores at the Dawn of the Twenty First Century*] (NATO Defense College, 2003). His works have appeared in the *Journal of North African Studies, Center for Contemporary Arab Studies Occasional Papers Series, Center for Muslim-Christian Understanding Occasional Papers,* and as book chapters, among other publications. He holds a PhD in Political Science from the University of Paris I-Pantheon Sorbonne (1996).

Index

www.ingramcontent.com/pod-product-compliance
Lightning Source LLC
Chambersburg PA
CBHW070918270326
41927CB00011B/2627